Paris Under Water

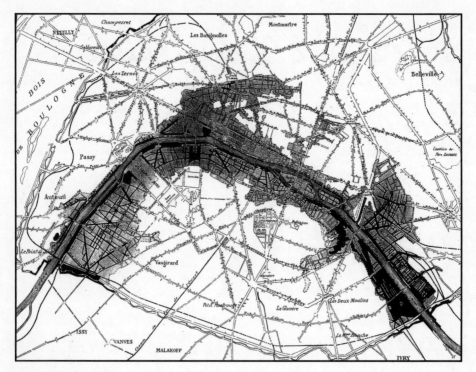

Map of the flooded area in January–February 1910.

Paris Under Water

HOW *the* CITY *of* LIGHT SURVIVED *the* GREAT FLOOD *of* 1910

JEFFREY H. JACKSON

palgrave
macmillan

For Ellen

Contents

List of Figures

FIGURE 1. Cover Illustration. The Eiffel Tower was surrounded by water when the Seine flooded the Champs-de-Mars.

> SOURCE: Charles Eggimann, ed., *Paris inondé: la crue de janvier 1910* (Paris: Editions du Journal des Débats, 1910). Courtesy of W. T. Bandy Collection, Jean and Alexander Heard Library, Vanderbilt University.

FIGURE 2. Frontispiece. Map of the flooded area in January–February 1910.

> SOURCE: Commission des Inondations, *Rapports et documents divers* (Paris: Imprimerie Nationale, 1910).

FIGURE 3. Prologue. The flooded courtyard of the Palais Bourbon, home of the National Assembly.

> SOURCE: Charles Eggimann, ed., *Paris inondé: la crue de janvier 1910* (Paris: Editions du Journal des Débats, 1910). Courtesy of W. T. Bandy Collection, Jean and Alexander Heard Library, Vanderbilt University.

FIGURE 4. Introduction. Parisians measured the height of floods on the bodies of the statues on the Pont de l'Alma, especially that of the Zouave.

> SOURCE: Author's personal collection.

FIGURE 5. Chapter One. Rescue efforts, including boats and ladders, helped Parisians escape the rising water in their homes.

> SOURCE: Author's personal collection.

FIGURE 6. Chapter Two. Parisians established wooden walkways, called *passerelles,* so they could continue to move about the city during the high water.

> SOURCE: Charles Eggimann, ed., *Paris inondé: la crue de janvier 1910* (Paris: Editions du Journal des Débats, 1910). Courtesy of W. T. Bandy Collection, Jean and Alexander Heard Library, Vanderbilt University.

FIGURE 7. Chapter Two. Streets were ripped up, sometimes exposing the foundations of buildings.

> SOURCE: Author's personal collection.

FIGURE 8. Chapter Three. In the Javel neighborhood, an elderly woman, rescued by the police, hangs onto a makeshift raft for dear life.

> SOURCE: Charles Eggimann, ed., *Paris inondé: la crue de janvier 1910* (Paris: Editions du Journal des Débats, 1910). Courtesy of W. T. Bandy Collection, Jean and Alexander Heard Library, Vanderbilt University.

FIGURE 9. Chapter Three. Photographers, like those from the studio of Pierre Petit, captured the strange beauty of a city filled with water.

> SOURCE: Pierre Petit, *Paris inondé, janvier 1910: 32 vues* (Paris: Pierre Petit, 1910). Courtesy of W. T. Bandy Collection, Jean and Alexander Heard Library, Vanderbilt University.

FIGURE 10. Chapter Four. First responders and city workers lined the quay walls with sandbags and stones to hold back the water's force.

> SOURCE: Charles Eggimann, ed., *Paris inondé: la crue de janvier 1910* (Paris: Editions du Journal des Débats, 1910). Courtesy of W. T. Bandy Collection, Jean and Alexander Heard Library, Vanderbilt University.

FIGURE 11. Chapter Four. A little girl is steadied by police as she crosses a narrow walkway to be reunited with her father.

> SOURCE: Author's personal collection.

FIGURE 12. Chapter Five. The interior of the Gare d'Orsay became a favorite for photographers who focused on the light-filled archway inside the central hall. The electrified tracks sat under several feet of water.

> SOURCE: Charles Eggimann, ed., *Paris inondé: la crue de janvier 1910* (Paris: Editions du Journal des Débats, 1910). Courtesy of W. T. Bandy Collection, Jean and Alexander Heard Library, Vanderbilt University.

FIGURE 13. Chapter Six. Shelters run by the Red Cross, the Catholic church, and the government housed thousands of Parisians forced out of their homes by high water.

> SOURCE: André Taride, ed., *Paris et ses environs* (Paris: A. Taride, 1910). Courtesy of W. T. Bandy Collection, Jean and Alexander Heard Library, Vanderbilt University.

FIGURE 14. Chapter Seven. Women begin the arduous process of disinfection in the Rue de la Convention in the 15th *arrondissement*.

> SOURCE: Charles Eggimann, ed., *Paris inondé: la crue de janvier 1910* (Paris: Editions du Journal des Débats, 1910). Courtesy of W. T. Bandy Collection, Jean and Alexander Heard Library, Vanderbilt University.

FIGURE 15. Chapter Seven. Looters threatened lives and property, especially in the hard-hit suburban areas, but some Parisians took matters into their own hands to fight back.

> SOURCE: Author's personal collection.

FIGURE 16. Chapter Eight. Government leaders were very visible during the flood, bringing comfort and assistance to the city's residents. Police prefect Louis Lépine points with his cane to show President Armand Fallières the damage.

> SOURCE: Charles Eggimann, ed., *Paris inondé: la crue de janvier 1910* (Paris: Editions du Journal des Débats, 1910). Courtesy of W. T. Bandy Collection, Jean and Alexander Heard Library, Vanderbilt University.

FIGURE 17. Chapter Nine. The cover of *Le Petit Journal Illustré* offered a stirring allegory blending Marianne, the symbol of France, and Geneviève, the patron saint of Paris, to show both urban and national solidarity in the midst of disaster.

> SOURCE: Author's personal collection.

FIGURE 18. Epilogue. In November 1910 when the river began to rise again, anxious Parisians watched the water level on a newly installed gauge.

> SOURCE: *L'Illustration*, November 19, 1910. Author's personal collection.

Prologue

The flooded courtyard of the Palais Bourbon, home of the National Assembly.

A fierce wind blasted Monsieur Gautry in the face as soon as he stepped outside the Palais Bourbon in the early hours of January 27, 1910. He tucked his jacket collar and scarf up tight around his neck and pulled his cap down to block the chill and the heavy rain. After camping for several days in the basement of his workplace with colleagues, he was heading home to his family through the freezing winter night. At this time of year the Parisian streets were always cold, sometimes snowy. Tonight his journey would take him through a grim landscape never before seen in this city in modern times. After five days of flooding, Paris was under water.

Gautry was a stenographer's assistant in the National Assembly, running errands and carrying messages. The lavish corridors of power—marble walls and columns, high domes, gilded trim work, stunning murals—bustling with politicians, clerks, and bureaucrats were an exciting, sometimes inspiring place to work, even for a servant such as himself. For several days, the building had turned dark and cold, and everyone was on edge. Most of the normal routines had come to a halt, but the deputies continued to debate bills on the floor of the Assembly, and Gautry and a few others remained behind to serve them and their staffs. When the electricity fizzled out shortly after the floodwaters started rising, workers found the old oil lamps in storage and hung them up around the building. Their glow was dim and eerie, and the burning oil gave off acrid fumes. As water engulfed the entire structure, the seat of the French parliament was cut off from the rest of the city. For days, Gautry had watched politicians by the boatful slowly floating through the flooded courtyard or carefully crossing wooden walkways. Now, shortly before 5 AM, Gautry himself glided across the water, reaching dry land a few blocks away.

Receding behind him in the predawn darkness, even the imposing neoclassical façade of the Palais Bourbon, with its tall Corinthian columns, vanished into the gloom. Clouds covered the moon, and few streetlights remained in service, especially in this area adjacent to the Seine. Gautry had to feel his way along carefully, hesitating before each step to make sure his numb feet had found solid ground. Cobblestones dislodged from the road surface were scattered everywhere, along with other debris. Noxious smells filled the air, including rotting food and human waste from overflowing sewers and cesspools. His splashing steps echoed through silent, empty streets.

A mile-and-a-half journey through the lashing rain and standing water drenched Gautry's clothes. As he approached his building in the Passage Landrieu, near the Pont de l'Alma, just yards from the Seine, he could see just how much the water had risen since he'd left home a few days earlier. It was knee-deep in the hallway, and he struggled through a muddy pool to reach his apartment door. With his hand on the knob, Gautry heard the screams and sobs of his frightened children. No one was asleep.

When he pushed the door open, Gautry's panicked and sobbing wife shouted to him for help. Pieces of furniture floated around the room in more than two feet of water. Most of their possessions, bought with a lifetime of hard work and sacrifice, were ruined.

After stripping off his sopping wet clothes so that they would not weigh him down, Gautry waded toward his small, crying son. Lifting the boy onto his shoulders, Gautry dashed—practically naked—from the building. He set his son down in a safe place, but could not pause to stroke the child's hair and comfort him. He hurried back into the building, and this time grabbed his daughter. Freezing water splashed against his bare skin as he carried the girl to safety and set her down in the darkness next to her brother. On the third trip he picked up his wife and brought her to join their children. Nearly exhausted, Gautry returned to the apartment one more time to salvage some dry clothes. Anxious and shaken, Gautry's family was soaked to the bone and freezing cold. They were safe but suddenly homeless.

Gautry eventually found a room in a hotel on Rue Laborde, where the ground was slightly higher and the flooding less severe. It was clear across the city, but at least it was dry. Gautry rubbed his frozen skin with alcohol to try and bring a little life back into muscles tired from the sudden strain. From the window, he could watch other Parisians, also forced to abandon their homes, heading to emergency shelters and churches or to stay with friends and family.

Gautry and his family had survived their ordeal, but it wasn't yet clear whether his city would be so fortunate. Paris was the most modern city in the world, for decades the envy of visitors who marveled at its spectacular beauty. During these desperate days, the City of Light had never looked so dark.[1]

Introduction

Parisians measured the height of floods on the bodies of the statues on the Pont de l'Alma, especially that of the Zouave.

*F*loods have been a regular part of life in the Seine basin for centuries. Despite every attempt to use the land for human purposes, the water always tries to reclaim it.

In the ancient past, the Seine spread throughout the entire bowl-shaped valley that now forms the Paris region, and at one time, it split into two arms. To the south, the slightly wider branch roughly followed the river's present-day path. To the north, an arc of water swept across what is now the Right Bank, through Bastille, Ménilmontant, parts of Belleville, and lower Montmartre. It reached all the way to the present-day locations of Chaillot and L'Alma, just across the river from the Eiffel Tower. When these two branches flooded, the whole basin filled to become a lake several miles wide. Little by little, the northern arm of the Seine dried up, and by 30,000 BCE, it had vanished completely, leaving more or less the Seine we know today. Large parts of the Right Bank remained wetlands for some time. The neighborhood called the Marais—which means "the swamp"—was once a marsh adjacent to the river. It is no wonder that when the Romans first invaded the area inhabited by the Parisii tribe in the first century BCE, they chose to construct their city on the less soggy Left Bank. No wonder either that they named the city Lutetia, likely derived from *lutum,* the Latin word for mud.

The Seine's water has sustained human life in this region since the first settlement, around 5000 BCE. Some of the oldest artifacts ever discovered in Paris are dugout canoes found near what is now the Bercy neighborhood, just past the eastern point where the Seine enters the present-day city limits. Over the centuries, as the primary conduit for goods and people throughout the entire region, the Seine turned Paris into a bustling commercial center. It supplied the city's residents with food, water, military defense, industry, shipping, tourism, and art. The story of Paris is inseparable from the story of the river that forms its most basic reference point, dividing the city into Right Bank and Left Bank.[1]

The relationship between Paris and its river, however, has always been precarious. For all the life the Seine has nurtured, it has also brought destruction and death in the form of periodic floods. Bishop and historian Grégoire de Tours recorded a massive inundation by the Seine in 582 CE, spreading over hundreds of acres and even temporarily reactivating the ancient northern arm of the river that had long since dried up. In 814, in a book about miracles in the city, an anonymous author wrote that when "God wants to punish the people of Paris by water, he sends such a flood and overflows the river Seine like we've never seen so that the entire town is flooded and one can only move about by boat."[2] In 886, a flood tore apart the Petit-Pont, which crossed the river between the Ile de la Cité in the center of Paris and the Left Bank. "All of a sudden," described one eyewitness, "during the silent night the middle of the bridge collapsed, swept away by the wrath of furious waves that swell and overflow." Between 886 and 1185, the Petit-Pont was destroyed ten times by high water, and, as a testament to Parisian stubbornness, each time it was rebuilt.

For centuries, Parisians could do very little except appeal to a higher power. In 1206, when nearly half the city flooded, the people cried out for church leaders to invoke the heavenly help of Geneviève, the patron saint of Paris. The bishop, Eudes de Sully, removed Geneviève's relics from the abbey church at the top of the Left Bank hill, which is today the site of the Panthéon, and led a somber procession of Parisians down the incline. Sainte Geneviève, long revered for having rallied Paris against an invasion of Attila the Hun in 451, now came to the city's aid in spirit. According to the official history, following the mass chanted at Notre-Dame with her relics present, the waters miraculously began to recede. Leaving the city's cathedral to escort Geneviève's remains back to the abbey, the large procession traversed the Petit-Pont. After the pilgrims had crossed over the water, just as the bishop replaced the reliquary on the altar, the Petit-Pont collapsed. No one was injured—the second miracle of the day.[3]

*O*ver hundreds of years, Parisians molded the course of the Seine in large part to help limit these floods. In the early fourteenth century,

King Philippe le Bel ordered the *prévôt des marchands*—the powerful city leader in charge of trade and shipping and elected from among the merchants—to raise the quay walls using cut stone and fortified towers, allowing him to cross the river without becoming stuck in the mud along the Seine's banks. Two centuries later, François I constructed additional quays, including those in front of the Louvre. Other expansions followed. Still the river flooded, and in 1658 reached its highest level ever recorded at just over twenty feet above normal.

The residents of Paris continued to manage the Seine to serve their purposes and save their lives. They dredged the river, built landings and ports, and created locks and canals, all to make it more usable and less dangerous year round, especially in winter when the water tended to rise. In the early eighteenth century, the Quai d'Orsay on the Left Bank was reconstructed and enlarged. The Canal de l'Ourcq was finished in 1823, and the Canal Saint-Martin opened in 1825, followed by a series of other waterways that allowed boats and water to bypass the city center altogether. The city's many bridges obstructed water flow during floods when they caught debris on their pylons, so some of these old structures were eventually destroyed, and new bridges were built with much larger arch openings. The river's tributaries—the Oise and the Yonne, as well as the Marne, which joins the Seine just outside the eastern city limit of Paris—were also channeled and dammed.

None of these solutions could stop the Seine's regular pattern of winter flooding with occasional high water at other times of the year. By and large, though, the floods that occurred by the second half of the nineteenth century were noticeably smaller than before. The centuries-old efforts to control the river meant that the water no longer reached the heights earlier generations had seen. By the turn of the twentieth century, most people believed that a catastrophic flood was highly unlikely and that the river had finally been tamed by human hands.

Some of the most important efforts to regulate the city and its river came under the leadership of Georges-Eugène Haussmann, a man whose faith in the power of engineering transformed Paris into a modern city in the 1850s and 1860s. Born in Paris to an Alsatian family steeped in business and politics, Haussmann worked his way up through the ranks of the civil service in the provinces and in Paris. Then, in 1853, the new emperor, Napoléon III, tapped Haussmann to become prefect of the Seine, the most powerful Parisian official in charge of the city and its suburbs. Given broader authority than earlier occupants of the post, including the title of baron and the office of senator, Haussmann was charged with rebuilding much of the urban space and making it the envy of cities everywhere. Paris would never be the same.

Much of today's Paris dates from his era. Haussmann's Paris comprised the new parks around the city; the new jewel-like opera house designed by architect Charles Garnier, with its exquisite façade beneath a copper dome and gilded statues; the mansard roofs and Beaux Arts decorations of chic apartment buildings along newly widened boulevards; and dozens of new plazas and squares. The city had been transformed, and there was also more of it than ever before. Haussmann had doubled the size of Paris by incorporating outlying suburban towns to form nine new *arrondissements* (wards or neighborhoods), bringing the number of these urban administrative districts to twenty.

Most people visiting Paris in the last few decades of the nineteenth century marveled at the spectacle that it had become. Wealthy Americans, who crossed the Atlantic to continue their education, have adventures, or go shopping, were particularly taken with the elegant new urban landscape. The luxurious department stores, which Émile Zola made famous in his novel *The Ladies' Paradise,* were cathedrals of commerce on Haussmann's new boulevards, with their high-domed ceilings, brightly lit interiors, and large picture windows displaying a seemingly endless supply of goods. In the 1860s, at the height of the renovations, one American sightseer—who knew nothing of Haussmann and gave the credit to the emperor—wrote in his diary: "The city is improved as no other ever was and perhaps could be by any other than the present Napoléon and he will thus, whatever his fate, leave the grandest monument to his genius and power the world has seen or ever will see."[4]

Napoléon III was only too happy to bask in the glow of *La Ville Lu-mière,* the City of Light. In 1867, even before the renovations were finished, he opened Paris to the world for an *Exposition Universelle,* or World's Fair, to show how modern and wealthy the city had become.

Supremely confident in his vision for reshaping the city, Haussmann applied an immense energy and the full powers of his office to the task. An early 1860s portrait by well-known photographer Pierre Petit shows a self-assured, relaxed Haussmann sitting in a velvet-covered chair with his legs comfortably crossed. In the buttonhole of his sober black coat, he prominently displays the rosette of the Legion of Honor. Rather than looking at the camera, he stares down at a piece of paper as if reading. Haussmann seems to want the viewer to believe that the photographer and his audience are not nearly as important as his own work.

Above all, Haussmann was determined to bring order to Paris. His aim was to make the city cleaner, brighter, healthier, safer, better for business and trade—in other words, more modern. Before Haussmann, Paris had been a lively place, but it was also smelly, dirty, and bloody. The waste left behind by the thousands of horses carrying people and goods through the streets was only part of the filth that people considered a normal part of urban life. Add to that the garbage, the cesspools, the rainwater from cemeteries leaching into the soil and producing sickening smells, the animals being butchered for sale in markets, and the food rotting from lack of refrigeration—not to mention fleas, rats, and stray dogs—and one can begin to imagine the challenges that Haussmann faced.

Modernizing the city entailed what many have called "creative destruction," the ongoing process of urban change in which demolishing the old opens up new possibilities for economic growth. For many, the costs of such dramatic change outweighed any potential benefits. Although he left in place more elements of the old city than is popularly imagined, the Paris that emerged after Haussmann had a very different look and feel. Parisians vigorously debated whether Haussmann's alterations were actually improvements, and many residents lamented the elimination of nooks and crannies in the irregular urban space that gave the city its special character. The extremely messy process of demolition, building, and renovation, which often left gaping holes throughout the city and scattered dirt and dust everywhere, lasted for years on end, further upsetting critics who watched entire swaths of Paris be destroyed before their eyes. The wholesale appropriations of property to make way for grand developments also angered many landowners. Finally Napoléon III, concerned that the entire project was undermining his own popularity, dismissed Haussmann in January 1870.

By altering the places where people lived and worked, Haussmann also unleashed a whole series of social changes at least as significant as the physical ones. As older, established neighborhoods were shattered to make way for new roads, upscale buildings with the latest amenities, or fancy department stores, working-class people were often priced or pushed out of the city center. With nowhere else to go, many relocated to the edges of Paris, either to the outer ring of *arrondissements,* especially to the northeast, or to the suburban towns just outside the city.

In the last decades of the nineteenth century, as Parisian industry expanded dramatically, the suburbs became the place where factories, making everything from chemicals and rubber to automobiles and glue, located in search of affordable land. Workers had already begun to move there to find jobs, a trend amplified by Haussmann's renovations along with steady immigration from the provinces. By 1900, the suburbs (*les banlieues*) accounted for 26 percent of the population in the greater Paris region, and that percentage was rising.

These towns created much of the wealth that made life in the modern city possible, but they didn't always benefit from the urban infrastructure that Parisians enjoyed. Suburbanites who still worked in the city faced long commutes, and the new subway system, which did not link up to other rail lines, provided no help. Although some of these areas around Paris were prospering in their own right by the turn of the century, many still lacked modern amenities such as running water, sewage, and electricity. No wonder that many suburban areas would start to be known as the Red Belt, as the growing strength of a militant, organized labor movement gave a voice to the working classes there, and as the Socialist and Communist parties gained most of the votes.[5]

The growing middle class and the working class lived much farther apart than they ever had before. For the bourgeoisie, physical distance from poorer areas was a visible sign of success that also made them feel safer and often enabled them to ignore persistent urban poverty. For the less affluent, life had often changed for the worse, creating a sense of anxiety and resentment beneath the surface of the beautiful city that Haussmann had created.

The baron's renovations were most visible above ground in the streets and buildings. But just as important was what Haussmann did below ground, renovating the city's plumbing. Water had always been the key to the city's life, but the mid-nineteenth-century Seine was thoroughly contaminated with runoff from streets and cesspools. Even if filtered, it was not good enough for the model city Haussmann was fashioning. In addition, the pipes running throughout Paris had proven insufficient to supply the growing metropolis.

Haussmann called on Eugène Belgrand, his chief of water services, to provide the city with plenty of fresh water. Belgrand engineered aqueducts to connect the city with a series of springs in the surrounding region. Within a few years, Parisians drank water that was cleaner than at any time in the past. Haussmann had doubled the city's population, but by the time he left office in 1870, the amount of water at every resident's disposal had also doubled.

Once they had supplied more fresh water to the city, Haussmann and Belgrand had to envisage how to get it out again as waste. The city already had an extensive system of drains and sewer pipes, but these became vastly inadequate for the growing metropolis with its expanded water supply. In the 1850s, fewer than 100 miles of sewers ran below the 260 miles of streets, and heavy precipitation rendered these nearly useless, in large part because they were simply too small. These early sewers were built so that a man could climb in and clean them, but rarely any larger. Near the river, the collectors that gathered waste from several tunnels and redirected its flow through the underground system were susceptible to the Seine's regular winter flooding. Belgrand engineered larger tunnels fitted out with rails so that mechanical cars, filled with cleaning crews, could pass through.

Before Haussmann's renovations, much of the city's human waste—sometimes referred to as night soil—still had to be removed manually from buildings and collected in cesspools. Some of this filth continued to be buried illegally in gardens or courtyards because the cost of hiring men to cart it away at night was more than many landlords could afford. All the new sewers were capable of handling some wastewater from buildings, as well as the massive amounts of storm water that ran off from the street. In 1894 the city began requiring all household water, including human waste, to go into the tunnels below ground. *Tout à l'égout,* the government proclaimed (everything into the sewer). By 1903, for the first time, the number of homes connected to the sewers exceeded those still using cesspools. All the refuse was then redirected west, to be deposited into the waters of the Seine downriver from Paris.

The emphasis on supplying clean drinking water and removing waste was based in part on the constant threat of disease. Like much of Europe, Paris periodically suffered through massive cholera outbreaks. Over eighteen thousand people had died in 1832, and more than sixteen thousand perished in 1849. These memories were fresh in Haussmann's mind when he came to office. Although illness killed fewer people over the years, death by cholera, typhoid, and other infectious diseases was a common fact of life in most nineteenth-century cities.

For hundreds of years, people believed that foul air, stench, and vapors—all labeled miasmas—made them sick. Theories of disease were slowly beginning to change in the second half of the nineteenth century as some physicians challenged the idea that illness came from odors and instead began embracing "germ theory." The belief that microorganisms lay at the root of sickness was made famous in the 1860s and 1870s by the French chemist Louis Pasteur's creation of a vaccine for anthrax and the introduction of pasteurization to kill disease-causing microbes. When the Seine flooded in 1876, however, Haussmann had hung posters throughout the city instructing Parisians how to clean their houses, posters that primarily recommended burning a large fire in the doorway with all access points to the house open in order to "clean the air."[6]

Haussmann's and Belgrand's interest in the sewers was at least partly an effort to circulate more water through the city in an effort to make it cleaner and safer. Using a common mid-nineteenth-century analogy for the city, Haussmann himself described it this way: "The underground galleries, organs of the large city, would function like those of the human body, without revealing themselves to the light of day. Pure and fresh water, light, and heat would circulate there like the diverse fluids whose movement and maintenance support life."[7] The city was an organism that needed a constant flow of refreshment and a reliable way to remove its waste and promote health. Haussmann left office before the renovation of the sewers was completed, but by that time he had quadrupled the number of miles of sewer lines below the city streets and rebuilt old lines to be larger and more effective.

By the turn of the century, residents knew that if the Seine ever rose too high, the sewers would carry it away. They also trusted the men of the Hydrometric Service to sound the alarm. Under Haussmann's orders, Eugène Belgrand had created the service in 1854 to measure the river's level and study its patterns. Until his death in 1878, Belgrand ran the agency himself, directing his engineers to analyze the water depth, rainfall, and meteorological conditions every day with great precision. Doing so enabled Belgrand to refine his growing understanding of the river and its movements, and he used these and other data to write several influential books about the Seine that remained crucial for shaping Paris's riverfront development even after his death.

The agency Belgrand crafted could forecast high water in the Seine river basin with a great deal of accuracy. Information collected during previous floods allowed them to build mathematical prediction models. However, even with these sophisticated formulas, engineers could give Paris no more than approximately twenty-four hours advance notice of a flood. For these scientific calculations to be truly useful, even under normal conditions, these engineers needed an intuitive sense of what the river might do, a knowledge based on personal experience.

Haussmann had unleashed the forces of urban change and development, and the next generation of builders would continue the process that he and Eugène Belgrand had begun. By sometimes ignoring their predecessors' wisdom, however, later engineers inadvertently increased the risk of disaster. Belgrand had carefully studied the Seine for years and wrote extensively about its history and its patterns. He understood the power of its waters. Knowing the river's tendency toward flooding, Belgrand proposed raising the level of the quay walls on the eastern side of the city where the Seine enters Paris, and downriver where it exits, to accommodate the seasonal high water and prevent it from overflowing the walls as it had in years past. Engineers did raise the quay walls, but never to the height Belgrand had recommended. Doing so would have obstructed views of the river and of the beautiful buildings that lined the banks. In the end, aesthetics triumphed over engineering, and Paris was left vulnerable.

Though the Seine remained crucial to the city's functioning, it began to fade from many people's imaginations, overwhelmed by the human creations that rose above it. In the 1830s and 1840s, guidebooks and novelists still dwelled on lavish descriptions of the river as central to the Parisian experience. But by the 1870s and 1880s, although the Seine was still important for trade and transportation, more modern developments like the railroad eclipsed it. When depicting urban life, artists showed broad avenues and new bridges rather than the ancient waters of the river. When late nineteenth-century painters did create water scenes, they tended to travel to the coasts, as Claude Monet did for *Impression, Sunrise* (1872), or to the recreational islands and towns outside Paris. Georges Seurat went to a popular site downriver from the city for his *Sunday Afternoon on the Island of La Grande Jatte* (1884–86). Pierre-Auguste Renoir journeyed a short distance out of Paris to the town of Chatou to paint his *Luncheon of the Boating Party* (1880–81). The river, especially beyond the city's borders, was still an important site of leisure and pleasure, but it was no longer the most fascinating feature of the urban core, in part because it was thought to have been tamed.[8]

Haussmann left office shortly before the outbreak of the Franco–Prussian War of 1870–71, the short but humiliating conflict born out of the breakdown of the great balance of power in Europe. When correspondence showing supposed insults between the Prussian king and the French ambassador became public, angry citizens of both countries cried out for revenge. France declared war on Prussia in July 1870, but soon the other German-speaking states rallied to the Prussian side, and thousands of men went off to fight. The French suffered swift defeats at the hands of invading armies from the east, including the capture of Emperor Napoléon III and the collapse of his government. The Prussian army laid siege to Paris at the height of the conflict for almost four months, nearly starving the unyielding capital into submission until the belligerents reached an armistice. Once the peace treaty was signed with the newly created German empire, France was forced to give up the Alsace-Lorraine territories in the east.

The Franco–Prussian War and its aftermath changed the relationship between Parisians and their government. Many residents felt abandoned by the defeated Napoléon III and the French army, which had failed to rescue Paris from the Prussians sitting just outside the city. After the hostilities with the invaders ended, radicals—especially in the northeast districts of the city where workers had settled after being displaced by Haussmann's developments and had suffered from the growing gap between rich and poor—seized the opportunity to declare Paris an independent city-state in 1871. Joined by increasing numbers of residents as well as some local army units, they created what was known as the Paris Commune. At the same time, a new national government, the Third Republic, had formed in the wake of Napoléon III's capture, and the capital's secession provided this young democracy with its first crisis. Under the direction of Republican leaders, the army retook the city, street by street, executing the rebels throughout Paris in a brutal show of force that came to be remembered as "the bloody week." The Communards who were not killed were exiled to New Caledonia in the South Pacific. The grave political and cultural divisions created during those years would last for decades.

In the wake of the Franco–Prussian War and the repression of the Commune, the new government worked hard to establish its legitimacy. By 1870, at the birth of the Third Republic, proponents of several political traditions each claimed to be France's legitimate government. The monarchists, supported by much of the Catholic Church, harkened back to the Bourbon family's rule that had ended with Louis XVI's beheading in 1793. The Bourbons had been restored in 1815 but were overthrown in 1830 by another branch of the royal family, the Orléanists, who also laid their claim to power. The Bonapartists, including both those loyal to the memory of Napoléon I and the more recent devotees of his nephew Napoléon III, represented another powerful faction.

The Republicans, who paid homage to the First Republic of 1792 and the Second Republic of 1848, grew in strength. There were also socialists, anarchists, and other radicals, many of whom drew inspiration from the ideals of popular government that had driven the abortive Paris Commune and called the more centrist Republic into question. At the same time, Catholics were furious over the state's growing desire to curb the church's influence in everyday society that would later culminate in the legal separation of church and state in 1905. New groups on the far right, preaching French superiority in a growing struggle between nations and races, preferred rioting and violence to voting and dialogue and were changing the tenor of French politics. Anti-Semitic politicians stoked fears about foreign conspiracies undermining French culture. Small shopkeepers, fed up with the government's failures to meet their needs and angry over the economic slump of the 1880s, abandoned the Republic for the radical right.

Challenges to the Third Republic had even come from within, including from its former army commander and first president, the monarchist sympathizer Marshal Patrice de MacMahon, as well as the

populist rabble rousing General Georges Boulanger, both of whom provoked political crises by challenging the legitimacy of the government.
Growing social conflict caused by industrial and economic change,
along with numerous competing parties and ever-shifting coalitions,
only added to an extremely complicated and volatile political landscape.

Frustrated with the divisiveness of politics, many Parisians found
less and less meaning in the Republic's principles, derived from the
French Revolutionary motto *"Liberté, égalité, fraternité"* ("liberty,
equality, fraternity"). Adding to their disillusionment was the fact that,
in the aftermath of the Commune, Paris had lost the right to participate fully in its own self-government. National troops occupied the city
until 1876, essentially ruling Paris by martial law and enforcing strict
curfews and censorship. The government simply did not trust Paris to
run its own affairs, using instead the bureaucracy and the military to
keep the city in check. The prefect of the Seine had long been appointed by the national government, and after 1871, so were the local
officials who administered the day-to-day operations of the municipal
government throughout the city's twenty *arrondissements*—they answered to the prefect, not to the people. Although the Parisian population elected a City Council that retained an important voice in local
politics, the prefect of the Seine was really the one in charge. (Parisians
themselves would not again elect a mayor until 1977.)

Just as Napoléon III had done in 1867, officials of the Third Republic
used a world's fair to bolster their legitimacy by showing how wonderful life could be under democratic leadership. In 1889 the government
hosted a fair to commemorate the centennial of the French Revolution
and erected the Eiffel Tower to rise high above the city as a celebration
of the power and beauty of modern engineering.

At the dawn of the new century, the Third Republic once again invited the world to its capital city to wonder at progress and innovation.
From April to November 1900, through the warm spring and summer
months and into the cool of autumn, more than fifty million people ar-

rived in the French capital to experience another *Exposition Universelle*. With dozens of exhibition halls, the fair stretched along both banks of the Seine, right through the heart of the city. Spread out on the river's Left Bank, the main grounds covered hundreds of acres, from the Esplanade des Invalides, in the shadow of Napoléon's final resting place under the majestic gold dome of the Hôtel des Invalides, all the way to the Champs-de-Mars, with the Eiffel Tower rising overhead.

Visitors to the fair in 1900 entered a glittering vision of the future, its displays proof of humanity's power to refashion the world. As they arrived at the entrance near the Place de la Concorde, they saw a monumental gate flanked by two towers and French flags waving in the breeze. An immensely ornate cupola and a statue representing Progress topped three enormous and intricately constructed arches painted a patriotic blue, white, and red. This was the gateway to another world. Flushed with excitement, throngs of eager tourists—men, women, and children from across the globe—moved through thiry-six ticket booths designed to admit sixty thousand people per hour. After exiting, they crossed the Pont de la Concorde, the Seine flowing silently beneath their feet, and arrived at the main fairgrounds on the Left Bank.

What they found there left many visitors awestruck and probably unsure where to go first. Stunning new buildings had been built just for the exposition, including to the east a fully electrified train station, the soaring Beaux Arts style Gare d'Orsay. The Pont Alexandre III, one of the fair's most visible symbols of human advancement and technological prowess, was the first bridge in Paris to span the Seine in a single tremendous arch, a blend of engineering and artistry on a monumental scale. The luxuriously decorated white bridge with gilded ornamentation allowed Parisians to keep the Seine safely underfoot as they crossed between the major exposition sites. The halls under the arching glass and steel Art Nouveau dome of the Grand Palais—another spectacular building created along with the Petit Palais specifically for the exposition—were packed with art from France and around the world. Near the fairgrounds, throngs of tourists stood shoulder-to-shoulder at the Louvre to see such masterpieces as Leonardo's mysterious *Mona Lisa* or the dramatic ancient Greek sculpture *Winged Victory of Samothrace,* which had been discovered not quite forty years earlier and was a striking recent addition to the collection.

The sensation of grandness and excess was precisely what Alfred Picard, the commissioner general of the committee that planned the exposition, wanted visitors to experience at the fair. Picard and his team began planning the fair in 1893 with millions of francs at their disposal. He had written the definitive report on the 1889 Exposition, so he was already quite aware of the administrative issues that he would face in preparation for 1900. Born in Strasbourg in 1844, Picard was an engineer by training, a graduate of the prestigious Ecole des Ponts et Chaussées, and one of a generation of mid-nineteenth-century men, including Gustave Eiffel, who believed unwaveringly in the power of technology to manage the world. Picard built railroads and canals throughout France in the 1870s and 1880s. His training and practical experience showed him how water flowed and how it might be controlled, and he spent a good portion of his early career trying to accomplish that.

Inside the Gallery of Machines and the Palace of Electricity, visitors saw thousands of new inventions and products, including novel types of furniture, fabrics, and consumer goods, the latest innovations in metallurgy, agriculture, optics, and building technology. Millions saw their very first automobile there. Fairgoers could enter one of the pavilions installed by over forty countries along what was dubbed Rue des Nations. Or they could view the Celestial Globe, an enormous sphere some 145 feet in diameter resting on four stone pillars. When lit up at night from within, the orb shone throughout the fairgrounds. Later they might climb on board the huge Ferris wheel, which on each revolution showed hundreds of people the sights from a height of nearly 350 feet. Many attended the events at the second Olympic Games, also held in Paris from May through October of 1900.

One American journalist, writing for the *Philadelphia Inquirer,* could not contain himself when he described the scene for his readers back home: "Recall to your mind's eye all the most dazzling stage transformation scenes you can, and spread them out before your imaginative gaze and the result would be as the dying embers of a cigarette in comparison with the scene that blazes [at the Exposition]. . . . It is as if a city of palaces devoted to the manufacture of planets, ordinary stars, starlets and comets, all studded with precious stones, was working on double time in conjunction with a special plant for the production of rainbows."[9]

Day and night, visitors were dazzled as colorful electric lights lit up the grounds, creating a scene of pure fantasy come to life. Everywhere they looked, they saw the wonders of electricity on display since it was one of the major themes of the exposition, and many of the exhibits used it to full effect. In the evening, huge crowds gathered to watch and cheer the spectacle of thousands of red, blue, yellow, and white lights switching on simultaneously at the Palace of Electricity. The fountains outside the building turned pink and blue with special illuminations, transforming ordinary water into an astonishing liquid light show. Thousands of bulbs twinkled along the façade of the Trocadéro Palace, across the river from the Eiffel Tower, and dozens of other buildings. An electric-powered tour boat hummed along the Seine, where passengers might look out across the water sprinkled with reflections of the exposition's lights dancing on the surface of the river's nighttime blackness.

The electric-powered moving sidewalk soon became the talk of the fair. Although intended to be purely functional, carrying people along the edge of the fairgrounds, the sidewalk developed into a popular attraction in its own right. Fairgoers were thrilled by the sheer amusement of the *trottoir roulant*. Some stood and enjoyed the smooth ride in silence, holding onto the railings and gazing out across the Seine that flowed just alongside the walkway. Others, especially the boys and girls, jumped on and off, playing with this new experiment in motion. In October, one woman supposedly gave birth on the moving sidewalk and named the baby boy Trottoir Roulant Benost.[10]

To get from place to place throughout Paris, fairgoers could also sample another new transportation option since the city had just inaugurated the Métropolitain, the electric subway—only the fourth such underground train system in the world. The Métro was an immediate hit with fairgoers and Parisians alike. The journalist from the *Philadelphia Inquirer* complained that he simply gave up trying to take a ride, "owing to the crowd waiting for trains so great that it extended up from the subterranean platforms to the street entrances."[11] Eight of the eighteen Métro stations opened in the middle of the exposition on July 19, 1900, with the remaining ten completed later in the summer. When visitors boarded the train running from Porte de Vincennes to Porte Maillot (what is now called Line 1), they whizzed underneath the heart of the historic city just parallel to the Seine, down the Champs-Elysées, to the Place de la Concorde, the Tuileries, the Louvre, to the Marais, and beyond. In 1900, about 15 million people rode the Métro. By 1909, more than 300 million did so. Moving through the city was far faster and easier than ever before, a sure sign of further progress to come.

Opening the *Exposition Universelle,* Minister of Commerce Alexandre Millerand proclaimed: "The machine has taken over control of the entire world. It is replacing workers, employing them in its service and expanding the relations between the peoples of the earth. Even death itself has retreated before the victorious advance of the human mind." Millerand expressed the widely shared belief that the range of human endeavors on display at the event could transform the world. Part of that hope for a better future was the feeling of international cooperation that the fair also represented. "The more the international relations resulting from the diversity of human needs and the ease of exchange become intertwined," Millerand told the crowd at the opening ceremony, striking a note familiar to progressive reformers on both sides of the Atlantic, "the more reason we have to hope and trust that the day will come when the world realizes that peace and the honorable struggles of human labor reap greater benefits than rivalry."[12] French President Emile Loubet put it another way in his opening speech, celebrating "peace and progress."[13] In the world of the future, scientific innovation and prosperity would even eliminate the threat of war.

For those who wanted to preserve the vision of the future that the fair offered, visitors could purchase any of the hundreds of postcards sold throughout Paris. During the months of the fair, photographers with lightweight, portable cameras toured the city, snapping shots of the exhibition's wondrous offerings and the crowds that came to visit, as well as documenting many of the city's most beautiful vistas, monuments, and architecture. Some postcards depicted ordinary scenes of life on the streets of Paris as people strolled the boulevards or went to the market. All of the postcards of the fair showed the city at its best, as a glittering, modern metropolis built by Parisian hands, ready to enter the new century. The images depicted a future firmly under human control. However, for all the new technology and modern science on display at the *Exposition Universelle* or in the photos, two momentous forces remained beyond the power of human invention: the weather and the Seine.

Despite the attractions at the fair, the city's most beautiful and historic vista remained the river, flowing right through the fairgrounds and offering a quiet respite from the crowds and noise of the pavilions. In contrast to the futuristic utopian vision on display at the fair, the Seine's ancient presence spoke of a deep history rooted in the land. The water was usually more than 30 feet below the street-level quays. A series of stairwells and ramps led down to broad stone embankments, which in most places bounded the river on either side. Many were wide enough for trucks to load equipment onto the numerous boats that tied up, one after the other, parallel to the bank. They also provided a beautiful spot for picnicking, promenading, or just watching the water. Seen from the level of the river, the city far above appeared to be only rooftops and sky, as the busyness of the crowded streets vanished behind the tops of the high walls. From the embankments, the Seine was close enough to touch. The straight, regular lines of the hewn stone walls offered a clear boundary between the human-built dominion of the city and the natural force of the river—and an illusion of protection.

Part One

WATER RISING

Chapter One

the SURPRISING RISE
of the SEINE

76. PARIS — Inondations de janvier 1910 — Quai des Grands-Augustins   C. M.

Rescue efforts, including boats and ladders, helped Parisians escape the rising water in their homes.

The first day of 1910 was unusually sunny and warm. Paris was generally cold and rainy at this time of year, so the mild weather was an especially welcome change. Parisians, along with hundreds of visitors from the suburbs and provinces, had stayed out late the night before, filling the brightly lit boulevards and warm cafés as they celebrated the new year. As the temperature reached 43°, people in the streets wished one another a happy 1910.[1]

Elsewhere in France that day the scene was not as bright. A few hundred miles to the west of Paris, the sea was churning off the coast of a windy and rainy Brittany. A low-pressure system began to move eastward across the English Channel toward Paris, adding more rain to the soil of northern France and the Low Countries, already saturated from several weeks of unusually high amounts of winter rainfall. In villages along the coast, wind began to rattle people's windows and doors.

By the second week of the new year, water from rising rivers began overflowing the banks of the Seine and its tributaries, washing through the small towns and villages upriver to the east and south of Paris. The water's full destructive force was unleashed on Friday, January 21, in the small mining town of Lorroy, 50 miles southeast of Paris on the Loing River. New rains engorged the Loing, one of the many waterways that feed into the Seine, causing it to run faster and stronger than most people could remember. The mines that undercut the region's rocky terrain had already destabilized the earth, and now the surging water weakened it further.

The men of Lorroy made their living digging coal from the hill just outside the town. Workers then loaded the coal into boats that floated down a man-made canal to the Loing River, eventually reaching Paris and beyond. Canals like this one were important to the economy because they allowed for the quick and easy transport of this valuable commodity. Under the rainy conditions, however, the canal had filled to overflowing and, according to press accounts, was adding more and more water to the drenched town and the land around it.

Each day these miners, black with coal dust, went home around one o'clock to join their families for lunch. On January 21, they trudged through wet and muddy streets, rain pelting them the entire way. While they were eating, without warning, the village began to shake violently. Plates and cups rattled on tables, and furniture slid across rooms. Screaming with fear, children scrambled to hide beneath the tables.

A huge mass of saturated soil on the hillside was dislodged by the strong pull of water and gravity, and it roared down the slope, bending over the trees in its path. No one had time to react as the avalanche tore downhill, crashing into several village homes with families still inside. Smashed by the force of mud and rock, wood and glass went flying, and doors were blown off their hinges.

When the terrifying landslide was over, the residents of Lorroy whose homes had been spared ran outside to inspect the damage. They gazed at their neighbors' ruined and half-buried houses, unsure whether the people trapped inside were alive or dead. The hillside above, previously covered with plants and trees, was a muddy gash in the landscape.

Local police and firefighters raced to the scene to join the victims' friends and families in the search for survivors. Hundreds of bystanders sobbed as rescuers shouted orders to one another about where to dig. They furiously scraped away the mud with picks, shovels, and bare hands, stopping only to listen for cries for help. Soldiers stationed at a nearby army base heard reports of what had happened, grabbed their equipment, and rushed to join the rescue efforts. Everyone labored throughout the rest of the cold, rainy day, refusing to rest until they recovered as many townspeople as they could. At nightfall, the rescuers lit bonfires and torches and pointed the headlights of cars at the mountain of rubble and soil so that the work of digging out the dead and wounded could continue.

In the middle of the night of January 21, while the people of Lorroy were still digging in the rubble by firelight, the residents of Troyes, an ancient Roman-era village located some 100 miles upriver from Paris on the Seine, heard the river's churning waters roll over its banks and pour through the streets. The rushing water and cries of danger wakened most people from their sleep. Many leaped from their beds, half-dressed, and fled through the black night for higher ground. They stood by, powerless, as the Seine washed away their homes. When dawn came, the people of Troyes gathered around what remained of their town and stared in disbelief. The force of the water had ripped away the walls and roofs of many homes and shops, leaving some buildings barely standing.

Back in Lorroy, as daylight returned on January 22, residents could see that the landslide had reduced these modest miners' homes to little more than ramshackle piles of timber. The people of Lorroy foraged through what remained of their belongings, scraping the mud off anything they found intact. The powerful force and weight of the avalanche had crushed seven people to death and wounded many more. The winter weather and raging floodwaters of 1910 had claimed their first victims from among some of France's most vulnerable citizens.

As the frantic digging and rescue efforts continued throughout the following day, men from the Paris newspapers arrived, asking questions and jotting down descriptions of the scene. Photographers carrying box cameras moved through the rubble, finding good spots to unfold their tripods and set up their equipment. Their shutters clicked hundreds of times, capturing the nightmarish landscape. The photographs they took could not show the extent of the destruction and suffering, but they would at least carry a fragment of the shocking story back for Parisians to see. The caption under one group of photographs that appeared in the popular weekly magazine *L'Illustration* said it all: "The total annihilation of the hamlet of Lorroy in Seine-et-Marne."[2]

Meanwhile, downriver in the capital, Parisians had been going about their daily business, largely unconcerned by reports of flooding in the towns and villages upriver. On Friday, January 21, as on most days, the banks of the Seine were bustling. Pedestrians marched down the quays, umbrellas raised, on their way to offices or to make social calls, or just out for a walk even on a rainy January morning. They sloshed through the puddles that day, as the smell of smoke from charcoal and wood fires wafted in the brisk air. In the January chill of short, gray days and long, cold nights, Parisians had been hunkering with their families by their fireplaces or stoves, trying to keep warm.

Since the middle of January, they had read in their newspapers about the rising water upriver. Those who took the time to think about the news must have realized that the surge of water wreaking havoc in the villages miles away would soon reach the capital.

Most Parisians, however, had plenty of other things on their minds. The year had barely begun, and the twelve days of Christmas were just finished. The National Assembly had resumed its session on January 11 to continue a heated debate about the secularization of the schools as part of the official separation of church and state declared in 1905. Arrangements for legislative elections were well underway, and political parties were preparing their lists of candidates to present to voters. Most people paid less attention to politics than to the steady flow of sensational stories published by the mass press, especially ones about criminals infiltrating the army or murdering policemen. On January 14 many of the city's children and their parents were thrilled by the opening of the Victor Hugo skating rink on Rue Saint-Didier, not far from the Arc de Triomphe.[3]

In the midst of all this activity, the Seine in Paris was already rising. Even those Parisians who noticed the swelling waters were not likely to have been alarmed. The river always climbed at this time of year. In fact, by mid-January the Seine had already risen and fallen twice. As a result of the especially rainy winter, the river had ascended several feet above its usual height at the beginning and again at the end of December 1909. The Seine's level began descending just after that sunny New Year's Day, and any danger from these small floods seemed to have passed. Since the December floods had not created a problem, no one was too worried now. A cartoon in *L'Illustration* captured the mood of January 21. It shows a comfortable bourgeoisie gentleman and his wife reading the newspaper. "The Seine is rising," she tells him. "*Eh bien,*" he retorts flippantly. "Let it rise."[4] Accustomed to winter rain and snow, most Parisians continued with their ordinary business.

Those who took a few moments on that rainy Friday, January 21, to lean over the bridge railings and watch the river below would have observed teams of engineers hard at work, something that newspapers were also beginning to report. The Seine was again making its way up the quay walls, and by the third week in January, the river had reached several feet above its normal level. Inspectors walked along the length of the quays, looking up to examine the walls and reinforcing them with stone and sand where necessary. They viewed this largely as a precaution. A portion of the Quai de Valmy, which borders the Canal Saint-Martin on the Right Bank, had sunk the day before, according to the daily police log, collapsing part of the sidewalk and leaving a gaping hole several feet deep.[5] From time to time, Parisians had witnessed such cave-ins, especially in areas built over one of the many passages running underneath the streets. City engineers and police had been quick to arrive on the scene, and by January 21 everything was under control. Parisians had faith that their city's infrastructure would protect them.

Paul W. Linebarger, an American federal judge who left Paris that day for Le Havre to catch a ship back to the United States, later remembered Parisians eyeing several crews of busy workmen along the river's edge as they inspected and shored up the various quay walls. "They watched with an idle sort of interest that showed they had no idea that the overflow of the river would be so great as it has turned out to be." Similarly, Mrs. M. L. Nuttall of New York, on her way to catch the same ship back to America, saw how Parisians reacted to the rising water. "As a matter of fact, the concern of the people was so slight that many of them appeared to treat the activities of the government engineers in strengthening the river banks as something like a joke."[6] She remembered how the Parisians who gazed at the rising water even teased each other about not getting their feet wet.

When Parisians wanted to know the level of the Seine, they went to the Pont de l'Alma to look at the enormous stone statues, some twenty feet tall and standing on pillars attached to the bridge, of four soldiers, two facing upriver and two downriver. These soldiers seemed to watch over the city, ready to defend against danger from either direction. One of them was a Zouave, a proud colonial soldier in uniform with his cape flowing behind him, holding his rifle by its barrel tip. He stuck one foot forward as he stared watchfully across the Seine, his bearded chin pointing upward, as if poised to spring to action. By January 21 the water was lapping against the ankles of his boots, about six feet above its usual level. But Parisians knew that the quay walls through the city's center were much taller, reaching to a height well above his head.

Anyone who lingered a few minutes longer on the banks examining the Seine that day would have witnessed some ominous signs. The water was moving at an extremely high speed, much faster than usual, approaching fifteen miles per hour. The powerful eddies traced strange patterns on the surface that foamed white in places. The normally busy river became strangely empty as river traffic, from barges to transports to tugboats, gradually came to a halt. Newspapers were reporting that navigation was clearly unsafe. Even stranger were the large quantities of debris charging down the swollen river. As the Parisian daily paper *Le Matin* described it: "Planks, boxes, barrels, beams, debris from barges, tree trunks come at an indescribable speed shattering against the bridge supports."[7] The occasional loud crashes could already be heard far from the banks, like small explosions echoing through the city.

Even as Paris went about its busy day, some city engineers who sensed the danger started to pick up the pace of their work along the Seine. As fast as they could, they used sandbags to build up the walls in the Auteuil neighborhood on Paris's western edge. Despite their efforts, during the afternoon several sewers in that district began backing up, silently overflowing into basements in streets like Rue Félicien-David, which runs parallel to the river. It was the first sign that the renowned engineers of Paris might finally have met their match.

The task of keeping order in the city fell directly to one man, the prefect of police. His jurisdiction extended far beyond simply combating crime. The prefect managed public health issues, oversaw city cleaning, fought epidemics, and ensured that Paris had adequate food supplies. He also directed the fire department, regulated street traffic, and monitored the movement of trains. Under his direction, the police regularly spied on political groups suspected of engaging in seditious acts and labor organizations planning strikes. Given the breadth of his job, the prefect of police was one of the most powerful men in the entire city, second only to the prefect of the Seine, the position that Haussmann had occupied. As a result, most prefects of police served a very short time since they were potential rivals to elected officials. Of the 78 prefects who had held the job since its creation in 1800, only three served for more than ten years. In 1910 the man in that post was Louis Lépine.

Born in 1843 in the provincial city of Lyon, Lépine was studying law in Paris at the outbreak of the Franco–Prussian War. Joining the fight, Lépine served as a sergeant-major at the city of Belfort, southwest of Strasbourg in the Alsace region. The French army defended Belfort against numerous attacks and survived a Prussian blockade for months. Once the peace treaty was signed, Lépine and his fellow soldiers who had protected Belfort were forced to surrender it to the Germans, along with the rest of Alsace and the neighboring Lorraine region. Lépine earned a medal for his valor.

After the war, Lépine completed his training as a lawyer and entered government administration, working his way up through the ranks. His first appointment as police prefect in Paris lasted from 1893 to 1897. Then for less than a year, he served as the governor general of the French colony in Algeria. Lépine was a man who refused to tolerate disorder of any kind, including in Algiers where Muslim–Jewish tensions, in Lépine's view, required a firm hand. A short time later, Lépine was recalled to Paris and took up his old job.

As the head of the police force from 1899 until his retirement in 1913, Lépine kept his finger on the pulse of the city, developing a reputation as a hands-on leader and earning the nickname "the prefect of the street." This was especially true during an emergency, but even on a daily basis he was out and about in the city, observing people and making himself familiar to Parisians. Lépine was a small, wiry man, with a large forehead, steely eyes, and a stern gaze. A thick mustache and goatee framed his pursed lips. He displayed stoic calm when facing down crowds of strikers—whose angry protests in the streets became more and more frequent in the late nineteenth century—with only an umbrella to defend himself.

At the time Lépine first became prefect, the police had become infamous for corruption and mediocrity, and few of the city's residents liked or respected them. Lépine wanted Parisians to love their police, starting with him. He wrote in his memoirs: "A prefect who no one knows, whose silhouette is not familiar, whose face no one recognizes in the cartoons in the newspaper, with whom no one rubs shoulders in the street, with whom no one exchanges ideas, this prefect can have all the qualities in the world, but for the Parisian, he lacks the most important one: this is not his man."[8] Lépine wanted Parisians to see him as their man, the one who could keep them safe.

In his fierce dedication to his duty, Lépine was Victor Hugo's real-life Inspector Javert, from his famous novel *Les Misérables*. Like Javert, Lépine was unyielding as he enforced his vision of the law single-mindedly with the same the military rigor he had learned during the war. Lépine sought to make Paris safe and proper, but only on his own terms. He sent his troops into the streets to fight prostitution, panhandling, vagrancy, and moral offenses. In the ten years between 1902 and 1912, the police would arrest more than 46,000 vagrants, nearly 2,300 beggars, and over 3,000 unlicensed peddlers. In 1907, Lépine unleashed a war against obscenity. His agents seized photographs, cards, engravings, newspapers, films, and numerous other items deemed to be pornographic or an offense to public morality. The prefect made Paris more orderly, but only at the cost of many people's personal freedom.[9]

As part of his quest to improve law enforcement in Paris, Lépine introduced novel ways of dealing with crime. In the process, he broadened the reach and power of the police force during some of the city's most turbulent years. He created a corps of armed bicycle policemen who could move quickly and easily, especially to the still-dangerous outer quarters of Paris where gangs of ruffians lurked. He experimented with sulfuric acid capsules that could disperse a cloud of poisonous gas and drive criminals from their hiding places. He also installed telephones around the city, accessible only to the police, so they could communicate directly with headquarters. In 1900 Lépine created a river police force to regulate traffic on the Seine, just in time for the Exposition. In 1912 he would establish Paris's first detective training program to turn the work of police investigation from guesses and hunches into a clear and codified science with distinct methods and professional practices, including matching fingerprints and identifying the patterns of tire tracks. Lépine asked detective Alphonse Bertillon, famous for his scientific approach to police work, to lead the training program. As head of the criminal records office, Bertillon had developed a system of identifying criminals based on facial features, using an archive of mugshot photographs to keep track of Paris's dangerous inhabitants.[10]

The square across from police headquarters in Paris now bears Louis Lépine's name, as does the yearly competition, the Concours Lépine, which he founded to showcase new inventions and which still reminds Parisians of Lépine's desire to promote science and economy in the city.

On Friday, January 21, 1910, Lépine entered a short note, at once mundane and ominous, into the police log. Water from the rising Seine had entered the unfinished construction of the new, privately owned Nord-Sud subway (now Métro Line 12) from what seemed to be a breach in the sewer not far from the nearby Gare d'Orsay. This line was destined to become a major north–south thoroughfare, carrying passengers underneath the river between the National Assembly building on the Left Bank and the Place de la Concorde on the Right Bank. Lépine sketched the scene with calm detachment: "Water from the Seine has flooded some of the walkways. Their collapse has produced some damage."[11] Repairmen from the sewer service, he noted, were on the scene. Perhaps Lépine realized that this minor cave-in could lead to larger problems, especially if the volume of water grew. But if he had any such concerns, Lépine omitted them from his daily report.

Based on what the Hydrometric Service knew about the patterns of France's rivers, its agents expected floods during the winter of 1909–1910. Exceptionally high rainfall the previous summer had saturated the soil, elevating groundwater throughout the region. Warmer than average temperatures caused the snow to melt quickly, and the extra moisture further engorged already swollen streams and rivers. When the Seine rose several feet above normal in late November and early December 1909, the Hydrometric Service had accurately sent word downriver so that Paris and other towns might take the necessary precautions. The service's success seemed to corroborate its promise that floods could be predicted and understood. However, the magnitude of the rising rivers in January 1910 took everyone by surprise, especially the Hydrometric Service.

As a general practice, the numerous observation stations upriver and down kept in constant touch, sharing data through a series of daily bulletins, each one passing along its readings to the others in the network. When engineers at upriver stations noted unusual conditions that indicated rising water—such as a heavy rainfall or a rapid snowmelt—they sent word downriver by postal bulletin or telegram. Readings were taken only once every few hours.

Floods sometimes stressed the system and made communication more complicated. To reach the equipment at measuring stations and take a reading, an engineer sometimes had to climb down a ladder to a platform located in the river. When the water was high, and especially when its flow was fast and churning, that task became dangerous. One wrong step and the engineer could be swept away by the current. Once he took the reading, he might then have to climb another ladder, which itself could be blocked by mud or floodwater, to a telegraph transmission station in order to send his bulletin. Some flood measurement stations had no telegraph nearby, so reports had to be sent through the mail.

With ordinary floods, measurements normally sent by telegram at 7 AM might be held up by at least an hour or more because of traffic on the lines. When delays mounted along the river, they set back any definitive prediction of the water's height downriver. If the water rose quickly enough, even a brief pause in communication might render the estimates provided by the service obsolete by the time stations downriver received them. By mid-January 1910, the rain was falling at an alarming rate. The Seine's rapid rise caused so much water to pour through the river's channel between readings that the service could not predict the flow with any accuracy. Their numbers were largely meaningless.

By the third week of January, the system began to break down. Measuring stations at Nemours, Toucy, and Bléneau, on the Loing River in east central France, were unable to report any readings for January 20, 21, and 22 because the raging flood waters had broken the nearby telegraph lines. Working lines overloaded with messages prevented the service from sending data through. The government's official report would later express frustration that their reliance on technology failed at the very moment it was most needed: "Without news of the water's movement, the service that announces floods is like the army officer in charge of a campaign who has no idea where to find the enemy or his own troops."[12]

The job of calculating the water levels usually fell to Edmond Maillet, one of the service's most trusted and gifted engineers. For the previous eleven years, Maillet had been the one who pored diligently through the reports and produced the official forecasts of the river's height. In all his years of experience, Maillet noted that he had never seen a flood in Paris above the 4.60-meter level (just over 15 feet), as measured at the Pont d'Austerlitz, shortly beyond where the Seine enters the city. Floods were inevitable, but he and his colleagues never expected one that could overwhelm the city. On January 16, 1910, as the water was mounting, Maillet failed to report to work. Pressing personal circumstances—of what kind remains unknown—kept him away for two weeks, and a less-experienced engineer took over the task of predicting the Seine's height. News from upriver about the magnitude of the rising water approaching the city was spotty and incomplete. Maillet, the one man in the Hydrometric Service with enough experience to fill in the gaps left by the science and make a realistic assessment, was absent.

Throughout the day of January 21, only the experts and engineers found much to worry about. That night, when they realized that the clocks had stopped, ordinary Parisians saw the first ominous sign that something was not right. Paris's compressed air service—which supplied the postal service's message delivery system through a series of pneumatic tubes, ran elevators and cleaning systems, provided ventilation, and moved factory motors—also ran many Parisian clocks, both on the city's streets and in numerous homes. When, on the evening of January 21, rapidly rising water submerged the plant that pumped the air out to the city, in many parts of Paris time itself came to a halt, at 10:53 PM.

The massive volume of water that had ravaged Troyes and Lorroy earlier that day had reached Paris. What had been the slow upward creep of the Seine during a normal winter runoff turned into a rapid assault on the city as the pace of the rising water now quickened. Overnight, the Seine jumped to nearly ten feet above its normal level, reaching the Zouave's knees—a rise of about four feet in a single day. Comparing this flood to the scientific data on file, one French geographer summed up the uniqueness of what he saw happening: "Never has the Seine risen faster."[13]

Snow fell throughout the morning of Saturday, January 22, and turned to steady rain in the afternoon, a pattern that would be frequently repeated throughout the flood as high temperatures across the region hovered around 39° Fahrenheit, several degrees above normal. The precipitation that might otherwise have resulted in a significant accumulation of snow instead fell as heavy rain or fell as snow and then melted during the day, pouring into the already swollen river.

In the western part of Paris, engineers began constructing a clay wall parallel to the river, running the length of Rue Félicien-David but to no avail. "Our work became ineffective even before we had finished," they noted in their report. "The water came from the basements, filled the ground floors, and spilled out into the street even before the river directly invaded the street."[14]

The same pattern was occurring all along the Seine. As the water's surge coursed through Paris, it seeped into the land. Silently and stealthily, it began trickling into buildings from below, bubbling upward from the fully saturated soil. The volume of water pulsed through the network of underground tunnels: subway conduits, sewer channels, wells, and reservoirs. It poured into a labyrinth of old quarries from which men had carried stones in previous centuries to build the above-ground city, and into basements and crypts dating back to Roman times, often forgotten when newer structures were built over them. The swell of water grew hour by hour as runoff from the streets roared beneath the city, pushing into every nook and cranny. To everyone's surprise, the water was not coming over the quay walls but under them.

The morning of January 22, hundreds of people who lived along the river's path through Paris awakened with basements full of water as the Seine oozed and dripped through walls or shot up from drains in the floor. Soon water was gushing up from manholes and sewer grates into the city streets. With the Seine still rising quickly, many Parisians were suddenly forced to grab a few of their belongings, perhaps load up a wagon, and leave their homes in search of dry ground. As they looked for a safe place to wait out the flood, they were joined by hundreds of homeless Parisians, who under normal circumstances lived in makeshift tents and cardboard encampments underneath the city's bridges, sleeping on beds of straw and crumpled newspaper and building small fires to keep warm. Their crude shelters were being washed away too.

The neighborhood of Bercy, a working-class district located on the city's eastern edge just where the Seine enters Paris, was one of the first and worst hit areas. By January 22 its basements were completely flooded, its streets transformed into a vast lagoon. A collapsed support wall along the Quai de la Gare threatened to snap a supply line that brought gas from the nearby suburb of Alfortville into the city. In one street, the flickering gas lanterns on the tops of light poles became the only visible things above the surface of the water. When H. Warner Allen, the Paris correspondent of London's *Morning Post,* arrived in the neighborhood, he was shocked by what he saw. "The scene was indescribably desolate; a long row of cheerless houses three feet deep in water, as far as the eye could see."[15]

Since the early nineteenth century, Bercy had become one of Paris's important warehouse districts and a center for wine distribution. The Seine poured into those storage facilities, forcing dozens of wine barrels out into the main river channel and propelling many of them downriver. Frightened wine merchants yanked on rubber waders and slogged through waist-high water trying to wrestle the enormous casks back into their warehouses with long poles in an effort to save their stock. Inside the warehouses, many more casks bobbed and floated in several feet of water, crashing into one another as the current pushed them around. After only a brief soak in muddy water, much of the city's precious wine supply began to spoil. For warehouse owners and workers, those barrels of wine meant income and labor. For the rest of Paris, including those areas untouched by the Seine, they were nourishment—not a luxury, but a staple of life.

Near the wine warehouses of Bercy, several of the city's electricity generating plants hummed, including those that powered Paris's subway system. On January 22 short circuits in power plants at Bercy and at Saint-Denis, which lies just to the north of Paris, froze Métro Line 1, the most important east–west corridor, and Line 6, which sweeps in an arc through much of the Left Bank. Métro stations near the Seine filled up with water, some to the very tops of the tunnels. Police and subway employees hastily began erecting barricades of wooden planks across the station entrances above ground to prevent anyone from trying to descend. Hundreds of gallons of water cascaded down the stairs inside some stations, creating waterfalls.

With the Métro at least partially out of service, Parisians had to start improvising other ways of getting around. Women lifted their long skirts up to their knees (normally considered an immodest action) as they waded through streets. Young men grabbed onto passing cars and rode along on their running boards in order to keep their feet dry. Boats began floating through the streets, and police publicly reassured residents who lived near the river that officers would row them home if necessary.

Along the railings of bridges and the quay walls, hundreds of people from all walks of life gathered throughout January 22, leaning over to see and hear the torrent below. The rising Seine was shocking but thrilling too. In many places, the crowds were three or four deep, gasping and buzzing with excitement. Braving the winter cold, men and women elbowed their way up or waited their turn to move forward and glimpse the rushing river. What had at first been a casual oddity was becoming a genuine show. This was the age of mass entertainment in Paris: flashy music halls like the Moulin Rouge, sensational newspaper stories, the wax museum, early motion pictures, and visits to the morgue for a bit of gruesome fun. In a metropolis full of fantastic, sometimes chilling visual spectacles, the flood provided a frisson of real-life excitement and danger.

Yet, even watching the Seine could be risky. The morning newspaper *Le Matin* reported on January 22 that the pressure of the rising water threatened some of the quays and that a few were already buckling and collapsing. In addition, the paper stated, "A young girl Mlle. Olympe Courdy . . . who was walking at this moment on the Quai d'Ivry, was swept away in an eddy, and several passers-by had to intervene and rescue her from this dangerous situation."[16] In the town of Château-Thierry, located several miles upriver from where the Marne joins the Seine, young Edouard Brullefert wasn't so lucky, according to *Le Matin*. The boy "fell in . . . and was carried away. His body was recovered by soldiers before his mother's eyes."[17]

By evening, the Seine had reached the level of the flood of 1896, the biggest in recent years. The Hydrometric Service looked upriver and tried to measure the magnitude of the approaching water. All they could report to anxious Parisians was that the Seine's rise was nowhere near its peak. Snow mixing with rain aggravated the wet conditions with further wintry cold. Officials fearing for the public's health issued emergency orders to boil any water used for drinking and cooking.

The growing danger in Paris was soon well known around the globe. Events in Paris were always world news, and few things sold more newspapers than a disaster. Reports from the French capital were coming fast and furious, and foreign papers made the most of the story. In its report on the situation on January 22, the *Washington Post* told readers a highly sensational tale of "a score of corpses of persons long dead" that had been pulled from their graves upriver and were floating in the Seine, which was "black with wreckage."[18]

As Parisians prepared to face the worst their river might have in store for them, the rising waters of three major rivers—the Marne and the Yonne, as well as the Seine—were coursing out of control across much of northern France. Engineers patrolled riverbanks throughout the entire region, shoring up levees with sandbags where they could. People who lived in towns and villages along these rivers abandoned their possessions and homes. As *Le Matin* reported, "A veritable panic is spreading throughout the country. There are only tears, sobs, and ruins."[19]

Much of the source of the Seine's flood was quite far from Paris. The headwaters of the Yonne River, which feeds into the Seine, are located in the Morvan region of central France, on the edge of the Massif Central mountain range. Like Paris, the Morvan experienced an unusual warming trend that winter, causing snow to turn to rain or to melt on the ground and run into the channel of the Yonne. Rainy conditions farther north in the Yonne basin added more water to the river's swell. Occasional freezing prevented the full force of the water from heading downriver all at once, probably contributing to the relatively slow pace at which the Seine initially rose in Paris. The warmer temperatures then thawed the flow of the Yonne, sending an ever-growing volume of runoff downriver. A flood of the Yonne alone would not have been tragic. The real crisis for Paris began when the waters of the Marne, fed by its swollen tributaries, the Grand Morin and Petit Morin, also spilled into the Seine. The Marne joins the Seine just outside the city limits of Paris near the eastern suburban towns of Alfortville and Charenton, where some of the worst flooding occurred.[20]

The conditions that caused the flood had been building up for months. Groundwater levels and aquifers throughout the region were higher than usual due to the elevated levels of rainfall during the previous summer. Between June 1909 and the end of January 1910, France experienced 38 percent more rainfall than normal. The ground water in the Seine basin was usually just over fourteen and a half inches, but by the end of the summer of 1909, it was more than seventeen inches. "Almost everywhere," wrote the Académie des Sciences in its assessment, "the maximum runoff level for impermeable soil and the saturation point of permeable soil was nearly reached by November 1."[21]

A low-pressure weather system, stretching from Brittany up toward the North Sea, remained stationary from mid-January to the end of the month and brought with it heavy rains. Paris was not the only place affected by the bad weather, which also settled across Italy, Switzerland, and Germany, and much of the rest of the continent. "From nearly every place in Europe," reported *Le Matin*, "floods, storms, avalanches, and earthquakes are being reported."[22]

The geography of Paris played a crucial role in the flood as well. Paris is essentially a bowl: Its highest points in the north, Montmartre and Belleville, provide some of the best views of the entire city. A walk south down the hill does not flatten out until about half a mile from the river. Across the Seine, continuing southward, one climbs up again— for instance, to the Panthéon, the hilltop where the ancient Romans placed their forum, or to Montparnasse. The river lies in a narrow lowland between the hills.

Within that valley sit some of the oldest parts of the city. The thousands of square feet of nonporous paving stones, wood paving blocks, and concrete laid on streets, sidewalks, and buildings refused to absorb water, instead causing it to roll into the river. With the sewers nearing capacity by January 22, the very infrastructure of the city, which normally made life better, was now making the situation worse.

Bends in the Seine also complicated drainage during times of flooding. Paris sits at the first of six horseshoe bends in the riverbed, each looping back on itself in a 180-degree turn as the water heads downstream. Combined with the relatively mild grade from the city west to the ocean—Paris is only about 250 feet above sea level—this topography means that, once a large quantity of water reaches Paris, the land itself provides little incentive for it to move. That volume of water is great, since the entire basin covers an area of more than 48,000 square miles, filled with streams and rivers that feed into the Seine.

Not all of the water in Paris was where it appeared to be. The Bièvre (its name came from the Gallic words for "river of beavers") was a small tributary of the Seine that began near Versailles and meandered across the city's Left Bank. Although it originally emptied into the Seine near the present-day Pont de l'Alma and also across from Notre-Dame Cathedral (around the present-day site of Rue de Bièvre), in the twelfth century monks split the Bièvre and redirected it for irrigation purposes so that it also joined the Seine near what is now the Gare d'Austerlitz. Over time, the Bièvre became a crucial site for the city's tradesmen who relied on a fresh and regular water source for their work: dyers, tanners, butchers, beer brewers, and the famous Gobelins tapestry factory. By the mid-nineteenth century, more than one hundred factories and workshops used the Bièvre for their daily work.[23] That industry took an ecological toll on the Bièvre, which became a highly polluted waterway. By the turn of the twentieth century, in part to reduce pollution and modernize the city, the Bièvre was being channeled, paved over, and driven underground, a process completed in 1912.

Given the saturation of the soil throughout the Paris region, no one was surprised that the Bièvre flooded in 1910, just as it had in previous years during high water. Covering the Bièvre may have worsened the effects that year by removing another possible channel through which rainfall could be carried away. Even worse was the fact that in some places the Bièvre had been linked to the city's sewage system to help drain its contents. Now as the level of the Bièvre rose, it emptied more water into the already swollen sewers. The newspaper *L'Eclair* described the swelling tributary as it passed through the 5th *arrondissement* near the Place Monge: "The Bièvre has broken up the masonry covering. In places, the water squirts out. The architectural inspector has seen the danger himself. Evacuations have begun immediately. The director of the school in Rue de Buffon and the people in her family have been rescued from the roof. . . . All this flooding is certainly due to the Bièvre. . . . The sight of this entire neighborhood is disastrous."[24] By attempting to control the Bièvre, Parisians had inadvertently increased the possibility of flooding across the eastern portion of the Left Bank.

The other underground source of water was the marshy lake below the Garnier Opéra House, the building that became the pride of Haussmann's redesigned Paris. Construction of the building had been delayed for months in the 1860s while workmen pumped thousands of gallons of water from the worksite. This underground water source, perhaps a remnant of the Seine's long-dried-up arm and a function of the topography, enabled architect Charles Garnier to include a man-made reservoir underneath the building, which later became the location of the fictional Phantom's lair in Gaston Leroux's *The Phantom of the Opera*.

By January 22, the entire river basin, with its intricate network of streams and rivers, all of which connected to the Seine, could hold no more water. Scientists in France and elsewhere came to see that the land had played at least as big a role in causing the flood as had the weather because the normally absorbent soil was so thoroughly saturated. France was like a wet sponge that could hold no more. As a result, all along these swollen rivers, a cascade effect took over. Towns upstream received the first brunt of the water as it gathered force, bringing flooding throughout parts of northern France. Later, towns farther downstream would be hit. So the water in the devastated village of Troyes, upstream along the Seine, was already falling while it was still rising in Paris on January 22. Additional rain and snow kept the river flowing like a machine, working its way toward the Atlantic Ocean. The second series of rains, the journal *La Nature* argued, "was followed by a third, then a fourth coming at intervals that were close enough to maintain elevated water levels."[25]

All the rivers in the Paris region were flooding, as were ones in the Rhône, Rhine, and Saône basins in France. According to press reports, communication was seriously disrupted throughout the entire nation, and the military forced evacuations of residents from several regions. Near Dijon in the south, the river Ouche trapped people on their rooftops, and rising water stopped a train on its tracks. At Saint-Martin d'Auxerre, near the Swiss border, a mudslide left victims stranded on their roofs. In the town of Fontaines, near Lyon, telephone poles had been ripped up from the ground. This was clearly a national crisis.

Chapter Two

the RIVER ATTACKS

Parisians established wooden walkways, called passerelles, *so they could continue to move about the city during the high water.*

As dusk fell across the city on January 22, the gentle splash of oars from a boat cutting through water echoed against the walls of the empty buildings. The craft slid toward a darkened streetlight. The occupant tried to stand and lean forward, the boat rocking from side to side. He reached out to grab the lamppost. Fumbling in the dark, he ignited the fuel, producing a flicker, then a flame of warm light that glistened across the black surface of the water in the deepening night. He pushed his oars back into the water and rowed to the next lamppost to continue the job.

Despite the efforts of dozens of such men on the city's public works crew, the City of Light grew darker as the water rose higher. Gas street lamps throughout Paris needed to be lit and extinguished daily by hand. Under ordinary conditions, teams moved rapidly through the city with long poles to start and stop the flames. This became an impossible task during the flood: Without enough boats on hand, these crews could not reach every lamp. Inside the flooded zone, many of the streetlights remained lit for the duration of the ordeal as long as the gas lines remained intact. In other neighborhoods, where water broke or flooded the supply lines, lamps could not be illuminated at all. Paris became a patchwork of light and dark. Some neighborhoods were bathed in a dim glow while in others the long dark winter nights began promptly at sunset.

To provide as much visibility as possible, the understaffed municipal lighting service improvised by mounting smaller oil lanterns, hastily purchased from stores, on the out-of-service streetlights. They also retrieved older lamps from their storage facilities and reinstalled them around Paris. Some were fueled by oil, but the city also kept Lusol, a byproduct from the coke manufacturing process, on hand as an emergency lighting fuel if the gas or electricity failed. More than half of these replacement lamps were clogged and inoperable. When the harsh winter wind extinguished them, they had to be relit—if someone had the time to do the job.

Keeping the city illuminated was a never-ending chore. Two workers from the lighting crew, Hector Ravaux and Auguste Delahaye, toiled to make sure that the 13th *arrondissement* didn't go dark. Ravaux navigated by boat the quays along that portion of the Seine near Bercy and was sometimes tossed about in the river's strong current as he tried to assess the situation. These men supervised the temporary lines being installed to keep gas coming to the regular lights in the area and kept a close eye on the makeshift levee built to prevent further rupturing of gas lines. When the lines did break, they hurried to install temporary lanterns, and when those failed to work, Ravaux and Delahaye hunted down new ones to replace the faulty fixtures. They were just two of dozens struggling against the gloom.[1]

Parisians living in the darkened neighborhoods feared for their safety, so police started guarding these areas with extra vigor. One Parisian journalist who tried to drive his car through black streets recalled: "The diligent soldiers barred the entry to the flooded streets. In the headlights, their bayonets gleamed. 'Where are you going?' . . . And these were deserted, darkened, desolate streets."[2] He encountered several similar patrols in the areas without streetlights.

The sudden darkness in the city brought back frightening memories of the siege of Paris during the Franco–Prussian War, when fuel supplies ran low and the city's lights dimmed. By the end of November 1870, nearly everyone had been cut off from the gas supply. Novelist Théophile Gautier wrote of the sense of stillness in the besieged city as he walked by the Seine: "Along the quay there is a silence as a death, a solitude that is terrifying. . . . The street-lamps at half-pressure, spot the darkness with scanty red dots, the reflection of which lengthens and melts in the river like a gout of blood."[3] These words, from 1870, could have been written again forty years later under the siege of the flood.

The French army permanently stationed a garrison of troops just outside Paris. In 1910 the senior military commander in the Paris region was General Jean-Baptiste Jules Dalstein, a career officer who had trained as a military engineer. He had distinguished himself by helping to build fortifications along the border between France and the

German territories near his hometown of Metz in the Lorraine region. In 1870, those fortifications could not stop the invading troops during the Franco–Prussian War, and Dalstein was captured and held prisoner. Later, he served in the French colonies of Algeria and Indochina, working his way up through the ranks. He took command of the engineering troops in the Paris region in 1899, earning the respect of more senior officers as well as politicians and gaining numerous awards from the French government, including the Legion of Honor. In 1906, at age 61, he became the commander of the Paris garrison and made a dramatic public debut on horseback in full dress uniform and sporting an enormous white mustache, to great public acclaim as he reviewed the troops at the Longchamps racetrack just to the west of Paris. The men under his command often played an important role in diplomatic and ceremonial functions as an honor guard for visiting royalty or dignitaries. Dalstein was sent as a representative of the French government to the wedding of the Spanish king. During the flood, however, diplomacy and ceremony would give way to action, and Dalstein's engineering background would prove extremely useful.[4]

At the request of police prefect Louis Lépine and other city leaders, General Dalstein sent his troops into Parisian streets to assist local authorities in calming the population. To coordinate the military's efforts, Dalstein divided the flood-ravaged area into five districts, placing each under the supervision of a senior officer. Orders were sent to naval bases on the English Channel and the Mediterranean, and French sailors began preparing to relocate temporarily to the capital with boats and supplies from the coasts.

By Sunday, January 23, parts of the city sat two or three feet underwater as the Seine continued to mount. The river had risen nearly two more feet since the previous day and measured approximately twelve feet above normal. The Seine was now tickling the Zouave's thighs and was still rising. A heavy snowfall blanketed the city. Authorities repeated their warnings that the water supply might be contaminated and that all water should be boiled before drinking or cooking. Police began requiring some residents in the hardest hit areas to evacuate. In the Rue Félicien-David on January 23, a man roamed through the streets hawking photographs of the high water as a souvenir for those who wanted to remember the still-unfolding drama.[5]

Reports in the press from the meat market at La Villette suggested that food was already becoming scarce and that prices were beginning to rise. Gardens and farms in the towns outside Paris normally supplied part of the city's fresh food, but those were now among the most devastated areas. As the farmers in these villages lost their livelihood, Parisians lost an important source of food. Throughout the flood zone, dry goods merchants, butchers, bakers, and other food vendors who stored their stocks in basements were now wiped out. High water forced a butcher named Monsieur Brez to close up shop in Rue Saint-Benoit and to move into a hotel, forfeiting some 500 eggs, along with meat, poultry, and wine,

Streets were ripped up, sometimes exposing the foundations of buildings.

a total value around 250 francs. He lost the income while the neighborhood lost both the provisions and nourishment.[6]

On January 23, the historic Latin Quarter was rapidly becoming a swamp as water rose from drains and the Métro. Portions of the Boulevard Saint-Germain above the subway lines were buckling and collapsing under the water's weight. Engineers rushed to fill holes in the quay walls at strategic locations, but a sinkhole near the Quai d'Orsay threatened gas lines. When crews turned off the gas supply to shore up the walls, they hung oil lamps to illuminate the walkway and the beautiful gilded decorations of the Pont Alexandre III.[7]

In the daily press, reporters recounted numerous tales of police and firefighters patrolling the streets on foot and by boat listening for shouts and cries for help. When they found someone in distress, these first responders plucked people from rising waters or from upper-story windows. The Paris correspondent for the London *Morning Post,* H. Warner Allen, crisscrossed the streets of the flooded city, recording what he saw. "I watched a rescue party row back with difficulty across the river," he wrote. "They had saved a few pathetic sticks of furniture and a great mattress, which, as its owner with exultation pointed out to the sympathetic crowd, was perfectly dry. A covered cart was in waiting, but the inside was already full and the mattress was hoisted on to the roof. Alas! for the vanity of human exultation! Hardly had it been tied in place when a storm of torrential rain swept down and drenched the mattress and its poor despairing owner as thoroughly as though they had fallen in the Seine." Despite some successful rescues, the scale of the devastation that Allen witnessed was overwhelming. In the heavily flooded Bercy neighborhood, Allen saw "a punt conveying a workman to his flooded home, poled slowly along by two policemen and bumping monotonously against the poplars and sunken railings."[8]

Although police and soldiers helped many escape, some Parisians attempted to flee on their own, grabbing pieces of wood or debris to fashion makeshift rafts. Newspapers told sensational stories of people attempting to travel through the high water in the city streets and drowning, although on January 23 the police records officially indicated only one death. That day, a dockworker had tried to help a woman through a flooded area at Porte de la Gare, and they both slipped and fell into a sinkhole. The dockworker was able to grab onto a tree, but she vanished into the water.[9]

As the Seine continued to spread out farther from its banks, expanding the flood zone, more Parisians found themselves trapped by water-filled streets. Throughout January 23 the sound of hammering echoed across Paris as police, soldiers, and municipal workers from the various services that kept the city running erected a complicated system of wooden walkways and footbridges, called *passerelles,* that would allow people to move around the city. Teams of men quickly joined planks together, balancing them on wooden sawhorses submerged in the water. On Rue du Seine, the corner grocer created a bridge from one side of the street to the other by lining up his display tables outside and laying boards across them. This practice was borrowed from the Venetians, who, surrounded by canals and the sea, live with the *acqua alta* (high water) seasonally as the tide peaks in wintertime. Not surprisingly, many people started comparing flooded Paris to Venice.

Some of these improvised walkways rose as high as six feet or more over the ground, and in places they stretched 300 to 500 yards or longer over heavily flooded streets. Along Rue de Javel, one of the most affected streets, the *passerelles* extended more than 2,600 feet. Where no stable ground remained below the water, workers began strapping the planks to barrels, creating pontoon bridges that floated on the water's surface.

By January 23 many *passerelles* soon looked like ordinary sidewalks in the city as people continued to go about their busy lives, making their way to work, to school, or to buy supplies as life carried on as usual. Well-dressed women even kept up their regular social calls. For Parisians who refused to evacuate, ladders and ramps reached up to the second-story windows of many buildings, connecting them to a *passerelle* below, thus enabling residents to enter and exit. Parisians living on upper floors could pass from the windows directly down to the *passerelles* and were often able to stay completely dry. Despite the benefits that *passerelles* provided, however, they could also create dangers as people sometimes fell off into the icy water.

The *passerelles* were the embodiment of a cultural trait that the French call *Système D*—the belief in the power of people to get themselves out of a scrape or a difficult situation. The "D" stands for the *débrouillard,* or the scrappy, clever "little guy." It is the French equivalent of what Americans might call "Yankee ingenuity" or "stick-to-itiveness," a sense of resolve in the face of tough odds. *Système D* speaks to a supposedly natural resourcefulness, inventiveness, and independence that has enabled the French to endure a tumultuous history.[10] During the flood, it meant the art of surviving. One man used two chairs to shuffle across a flooded area, advancing each chair in front of him to take the next step. Another adroit Parisian waded through the streets on stilts.

*B*y January 23 some of the greatest physical damage was taking place in the suburban towns where "the flood spread with extreme violence," as *Le Matin* had put it.[11] The devastation was so great in large part because these villages did not have Paris's tall quay walls to protect them from rising waters. In Paris, the Seine gushed up from below, but in the suburbs water cascaded over the tops of levees and barriers, flowing directly into the streets, some of which were still unpaved. Buildings there were often smaller and less able to withstand the force of rushing water. Many of the towns downriver lay within the horseshoe curves of the Seine and were therefore surrounded on both sides by the river bending back upon itself. As a result, water could come from two directions at once to menace the inhabitants.

Residents throughout the entire region were soon forced to improvise their own solutions. The town of Issy-les-Moulineaux sits just outside the southwestern boundary of Paris as the Seine exits the capital and begins to curve again to the north. With just over 16,000 inhabitants at the turn of the century, and its own sewer and tram systems, Issy had become an important manufacturing site. The people of Issy were no strangers to disaster: In June 1901, a terrible explosion at a munitions factory had killed seventeen people, including fourteen women who worked there, for whom a large public funeral was held.[12]

During the day of January 23 the town began sounding its warning horn, alerting residents to take action and preserve themselves and their belongings as water filled people's basements and the streets. Although Issy had an emergency flood warning system in place, word of the approaching deluge had not arrived by telephone or telegraph as they had hoped, but by the regular postal service. By the time the official notice arrived, so had the flood. At 11 PM, town council members toured the streets to assess the situation and witnessed the damage already done to people's homes. In Rue Diderot, residents were hauling furniture to the upper floors and walls were crumbling. Rescue services from Issy and nearby Vanves prepared for the worst. Monsieur J. Hubert, a photographer and publisher based in Issy, moved through the area, snapping hundreds of images of the rising water.

At 2 AM on January 24 the Seine topped its banks in Issy. In his memoir, Hubert described the moment when the Seine overflowed: "a furious wave that nothing could hold back rushed forward onto the plain. This was no longer just a matter of infiltrations, a torrent was unleashed, a deluge of rain kept falling." Waves rushed through the streets of Issy-les-Moulineaux, tearing wooden wagons apart. The church bells rang into the dark night as both a warning and a prayer.

Soon many of the small houses in Issy where the laborers lived were submerged, and the residents rushed to dress and flee, leaving behind their belongings and wading through waist-deep water in order to escape. By 3 AM on January 24, one hour after the Seine began to overflow its banks, the lowest parts of the village were already more than six feet under water. Familiar streets and landmarks had disappeared. Along one avenue, according to Hubert, "one could only see an immense sheet of water dotted here and there with lines of bare trees, gas lights still illuminated, a few roofs and the poles for the tramline." The electric lights went out, and the potable water supply vanished. The Seine infiltrated the home for the elderly poor, shutting down the kitchen and laundry.

Those who lived on the ground floor were soon moved to the upper levels of the building as the water continued to climb. The many factories located in the town were forced to close, leaving much of the population without work and unsure of when it would resume. "Their desolate eyes," Hubert put it, "looked out on the immense liquid plain, searching for the poor little house which used to shelter their family."[13]

Issy had fallen eerily silent and dark. The sudden and near-total shutdown of shops and factories meant that the streets were strangely empty. During the night, from time to time, a small flickering light could be seen on the street as someone made his way through the village carrying a torch. Soldiers began arriving to lend a hand.

Refugees arrived at the town hall in hopes of finding assistance on January 24, and more came during the following days. Officials set up seven refugee centers for the suddenly homeless, and empty spaces in town were put at the disposal of the local administration. People with extra rooms often welcomed flood victims into their homes. The nearby town of Montrouge offered to care for the children of victims, and parents tried to comfort their little ones as they were handed over to neighbors. Other towns sent clothes and supplies to Issy in a spirit of goodwill and charity. Yet charity could only go so far.

Although towns like Issy were certainly not destitute, they simply did not have the same resources as Paris. The flood soon began to reveal the basic inequalities between the many working-class suburbs and the wealthier city. When British journalist H. Warner Allen visited nearby towns, he was revolted by the sight. "From visits to out-lying districts," he wrote, "I retain a vague impression of thick black slime, abject shivering misery and great lakes of yellow water, with here and there the upper story of a house rising like an island from the desolate waste."[14] The magazine *La Vie Illustrée* agreed that the situation in the suburban towns was horrific as poorly constructed roofs that could not withstand the intense weather fell in, leaving hundreds without shelter. "This little house," one journalist lamented, "the dream of an entire lifetime's worth of labor, built for the calm days of old age . . . collapses under the unrelenting force of the water."[15]

From dozens of villages upriver and down, refugees were streaming into the capital by the thousands by January 24. Many went to stay with family or friends, who gave them a warm welcome. These exiles hoped that if their own towns could not provide them with enough resources, Paris could. Responding to the urgency of people's needs, Parisian public assistance offices offered aid to many suburban residents, but this help was forthcoming only if the flood victim could show that he or she had not also received an allowance from another town. That could be difficult to prove under the chaotic circumstances. Public assistance officers hesitated to distribute relief to the outlying communities, especially before the worst of the disaster was over, for fear of running out.

The town of Alfortville, just to the southeast of Paris, was particularly devastated by January 24. At the turn of the century, nearly 12,000 people lived in the town.[16] There was only one factory, so most people earned their living in the trades as jewelers, tailors, and carton makers. Located in an area known as La Bosse du Marne—*bosse* meaning "bump"—Alfortville consisted of a piece of land sandwiched between the Marne and the Seine that came to a point just at the place where the two waterways merged. In a flood, topography worked against the town since it could be easily cut off from Paris. When both rivers overflowed and the two bridges closed, many residents of Alfortville were essentially stuck. With only about 11 percent of the town's streets served by sewer lines, the water had nowhere to go, and large pools formed throughout the village. Many homes in Alfortville were immediately overcome by the floodwaters and turned into little more than piles of debris.

One resident told the newspaper *L'Autorité* how fast the water rose in Alfortville. When he went to bed on the night of January 23, there was already some water inside the house with more in the courtyard outside. It did not seem to have gotten much higher since that morning, so he found little reason to worry. The situation changed around 4:30 AM on January 24, when his dog leaped onto the bed crying. In the few hours that he had been asleep, the freezing water had risen nearly sixteen inches. When he jumped out of bed, it came up to his knees. He and his wife hastily made a *passerelle* out of crates and boxes and climbed out the second-story window with a ladder, bringing their mattress, sheets, pillows, and the clothes on their backs. At about 10 AM, he returned home to find the water up to the level of the dining room tabletop. He took a few clothes and left. "Now as of today we have no home, no furniture, no linens, and no work. . . . But our situation is not nearly as bad as so many people I know who have several children."[17]

That same day, the mayor of Alfortville was beginning to panic. "The situation is indescribable," he reported to the police, "and the help which we have waited for is not sufficient."[18] Political differences with the government before the flood had already led many in Alfortville to become active in socialist movements, and the disaster only exacerbated tensions as residents blamed the city for its failure to take measures to defend the bridges—and their homes and livelihoods—against flooding. (After the flood, local tradesmen would write to the government, begging for engineers to raise the height of the quay walls.)

In nearby Maisons-Alfort, which joins Alfortville to the east, some of the newly homeless camped out on the railroad tracks of the Paris-Lyon-Mediterranée line, huddling around their belongings. This town was also the home of the national veterinary school, which sat nearly on the banks of the Marne. When the waters began rising, the school doubled many of its important provisions in preparation for a possible flood. Nearby train lines and boat services stopped running, and students had a difficult time getting to the school. By January 24, the Marne was over its banks, and the school's basements had filled with water.

Despite the difficulties, professors and students continued to hold classes and dissections as usual, according to an account by the school's director, Professor Gustave Barrier: "Every face showed worry; people tore up their newspapers; everyone spoke of nothing but the flood, the ravages it caused, especially in the surrounding areas." Eventually Barrier called the students together and announced the suspension of classes. When he asked them to participate in rescue efforts, he remembered them breaking out into spontaneous applause. Such spirit would be needed as the flood forced the population of Alfortville and Maisons-Alfort to evacuate their homes. "There was no sadder spectacle," Barrier wrote, "than that of these poor people, freezing, soaking, covered with mud, searching for a new shelter, telling disturbing details of the ruins which they had abandoned."[19]

*G*uillaume Apollinaire lived in Rue Gros in Auteuil, in the 16th *arrondissement,* on the city's western edge. Already a well-known poet famous for breaking down old literary styles and experimenting with new forms, Apollinaire was part of the cutting-edge art scene, friends with Pablo Picasso, Jean Cocteau, Erik Satie, and Marcel Duchamp. Several years later, he would coin the term "surreal," which came to describe a new style of art that reveled in the irrational and unexpected. What he described in articles for the Parisian paper *L'Intransigeant* during the flood might also have fallen into that category.

At first, the sight of the rising Seine outside his window on January 23 did not worry Apollinaire; rather, it amused him, making him think of "a little village in Holland" where houses lined the canals and boats floated by peacefully. As he strolled through the neighborhood, however, his attitude changed. Water was already six feet deep in the basement of his apartment building, and his neighbors feared the worst. "In the Rue Gros, a crowd had gathered. The sun had disappeared. Instead of a boat, there was a cart in Rue Félicien-David where the sad residents were throwing pell-mell their most precious possessions." Parents were handing their frightened and crying children from upper-story windows down to friends and family below. Nearby a woman sobbed in despair as the water rose around her.

Later, as Apollinaire returned home, the "immense and furious" Seine washed away any remaining illusions about what was happening. In its quickening current, he saw "before my eyes a tree full of leaves and a black and red cow" being swept away. Thoughts of happy Dutch villages vanished as workmen hastily pounded boards across the door to Apollinaire's building to try to prevent the water from entering the ground floor. With the water so high, Apollinaire was unable to return home unaided, so a sewer worker lifted one of France's most famous men of letters on his back and carried the poet through the water.

Despite the workmen's best efforts, the Seine poured into Apollinaire's house during the night. On the morning of January 24, he heard his downstairs neighbors weeping and calling out to him. They begged him to let them store their furniture and personal belongings in his upper-story apartment. "And, shortly thereafter, there was a sad heap of beds, chairs, armoires, tables, linens, touching souvenirs of family. I hoped that the water would not reach the first floor." In the end, he, too, was forced to leave home and abandon his most valuable possessions—his books. Engineers erected a wooden walkway leading away from his front door. As snow fell, Apollinaire shuffled across the planks to a boat that carried him away to safety.[20]

Snow fell from a gray sky, turning to rain and then back to snow again, adding to people's misery. The barometric pressure began falling, a promise of even worse weather conditions to come. On January 24, the entire infrastructure of the city was shutting down. As *Le Matin* reported, "Factories are stopping, electricity and gas are going out, two thousand telephone customers are out of communication."[21] Water covered the train tracks that ran alongside the river, and stations started closing. The rail companies rerouted their passengers and cargo to less vulnerable stations where possible. Telegraphs stopped clicking, and businesses throughout the city locked their doors. Little by little, whole portions of Paris were cut off from the rest of France and the world.

Their fur matted with water and mud, rats had been coming up from their washed-out underground habitats in search of a bit of food or dry ground. Rats symbolized filth and disease, and as they appeared more frequently around Paris during and after the flood, some Parisians began to speak openly of a possible outbreak of disease, especially the dreaded typhoid, due to contaminated water. If that happened, with the city under water and flood-related injuries already filling hospitals, they worried it might quickly become an epidemic and decimate the population. The persistent fear of disease was based in part on a long history of sickness in the city. Paris had lived through great episodes of mass illness in the past, notably the cholera epidemics of 1832 and 1849, when waves of the dreaded disease had moved across the entire continent. Between July and October 1880, Parisians suffered through a mysterious "great stink" when a foul odor drifted over the city. Many blamed it on inadequate cleaning of the cesspools or the waste treatment plants outside Paris that burned the city's refuse. The overpowering smell returned in the summer of 1895, again raising worries about the possibility of sickness and death.[22] Now, in 1910, the sight of rats did not help ease people's fears, nor did the animal carcasses that still occasionally floated down the Seine, adding to the stench and to the feeling of filth permeating Paris.

Louis Lépine had been receiving reports from his police agents throughout Paris and its suburbs on January 24 and had toured Paris and the suburban towns upriver, surveying the damage and trying to anticipate what else could happen. He moved briskly through the city, wearing a heavy black overcoat and a bowler hat, his pants tucked into rubber boots, and using a cane to steady himself in the mud. More than anyone else, he frequently stood as the government's authority at the water's edge.

For a time, there were still a few signs of hope. The Métro's brand new Line 4, the system's primary north–south axis, was still running on January 24, so people could move about some parts of the city. Even these trains, which normally carried passengers underneath the river, were now forced to stop on either side and go back. Châtelet on the Right Bank and Odéon on the Left Bank were the new terminus points of what had effectively become two truncated lines. Riders wanting to reach the opposite bank had to exit the Métro, climb above ground into the cold and rain, and walk across one of the bridges to catch a train on the other side. Water was still pouring into the Bercy electrical plant, threatening a massive short circuit of the entire network. Soon the plant's basement filled with so much water that the generators shut down completely, and what remained of the Métro system came to a halt.

Even areas far from the river were feeling the adverse effects of the flood. The company supplying electricity in the city's northeast neighborhoods, along streets like Avenue Gambetta and Rue de Belleville, reported that it could no longer ensure their service. Problems mounted as basic infrastructure—electricity, transportation, communication—continued to break down.

By January 24, water had soaked and shut down three of the city's four garbage processing plants, so the tons and tons of waste that Paris produced could no longer be burned as usual. Sanitation officials hastily organized a contingency plan: Garbage that would normally have been incinerated at Vitry now went into the Seine, thrown from the Pont de Tolbiac on the city's eastern edge near Bercy. Waste that should have gone to two other furnaces went over the side of the Pont d'Auteuil. Nearly fifty men began carting the city's waste to the river, using rakes and shovels to lift stinking piles of half-rotten refuse over the edge. The remaining processing plant worked overtime. Men from the waste collection service formed emergency trash crews to assist with the regular collection. They sorted garbage to remove anything dangerous or combustible and then hauled those items to the edge of the city on horse-drawn wagons that the military had placed at their disposal. Once there, they burned the volatile materials, sending clouds of acrid smoke to hover over parts of Paris. All the rest of the waste went into the still-rising river. With the flooded incinerators out of service, garbage men would continue to jettison mountains of the city's foul-smelling rubbish into the Seine for days until officials finally ordered their work stopped for public health reasons.

As Parisians added their own flotsam to the debris already in the river, the stench in places became overpowering. Basements were frequently used for food storage, so decaying foodstuffs were added to the mix. By January 24, in Bercy, the air was so thick with the smell of rotting food in the warehouses and of garbage in the river that it was hard to breathe. Water lapped over the banks of the smaller of the two islands in the middle of the Seine, the Ile Saint-Louis. It had been created in the early seventeenth century when two islands, one of which was called Ile des Vaches (Cow Island) were joined by landfill. Large quantities of debris being pushed downriver by the water's flow crashed into a dock jutting out from a portion of the island. The wall attached to the pier was now threatening to collapse under the growing weight of the refuse being piled against it by the Seine. If the dock and wall fell, many of the island's buildings would quickly fill with murky water. All the refuse from so many additional sources caught on the bridges and clogged the already overtaxed drainage system. In some places, engineers rushed to install extra grates onto the drains to prevent rubbish from obstructing them.

Downriver, residents of the villages that were beginning to suffer from rising floodwaters also had to contend with Paris's garbage floating into their town. In a memo to city officials, a public hygiene expert, Doctor Heller, described the conditions in Clichy, a suburban town to the northwest of Paris. The Seine, he wrote, "has left on the bank a considerable deposit of household waste and mud along a stretch of at least 700 meters. This waste is beginning to putrefy and is giving off an already annoying odor which will soon be intolerable."[23]

Meanwhile, on the western side of the city, water was rushing through another working-class neighborhood. Javel, a lively industrial district, was famous for its disinfectant *eau de Javel,* a bleach that had been produced there since the 1770s. By January 24, Javel sat entirely under water. The Seine began rushing into streets, homes, and businesses that morning. Men who owned small boats launched their craft into the water, calling out "Ferryman! Ferryman!" and offered to take on passengers who were either trying to reach safety or stock up on food and supplies for the long haul. Within a short time, there were few other ways to get around the neighborhood. Describing the scene throughout the area, the parish newsletter from the Church of Saint-Alexandre de Javel compared these ordinary boats to Venetian gondolas, but the Parisian "gondolier" did not sing: "How could he sing in the middle of these ruins, at night when one could hardly hear anything but the howling of dogs interspersed with cries for help?"[24]

Across the entire region soldiers and local police forces were trying to preserve law and order, but problems were already emerging. On the night of January 24, upriver from Paris, in the town of Troyes—which had been hit hard by flooding three days earlier—a group of thugs broke the local curfew set by the police and attacked a policeman guarding a *passerelle.* The officer drew a bayonet to defend himself, but the burly men still tried to push past him. The situation came under control only after a police patrol arrived. According to the police report, "Numerous gunshots and shouts of 'Help!' were heard throughout the night." Authorities posted warning signs around the town saying that "agents had received the order to shoot at those who, during the night, do not obey the curfew."[25] The flood was beginning to tear communities apart.

The events of January 22–24 shocked and frightened Louis Lépine and others in charge, who perceived a clear immediate emergency across the entire region and with it a test of their leadership. In the midst of continuing the regular business already on their agenda, the members of the National Assembly arranged for a vote on January 24 to extend emergency credits to the first victims of the flood, thereby making immediate loans possible. In order to cast that vote, the elected representatives of the French people first had to cross the swirling waters. The Seine had surrounded the Palais Bourbon, cutting off the deputies' meeting place from the rest of the city. To reach the chamber, the politicians were forced to climb into boats, at the risk of soiling their gentlemanly suits, and float through the courtyard. Soon a wooden walkway linked the entryway to dry land. Although it was apparently quite serviceable, the president of the chamber, Henri Brisson, insisted on having the Palais Bourbon walkway rebuilt when he decided that the bridge being constructed for the nearby foreign ministry office was finer than his own.

When the National Assembly voted January 24 to provide financial assistance to the city and its surrounding regions, the lights in the Palais Bourbon were still working. Three of the pumps that kept the building's emergency generators dry were still operating. The next day, January 25, the electricity flickered and finally went off inside the building, as had happened bit by bit throughout the city.

Robert Capelle, a stenographer who worked for the National Assembly, had evacuated from his home because of the high water and was now living in the Palais Bourbon with a few other staff members, including Monsieur Gautry. True to his profession, Capelle dutifully recorded what was unfolding around him in a brief journal of life inside the government's headquarters during those days. Once Gautry returned to work after rescuing his family, he told the story to Capelle, who included it in his memoir.

Capelle's own home, a few hundred yards away on Rue de l'Université, had been flooded along with the rest of the neighborhood. By January 24, the emergency supplies of wine, coal, and potatoes that Capelle and his friends had gathered for their stay at the Palais Bourbon were completely waterlogged and useless, so Capelle went out into the snow, which had been falling all day long, and caught a pheasant and a rabbit. At least they would eat that night.[26]

With the waters of the Seine above the Zouave's thighs, Parisians recognized that this flood was the worst in recent memory. As temperatures plunged below freezing, numerous small icebergs floated amidst the debris in the river. Paris had become a strange and unfamiliar place by January 24. No one knew when this misery would end, but as the water continued to rise most people realized that they had not yet seen the worst of what the Seine could do to their city.

Chapter Three

PARIS UNDER SIEGE

In the Javel neighborhood, an elderly woman, rescued by the police, hangs onto a makeshift raft for dear life.

efore sunrise on January 25, the suburban town of Ivry to the southeast of Paris lit up with a roaring blaze. Water invading the Pagès, Camus, and Company vinegar factory mixed with the chemicals stored there to create a flammable gas. When those fumes caught fire, there was a sudden explosion, heard miles away in central Paris, and the factory went up in flames. "The sound produced by this explosion," reported the newspaper *Le Journal*, "made Parisians think that the Pont de l'Alma was being blasted apart with dynamite."[1] Such a thought was not far-fetched. Debris washing downriver from the Bercy warehouses and towns to the east frequently became caught on the decks of bridges and prevented the water from moving freely underneath. In desperation, General Jean-Baptiste Dalstein had considered ordering his troops to destroy the rubbish and open up the passageways under the city's bridges with explosives.

The local firefighters who arrived on the scene at Ivry struggled to reach the burning factory, but the deep water around the building blocked their path. They could only watch as the building glowed hotter and hotter as a result of the large quantities of alcohol and various chemicals inside. The area around the vinegar factory was now extremely dangerous, and construction workers living at a nearby building site evacuated by boat to a temporary hospital.

Prefect of police Louis Lépine soon arrived with a team of Parisian firefighters to assist the men from Ivry, and they charged toward the burning structure through knee-high water. But then they hesitated: Everyone realized that in order to prevent another explosion inside the building they would have to hurry, but Lépine and Lieutenant Colonel Corder of the fire service did not want their men to be killed by another blast. They decided they had no choice but to proceed. "Men with battering rams quickly entered the building preventing a detonation that would have showered the entire area with debris and perhaps victims,"

Lépine later told the City Council.[2] The fire at the vinegar factory had been extinguished, thus averting a second explosion.

Two hundred people employed by the destroyed vinegar factory were suddenly out of work, but they were not alone. The newspaper *L'Humanité*, the organ of the Communist party, reported the rapidly growing unemployment to its readers. After the fire, "Ivry is in ruins. Factories are closed, and thousands of workers are now out of a job."[3] Workers throughout the entire Paris region were suffering. In some cases, the suspension of gas or electricity or the inability to move goods and people on the rail lines shut down factories. In working-class areas, lower quality housing was often more vulnerable to destruction, leaving many residents homeless as well as jobless.

One of the newly unemployed in Paris was a laborer, Jean Rapinat, who had worked for the Lalong construction firm as a bricklayer and stonemason. The company, which specialized in urban public works projects, including sewer and drainage construction—its letterhead proudly proclaimed the motto *"tout à l'égout"* (everything into the sewer)—was forced to close its builder's yard located in the heavily flooded Rue de la Convention in the 15th *arrondissement*. As the water rose, it also engulfed the construction site where Rapinat had been working in the nearby Rue Lourmel on January 25. When he filed for unemployment assistance, Rapinat's employer wrote a note verifying to relief officials that the business was shut down and that his men were temporarily out of work. Rapinat was now spending five francs a week to live in a hotel since his home had been flooded too.[4]

A short distance away from Ivry, the veterinary school in Maisons-Alfort had become a refuge for inhabitants of the southeastern suburbs by January 25, including people from nearby towns like Charenton and Alfortville. Many brought their animals with them. Soon victims were housed throughout the school's facilities. Under driving rain and snow that day, marines and soldiers floated slowly along the river, making sure to avoid debris, on their way to rescue people. The veterinary school was now an important operations base for the military effort.

The school's director, Professor Gustave Barrier, wondered how he could give shelter to all the refugees. In his memoir of the events, he described a sudden influx of people on January 25: "Half-dressed, soaking wet, stiff, starving, they had left their houses quickly, and everything they owned was gone. Babies cried; huge tears rolled down the cheeks of their parents too. Over here, a woman with eight children who doesn't know where here husband is; over there are more women being consoled by others."[5] The school's staff and generous neighbors handed out bread, soup, beans, and hot milk to the growing crowds in this temporary shelter. Professor Barrier also had to find space to bivouac and feed the troops. As the water rose, communications with the city were failing, and so were the means of transportation. The people who sought refuge in the school were again trapped by the water.

Police and soldiers along with Red Cross workers arrived at the school to render assistance, bringing food, beds, and medical care — much-needed relief for Professor Barrier, who had little experience dealing with emergency matters. As a veterinarian whose expertise was in horses, he was used to caring for animals, not people. "Access to the school from the Pont de Charenton," Barrier wrote, "has been cut off to pedestrians; one can only go this way by wagon, on someone else's back, or by . . . boat." Soon the options were reduced even further, as only boats were able traverse the high water.[6]

Throughout the day of January 25, the fourth day of the flood, Robert Capelle and other staff members of the National Assembly pulled oil lamps out of storage and hung them throughout the Palais Bourbon. Deputies were shivering as they rose to speak on the floor of the chamber during the ongoing legislative debates. Soon they began to cough and wheeze from the fumes generated by the oil lamps, their eyes watering and burning. Frustrated by these inconveniences, some members grumbled to one another that perhaps the Assembly should suspend its sessions. Others vehemently objected. If the Assembly refused to meet, they said, it would send a bad message to the people of Paris, frightening them even more at the very moment when they needed leadership. According to Capelle, one deputy declared: "When there is water in the amphitheater, we will climb onto the seats."[7] After all, their discomfort was nothing compared with what thousands of Parisians were suffering. Realizing the growing needs of victims, whose homes and businesses had been washed away all across northern France, the deputies continued work on the generous aid package already under consideration that would provide relief to those touched by the flood.

Parisians were continuing to labor from one end of the city to the other to fight the flood. Police and soldiers piled sacks of cement along the quay walls at the Pont de l'Alma on January 25 to prevent the water from overflowing. A portion of the Quai des Orfèvres on the Ile de la Cité collapsed.

Some of the debris sweeping through the city on the river's powerful current included casks of wine and pieces of furniture, which many Parisians saw as free for the taking. Risking life and limb, treasure-seekers tried to grab some of the river's loot with their bare hands. A correspondent for the daily newspaper *Le Gaulois* described how some people climbed over the bridge railings at the Pont de Solferino to pluck items from the raging water:

Men with huge hooked poles are on the watch for wreckage. . . . Lo! . . . a cask of wine. Precious, delicious beverage! Ready there with the pole! The chance of a lifetime! Gaily sails that cask [in] the angry stream, a burden of joy on the bosom of all this rage. Bump! The cask has collided with the glorious architecture of the Solferino. Ah, bah! The wretch with that hooked pole has missed! The cask goes bumping along beneath the bridge. Freed on the other arch, it bowls defiantly down the Seine. Off with you, precious thing, amid the cheers of enthusiastic Parisians! Bear your burden of delight to other shores, other gullets. An arm chair is next, then a bedstead, then . . . a grand piano![8]

Much of the debris, traveling at more than 15 miles per hour down the river's channel, was destroyed when it crashed into the bridge pylons with great force. The police hung posters by the Seine's banks reminding Parisians that, by law, anything recovered from the river must be turned over to the authorities within 24 hours. Nevertheless, for some of the people on the bridges, the temptation of gathering up these floating items was too great.

During the flood American writer Helen Davenport Gibbons weaved through Paris's flooded streets, trying to take in the extent of the damage and the strange spectacle of the river. No stranger to the city, as a child Gibbons had visited Paris many times with her family, and shortly after marrying, she and her husband moved there in 1909. Gibbons immersed herself in the life of the city, writing extensively about her experiences for American magazines and in her memoirs. She described her disbelief as she saw Paris drowning. "Although the newspapers warned us that they might be swept away," she reported, "the bridges were crowded with sightseers." Gibbons recounted the strange mood of the crowd, as she stood on the Pont d'Arcole near Notre-Dame, in which "the calamity was forgotten in the sport of watching huge barrels sucked one by one under an arch and jumping high in the air as they came out on the other side."[9] For the Parisians around her on the bridge, this was quite a show. Spectators sometimes cheered on pieces of garbage in a mock race to see which one would make it to the bridge first, laughing and shouting if their chosen debris won. American magazine *Current Literature* described a similar scene on another of the city's bridges: "Immense arm chairs were received with rapture and dainty ladies in furs, from the summits of automobiles, wagered gems and bonbons upon the results of races between upholstered sofas and great carved bedsteads."[10] Gibbons could only explain the phenomenon with a quip about human nature: "Curiosity is stronger than fear."[11]

At the Gare d'Austerlitz, water had blocked both the Métro and southbound trains leaving for Orléans. Across the river, the Gare de Lyon, from which trains also departed for points to the south, was swamped too. Just after the river started rising so dramatically, worried

Parisians began coming to the station by the hundreds, carrying what they could of their belongings, hoping to catch a train headed to drier locations. At first, a few of the older, steam-driven trains were still running, but by January 25 most sat empty, frozen in the station or the yard and surrounded by high water. For the lucky few who found a still-functioning train in those first few days, departing Paris first meant rowing out to the tracks in a boat and sloshing through the water to climb aboard. Passengers whose trains were canceled either went back home if they could or camped out, sitting on their luggage in the station, praying that something would move. Some train stations had become unintended emergency shelters. By January 25, around two hundred flood victims from Alfortville, including children, were huddled together in the waiting rooms at Gare de Lyon with coats wrapped around them, begging for assistance from the station's administrators. The superintendent wrote to Louis Lépine on that day, asking for help with these refugees from the suburbs "since the number of unfortunates coming to Paris is growing. . . ."[12] There was little else he could do. Nearly every train, subway, and tram line would be closed for days, even weeks.

More and more Parisians felt trapped by the rising water, causing extreme levels of distress. One anecdotal report, published in the newspaper *Le Matin* on January 25, described the case of a police agent living on a floating dock on the Seine that he oversaw as part of his official duties. He had been diagnosed with cancer and planned to live out his final days in the comfort of his familiar surroundings. When the water climbed so high that he would have been forced to leave his dockside home, he committed suicide rather than going elsewhere to die in an unfamiliar place.[13]

Throughout the city on January 25, an army of volunteers was hard at work trying to provide as much relief as possible in the midst of the disaster. The Royalist Committee of the 4th *arrondissement* was running a soup kitchen, open to all, from 9 AM until 7 PM every day. A shelter for some eight hundred children in the Faubourg Saint-Antoine had been completely flooded and was receiving donations after publicly asking for assistance.

Charitable organizations, especially the French Red Cross, had swiftly moved into action once the flood began to wreak its havoc, organizing the most significant private efforts to alleviate suffering with food and shelter, and funneling enormous donations from throughout France and the world into rescue efforts in and around Paris. Three unique groups made up the French Red Cross: The earliest, the Society for Aid to War Wounded, was founded in 1866 shortly after the Red Cross in Geneva, and its members had served during the Franco–Prussian War and late nineteenth-century colonial wars organizing ambulances, medicine, and relief to soldiers and civilians. Now this group brought its care and concern to the streets of Paris. Also part of the Red Cross were the Union of French Women and the Association of French Ladies, both organizations that were formed in the decades after the Franco–Prussian War. These groups provided upper- and middle-class women with opportunities to conduct charitable work acceptable to their social station and their expected role as nurturing mothers while also serving the nation.[14]

Cooperating closely with Louis Lépine, by January 25, these Red Cross groups had opened shelters throughout the city to serve as temporary homes, complete with beds and heaters, and they provided emergency soup kitchens and clothing distribution to the newly homeless. One reporter writing for *Le Matin* described what he saw in such a Red Cross station in the Grenelle quarter: "There were already thirty people quietly sitting, opening their mouths wide to eat the vegetable and bean soup and lifting . . . their big grateful eyes [toward the cook]."[15]

A reporter for *Le Temps* provided a glimpse of the busy activities of the Red Cross after he rode with a volunteer driver making his rounds. The man sped his truck full of supplies to the school in Saint-Ouen, a suburb north of Paris. He hopped out, flung open the back of the truck, and began to unload food, bedding, clothes, and other essentials for the fifty flood victims inside the temporary shelter, where members of the Union of French Women tended to them. Back on his route, the driver pulled his vehicle into another shelter run by the Society for Aid to War Wounded, which was handing out soup, bread, and meat to flood victims.

At the next stop, members of the Red Cross worked hand-in-hand with the Catholic group Sisters of Charity, distributing clothing to those refugees who had fled their homes with nothing but what they had on their backs. No one asked whether the needy who showed up were really victims of the flood. The women working in the shelter wrote their names down in a registry but asked for no other proof. An empty hall became a shelter, housing women, children, and the elderly, including a blind man and a paralytic. In another refuge the driver visited, a mother rocked her nine-day-old baby in its wicker cradle, a man with a broken leg sat nursing his wounds, and a little girl tried to amuse her brother by doing somersaults. Back in his truck, the driver headed to the suburb of Saint-Denis, where he dropped off a load of bread, meat, potatoes, and chocolate, and then he zoomed ahead to the next stop.[16]

The Society for Aid to War Wounded approached the task of rescue with military precision. Dividing the city and its environs into six sectors, its volunteers made daily rounds through each zone, taking special note of the particular needs. One of the group's wealthy benefactors, Duc de Camastra, placed the courtyard of his mansion at their disposal. From there, a dozen cars roared out to each section, transporting supplies that included bread, eggs, chocolate, gasoline, wool coats, shoes, and baby items. The society received more than 2,000 pounds of vegetables from one small provincial village. Vendors at the central food market sold meat at a discount to the society.

Within the first week, the Society for Aid to War Wounded alone set up more than fifty sites around the greater Paris region. According to one press estimate, at the height of the crisis the Red Cross handed out a hundred thousand loaves of bread every day. In the Red Cross hospital in Auteuil, volunteers added beds to the wards filled with the patients already under their care. Some of the newly arrived refugees who had fled suburban towns assisted in the Red Cross's workroom, where unemployed women prepared clothing to go to other refugees.

In conjunction with Catholic clergy, the Red Cross ran the shelters
at Notre-Dame-des-Champs as well as at other religious sites throughout the city. They staffed schools, including the veterinary school at
Maisons-Alfort, and military barracks that now housed flood victims.
The government printing bureau on Rue de la Convention became a
Red Cross refuge, and there was talk of converting the Panthéon into a
shelter if necessary. In his account in *L'Intransigeant,* Guillaume Apollinaire called those who worked day and night to run the shelters "angels" for what they did. Another poet, Comte de Sabran-Pontevès,
penned a verse in their honor calling them:

> the *stars* of France . . . workers of heaven,
> On a dismal horizon you are the rainbow.[17]

The school for the deaf installed forty cots in an empty space, and the
school for the blind accommodated several dozen more. The mental
hospital at Charenton offered many of its unoccupied beds to the
homeless and installed more in a dining room. The eastern suburban
town of Le Vésinet took in around nine hundred flood victims, and En-
ghien-les-Bains to the north offered to shelter and feed four hundred
people. Three hundred refugees from Alfortville traveled west to Mon-
treuil-sur-Bois to be housed in a school.

The Society of Saint Vincent de Paul and the Philanthropic Society distributed flyers throughout the city, listing dozens of locations
where people could find help: lodging at hospitals and temporary shelters, some dedicated to single women or those with children; food, including soup kitchens, bread, and makeshift restaurants serving women
who arrived with their children; and dry clothing. Each organization
had 25 locations in and around Paris where a person could get a hot
meal, and there were dozens more.

On January 25, large posters went up all around Paris on walls, on advertising columns, and outside government buildings, calling in bold letters for donations to be brought to the administrative offices in each
neighborhood. These posters argued for citywide social responsibility

across geographical and class lines. One notice posted by the local officials of the 4th *arrondissement* put the case plainly: "A large number of families are already without shelter, without provisions, and without clothing." The measures of the government would not be enough, it said, unless "each one of us provides his spontaneous assistance to the humanitarian spirit on behalf of these victims." Bring your donations to the town hall, the poster instructed, and a list of contributors would be created "as a testimony to the spirit of human solidarity in our *arrondissement*."[18]

The 8th *arrondissement,* which includes the Champs-Elysées, was one of the wealthiest districts in the city. Although it too was affected by the flood, it was certainly better off than many others. A placard bearing the imprimatur of its mayor appealed for all expressions of heartfelt public generosity: "An unprecedented catastrophe has upset Paris. The disaster becomes more unsettling each day. The calm and courage of the entire population is admirable. But we must all hasten to come to the aid of the unfortunate victims of the flood. The more fortunate *arrondissements* must subsidize to a great degree the urgent needs of those who do not have the same resources. This is the duty of the 8th *arrondissement*."[19]

Posters told residents that the whole of Paris was in danger, not any one particular neighborhood. The fate of the entire city was bound together, regardless of whether their *arrondissement* had been touched by the waters.

Even in the midst of the flood, the regular duties of the police continued. Louis Lépine's agents did not stop observing the actions of unions, striking workers, and political radicals. They still arrested criminals, responded to robberies, and attended to domestic disputes and assaults just as they did on any given day. They arrived at the scenes of fires to provide security and assistance as always. The city's flooding only added more work and stress to an already busy police force trying to keep order in a big city. To make matters worse, on January 25 the basement of police headquarters began to fill with water.

That day, Lépine traveled with several other officials to the Javel quarter to inspect the damage. Among them was Armand Fallières, the grandfatherly 69-year-old president of the Republic. Fallières had already weathered many tumultuous years at the highest levels of power. An ardent Republican who believed in the power of law, science, education, and reason, he had served for years in the National Assembly as one of a generation of reformers that moved French politics toward the center, away from both the conservative policies that dominated at the founding of the Third Republic and the radical politics that sought to overturn the government altogether. As minister of public instruction in the 1880s, he had helped institute significant changes that made public education in France free and mandatory, and also secular. This was a direct challenge to the Catholic church's longstanding role in training French youth and fueled a growing battle over the role of religion in society. In 1906 the National Assembly elected Fallières to the presidency.

Despite his age, the white-haired Fallières made regular visits throughout the flooded areas by boat, car, and sometimes horse-drawn wagon. As the president arrived with his entourage in the flood-soaked neighborhood of Javel on Tuesday, January 25, he knew that the Seine was now encircling the Zouave's waist, some fourteen and a half feet above normal. After climbing out of the car, Fallières and Lépine waded through knee-deep water and mud to inspect the desolation. Residents were furiously evacuating their homes, packing as much as they could in suitcases and trunks and loading them onto wagons, but still leaving things behind. Crying women sloshed through the streets balancing children on their hips and wondered aloud through their sobs what would become of them and their families. Fallières and Lépine were deeply shaken by the scene.[20]

Later that day, on a visit to the suburban town of Charenton, just east of Paris, Lépine guided the president and his party around the flooded area, pointing his cane in the air to show the course of the water's progress. "Do you think," Fallières asked Lépine, "that the damage is worse here or in Paris?" Much worse in places like Charenton, Lépine asserted. Paris had the men, boats, and tools, he said, that were sadly lacking in the suburbs. "Poor people live in this area, and they have neither shelter nor resources." As Lépine and the president slogged through the mud, they heard cries for help coming from an upper floor of a building surrounded by water. "How horrible!" Fallières exclaimed, and asked people to go to the aid of the person in need. Lépine ordered his men to hurry, and the agents ran off to find the flood victim who was calling for help. As the president and Lépine were returning to the car, they heard other voices crying out, "Don't forget us! Help us!"[21] Their shouts did not fall on deaf ears.

For all the hard work of those helping the suffering, though, many Parisians were already becoming confused about whom to turn to for assistance, especially since there was not always a clear sense of who was in charge. At the local level, the prefect of the Seine and the prefect of police worked closely together, but their jurisdictions overlapped. At the national level, the ministry of interior oversaw internal security matters, but General Dalstein's military troops were also working to rescue victims and provide safety. Soldiers were helping to build *passerelles* and deal with other emergency engineering questions, but that caused them to venture into the territory of the national ministry of public works. Police, soldiers, sailors, firefighters, public assistance workers, men who worked in the Métro and the sewers, road crews, and teams from the water, gas, electric, telephone, and telegraph services all answered to different supervisors. Paris was becoming an exercise in controlled chaos.

The night sky on January 25 was clear and bright with starlight, and a full moon danced across the water's moving surface. Despite the damage caused by the flood, the beauty of Paris still shone through, especially after dark. Light from the emergency oil lamps and the few remaining electric bulbs sparkled on the expansive Seine. The river now spread out like a vast, watery plain across large stretches of the city, erasing the clear distinction between the Right and Left Banks. Where water on one side of the quay wall and cobblestone on the other

Photographers, like those from the studio of Pierre Petit, captured the strange beauty of a city filled with water.

once clearly defined the river's edge, the streets had now vanished, and the Seine lapped against the walls of buildings.

In the daylight of the following morning, January 26, everything about the rising river seemed ominous and strange. The color of the racing water had turned a murky shade. The very look of the river—muddier than usual, frothy in places, and filled with debris—told of a great disaster. The *New York Times* called it a "filthy, yellow monster gnawing into its [the city's] very vitals."[22] The newspaper *L'Intransigeant* described one old ruffian, the sort normally dismissed by passersby, who cried out "It's the end of the world!"[23]

British journalist Laurence Jerrold, the Paris correspondent for London's *Daily Telegraph,* walked alongside the river, observing the bloated Seine's power firsthand: "The yellow stream, yellow like the Rhine at Cologne, tore along beneath us as the Rhone rushes out of the Lake of Geneva. . . . It whirled on, this flat country Seine, with the force of a mountain torrent, as fierce and fast as the blue Aar at Berne, but yellow and muddy, for it carried every kind of refuse and ruin with it. Yet it was beautiful!"[24] Jerrold expressed the same mixture of attraction and repulsion as did the large crowds of Parisians who were still coming to the bridges and riverbanks on January 26 to be entertained by this once-in-a-lifetime event. The London *Telegraph* correspondent reported that not since the world's fair in 1900 had he witnessed "such a dense assemblage of well-dressed people on the bridges or near the quays."[25] French journalist and chronicler of the day, Jules Claretie, had a slightly more somber memory of people lined up along the Seine's banks that harkened back to the Franco–Prussian War. "These crowds," he wrote in *Le Figaro,* "will revive in the minds of all who passed through the great siege the painful memories of those tragic days when just such black throngs lined the riverside to see boats bringing back wounded from the battlefields of the Marne."[26]

By Wednesday, January 26, a storm was raging across the north of France and the English Channel, bringing high winds, rain, and snow, and stalling much of the shipping traffic out of French ports. Fortunately, Judge Linebarger and Mrs. Nuttall, the two American visitors who had left Paris for their trip back home, had already set sail on the *Bretagne.* In the midst of their trans-Atlantic voyage, they began to receive wireless radio reports of what was happening back in Paris. One report that reached the ship started an on-board rumor about the near collapse of the Eiffel Tower. So disturbing was the news that the ship's French passengers began to fear openly for their families living in the flood zone, as well as for their city. When the ship finally docked in New York, reporters immediately quizzed Judge Linebarger, Mrs. Nuttall, and other passengers, since they were among the first eyewitnesses to reach American soil, to confirm the news coming out of Paris by cable.

Once released from quarantine, the anxious French passengers hounded American reporters to find out any news from home: What had been destroyed? How many had died? And what remained of Paris? As the *New York Times* put it, "They were not much comforted by the news they got."[27]

The reports about the Eiffel Tower, at least, were better than the passengers had feared. The city's most recognizable icon had not collapsed. Hydraulic pumps in its four pillars prevented it from sustaining much damage. The tower now rose from the middle of an icy brown lake that covered much of the Champs de Mars, once the heart of the 1900 fairgrounds. Just beside the landmark structure sat the Gare du Champ de Mars, the train station built for the 1867 Exposition. All around the snow-covered yard, buildings and dozens of rail cars full of abandoned goods lay submerged in water. What had only recently been a site of brisk activity was now eerily still. The tower looked much less striking adjacent to a lifeless station with debris floating through the water.

On January 26, sewers underneath the Post Office's main building near the Louvre overflowed, and water trickled into the central telegraph exchange in the basement. Suddenly, the 728 telegraph lines, including 32 devoted to international messages, were threatened, and Paris could soon be cut off from the rest of the world. Fast communication was so crucial for business in the modern age that in 1909 Parisian telegraphs wired some 33 million messages. Now the Seine threatened to reduce that number to zero. Maintenance crews hastily brought in sacks of cement to reinforce the walls while floodwaters doused heating devices and shorted out the electrical system. Firemen finally brought a functioning pump, but fears for the building's weakened foundation forced them to shut it off, and water flowed into the equipment. Communication to other parts of France as well as England, Belgium, Holland, Denmark, parts of Switzerland, and Italy were knocked out, and international trade was frozen. Under these conditions, foreign correspondents had difficulty telling the world what was happening in Paris. Since at least one trans-Atlantic line remained intact, one British reporter noted that he could send stories to London only by way of his paper's New York bureau, which then sent them back to Europe at enormous expense. Many anxious families had no way to send messages to let others know that they were safe.

On January 26 water overran the power plant for the city's trams, knocking out a great deal of their service. Tram cars moved in some areas of the city, but elsewhere Parisians now had to resort to other means. Horse-drawn omnibuses and carriages, although in dwindling use in the streets of Paris, were one of the few forms of transportation that could continue. These vehicles carried people through the streets in water that in some cases nearly reached the horses' shoulders.

$\mathcal{R}$ain and brisk winds continued throughout the day on Wednesday, January 26. The weather was seeping into the home of writer and philosopher Emile Chartier, better known to French readers as Alain, who noted in his journal: "Gusts of wind blew the rain against the windows, and even though the window was closed, there was the smell of rain, as if the window had been left open."[28] Snow coated the bare branches of trees and empty benches in the parks, giving a beautiful sheen to much of the city. Yet it only worsened the gritty mud and oily slush already gumming up traffic on the streets. As it slid below ground through sewer grates, the additional moisture and muck entered the overflowing conduits. The screaming headline of *Le Matin* that morning reflected the growing consciousness about the scale of the disaster, proclaiming it "A National Calamity."

Hôtel de Ville (City Hall) on the Right Bank, across from the Ile de la Cité, continued to function during the flood despite the difficult circumstances. Bureaucrats working for the municipal government behind the building's ornate sixteenth-century façade, rebuilt after its destruction during the Franco–Prussian War and the Commune, struggled to continue their duties as lights flickered and eventually went out. Phones rang off the hook until water destroyed the lines. For days, messengers ran past the statues of the dozens of historic Parisians that lined the front of the building, bringing updates from around the city.

The City Council met there in an emergency session on January 26, five days into the crisis. Representatives from districts across Paris climbed the grand staircase and filed into the council chamber to describe what was happening to their constituents and to urge colleagues to send help to their neighborhoods. Surrounded by the chamber's deep, wood paneling and the Napoleonic-era tapestries from the Aubusson factory that depicted the city's monuments, council members settled nervously into their seats to begin the session. Twenty-six feet over their heads, embedded into the ceiling, were the emblems of the dozens of communities that compose the Department of the Seine (Paris and its suburbs) for which this body was responsible, reminding them of just how many souls were in their charge.

At the beginning of the session, Justin de Selves, who since 1896 had held the powerful position once occupied by Haussmann as prefect of the Seine, rose to make a statement. De Selves was a Franco–Prussian War veteran from a wealthy tobacco-producing family in Toulouse. A career administrator and official with a lawyer's training and family connections to government, de Selves had served in regional prefectures, as head of the French postal and telegraph service and as a member of the French Senate. His receding hairline and strong jaw framed deep-set eyes that gazed serenely and confidently into the council chamber. "Gentlemen," the prefect intoned from underneath his large gray moustache. "Alas! I do not need to tell you about the disaster that has struck our region since you know about it all too well. We have taken every precaution and offered every kind of assistance within our power." Like most Parisians, de Selves believed that the city had been as prepared as it could be for an event like this. What Paris needed now, he said, was money. De Selves called on the City Council to approve 100,000 francs' worth of credit immediately to assist flood victims. There was much work to do.

"I have sent an expression of our gratitude to the military governor of Paris [General Dalstein, in command of the Paris garrison] to all the officers, and to the foot soldiers, who have risked their lives to come to our aid," de Selves told the City Council. "I am sure you would like to associate yourselves with these sentiments under the circumstances." The assembled lawmakers cheered, *"Très bien! Très bien!"*[29]

Then the president of the City Council, Ernest Caron, took the floor. Before the work of the day began, he declared proudly: "I want to let you know that we have been witnessing—from every part of the Parisian population, from the highest to the lowest on the social ladder—the admirable expressions of human solidarity demonstrated by the considerable donations of money and personal aid." Caron shared telegrams the council had received from officials in other cities, conveying the compassion of their residents. "Moved with great sorrow by the frightening ravages of the Seine, the municipality of Toulouse," he read aloud, "reminded by the misfortune of its own experience, addresses its deepest sympathy."[30] Caron had replied with Paris's gratitude for such expressions of solidarity, and a feeling of good will filled the chamber. In its hour of need, Paris would not be alone.

Among the council members sat Louis Lépine. The flood was a direct challenge to his hard work. "The prefect of police has the floor," President Caron called out from the rostrum. After adding his voice to the expressions of thanks made by de Selves and Caron, Lépine changed the tone of the discussion. "Words must now become acts: That's why I am here." The suburbs were already hard hit, and now Paris would continue to feel the full brunt of the still-rising water rushing downriver, Lépine asserted. "At this very moment, Paris is being threatened. We can assure those who live in the flooded streets that they will be rescued, supplied, and hospitalized as necessary." Still the resources that Lépine had on hand were simply not enough. "I will ask the minister of the navy to make more boats available to me. I will have them tonight or tomorrow morning at the latest."[31] Lépine's request couldn't have come too soon. Many in the city were starting to feel waterlogged and overwhelmed by events, to the point of giving up. *Le Matin* reported of the mood on January 26 that "people aren't struggling against the water any longer, they just watch it come. Paris is keeping quiet."[32]

But Lépine was not the sort to keep quiet. With sixty boats already in use, he had sent an order requisitioning any available craft docked at the La Villette basin, part of the canal system in the city's northeast quadrant. He commandeered the rowboats from the lake in the Bois de Boulogne, the ones Parisians would normally take out for a leisurely Sunday afternoon in the park. Lépine had also asked the minister of the interior to prepare several sizable buildings, such as schools and museums, which could be used as emergency hospitals, and to bring in heating devices and bed linens. "You are already aware," he told the council, "that I have already begun to use the former seminary at Saint-Sulpice." Lépine had turned into a shelter the beautiful late Baroque church with mismatched towers, just a few blocks from the heavily flooded Boulevard Saint-Germain.[33]

For all the goodwill that circulated in the City Council that night, however, serious problems were already surfacing, and the mood inside the chamber quickly became heated. Despite Caron's claims of solidarity, the council was forced to address growing tensions within the city. One angry council member, Monsieur Evain from the extremely damaged 16th *arrondissement* on the city's western side, accused the government of doing very little to warn Parisians about the impending flood. Once the water reached his neighborhood, he claimed, the administration was not as effective as it could have been. The help came much too late. "Beginning on Saturday, had we been able to cut the sewers off from the Seine, if pumps had been made available to us, we might have been able to dry out the Rue Félicien-David and hold back the disaster," he railed on the floor of the council chamber. Instead, he said, the people in his neighborhood were not provided with pumps. "For forty-eight hours we had nothing to help us but three pitiful boats that some individuals had to go and borrow."[34] In those boats, Evain claimed, the residents of his district had practically performed miracles on their own, saving more than seven hundred people. On at least one occasion, he told the chamber, a boat sank with five people aboard, including a pregnant woman.

In Evain's opinion, since Rue Félicien-David had proven vulnerable to flooding before, the administration should have taken precautionary measures much earlier. "This is not the first time that I have seen a flood during my time on the council. It is at least the third time." Deeply frustrated that his constituents had been left to fend for themselves, Evain shouted his disdain.

Several other members stood up as well. Why had their districts been ignored over the past few days? Why had posters announcing where to find emergency relief not been hung where they lived? When would boats arrive for their districts? "I demand that the administration put 100 troops, 8 boats, and 16 pontoon men at the disposal of the police in the 12th *arrondissement*," intoned Councilman Pierre Morel. "I don't think this is too difficult."[35]

Morel also denounced bakers who were raising the cost of bread from its average price of around 80 centimes to 1.20 francs, declaring that he intended to "bring the greatest shame" upon any price gouger, and he called on others to do the same.[36] De Selves also understood that the cost of food was becoming a serious concern as rumors of price hikes spread. Hunger, the prefect realized, could easily lead to the breakdown of law and order. Earlier in the day he had sent a confidential memo to the mayors of the twenty Paris *arrondissements,* warning them to stay alert to the possibility of illegal profiteering by bakers in their neighborhoods. If the situation warranted, he suggested, bread could be sold from the town halls.

Council members had limited administrative power on their own since the prefect of the Seine was really the one in charge, but such exchanges showed that they were beginning to question de Selves's leadership. By the end of the session, the council voted to approve 100,000 francs of immediate aid to victims, and 50,000 more were placed at Lépine's discretion for rescue work. While the council was in session, the Seine was pouring into the Hôtel de Ville. In the basement, the municipal printing office regularly produced the *Bulletin Municipal Officiel,* the government's publication that announced ordinances and declarations for the public record. The pumps could not keep pace with the flooding, so the printing presses were shut down, suspending for eight days the dissemination of important government information, although reports of the council's meeting that night were promptly reported in the press.

While the politicians were arguing, Guillaume Apollinaire ventured out into the streets again on January 26 to take stock of the human tragedy around him. He splashed through several inches of icy water, his feet quickly soaking as he walked across the square in front of the Church of Saint-Sulpice. He had come to investigate the improvised shelter that Lépine had opened. As he approached the building, a well-dressed woman arrived with tears rolling down her cheeks. "I don't have a home anymore," she cried, "and the town hall sent me here."[37] She and Apollinaire entered the seminary doors to find hundreds of others, in the very same situation, who now called the church home.

Apollinaire made his way through the dim corridors, poking his head into rooms to survey the scene. "Tonight, nearly 600 *misérables* are sleeping at Saint-Sulpice. A hat maker, his wife and their three children are sleeping with clenched fists." The chic Left Bank department store Le Bon Marché had donated mattresses and sheets to the shelter to try and put people at ease, but comfort was in short supply. "By a miracle . . . ," Apollinaire described the shelter, "a rainbow illuminated the tragic gloom of Paris: It was a rainbow of charity filled with grace."

Despite his lavish praise for this sanctuary, Apollinaire could not help being disgusted by its living conditions. As he moved into the darkness of the seminary, the stench overcame him. The dampness of the rain, river, and sewage clung to bodies and clothes, magnifying the ordinary smells of people now crammed into close quarters with few facilities for personal hygiene. All around, Apollinaire heard the sad moans of the dispossessed echoing through the shadowy hallways. "I looked at the single women. They slept on mattresses, these unfortunates. I heard the cry 'My God!' and one of them singing softly the refrain from a song . . . which would normally be happy, but the circumstances had made the words dismal." In another room, many of the single men spent another sleepless night contemplating their fate. Some wept. "Others who kept quiet looked at me with fear in their eyes. Others finally snored."

Apollinaire's wet shoes squished against the stone as he climbed the stairs to the second floor, where he found families with children in small rooms huddling close for comfort and safety in the dark and strange surroundings. They were given frying pans to cook a meal, and when finished, they set the still warm utensils in the hallway. Apollinaire passed by as one father put his used charcoal into a pan. The pitiable man explained to the poet: "You understand, I'm here for my little ones." Apollinaire seemed to have been touched by the remark. Turning to one of the volunteers who was helping to care for these refugees, he asked: "And tomorrow?" What will become of these homeless Parisians? "Most of the men will go to work, and most of the women will stay here sewing or taking care of the children," the shelter worker replied. Moving through the sleeping quarters on his way out, despite his sympathy, Apollinaire felt a sense of revulsion when he described the situation: "Terrible human odor!"[38] As he left Saint-Sulpice through its magnificent sanctuary, Apollinaire might have looked up at the enormous Eugène Delacroix painting of Jacob trying to wrestle his blessing from an angel, a fitting metaphor for a city still struggling for its salvation.

By January 26, boats became essential for moving throughout the city. Enterprising Parisians in several neighborhoods carried people from one side of a flooded street or square to another in an improvised ferry service. Sometimes as many as five or six people piled into a boat, launching out into a street that they normally crossed on foot. Well-dressed men in bowler hats and thick woolen overcoats frequently sat next to workmen in caps and cheap jackets. Boatmen, many of whom were probably river workers, propelled their ferries by plunging long poles into the water and pushing off the surface of the street below. Passengers sometimes wondered whether this act of kindness was a form of profiteering since the police usually reimbursed the boatmen. To quell any fears of exploitation, boats driven by police or sailors eventually replaced private craft.

For some people, these ferry services were their only lifeline. In one neighborhood, a man named Monsieur Coutant had been helping to organize the evacuation of nearly seventy flood victims, including numerous women, children, and sick people. "We had only one boat with three sailors who had worked day and night," an anonymous eyewitness reported to *L'Humanité,* but these men were called away to other duties. Now the responsibility fell on Coutant's shoulders as his increasingly desperate neighbors began to beg him for help. In frustration, Coutant told them, "I can't be everywhere!" Fearing for their safety, several people grabbed him by the collar and forced him to a boat so that they could continue to travel across the high water.[39]

Without boats of their own, many Parisians were reduced to struggling across the water on homemade rafts despite being fearful of falling in. Swimming had long been practiced for medicinal purposes among the middle class. By the turn of the century, medical reformers saw it as a way for the French to strengthen their bodies at a time when they feared that citizens were becoming weak and that the nation might be unable to survive should another war break out against Germany or some other foe. Swimming, nonetheless, remained largely an activity for those with leisure time, and many of the Parisians splashing about in the streets could not swim very well, if at all.

Dreading the water, people strapped together planks of wood, old crates, boxes, or any debris that would float, and they found a pole to push themselves along. Passengers on these makeshift rafts needed some luck to arrive safely at their destinations. In the Rue de Javel, an elderly woman crouched down on all fours on board one of these crude vessels, wrapped a shawl around her body, and covered her head with a scarf to block the chill. She fixed a deeply worried stare intently on her destination, praying for it to come faster as she tried to keep the fear at bay. The rickety, improvised raft underneath her was nothing but a thin plank tacked across two barrels. A policeman with a steady gaze and a long pole piloted this unstable raft, which seemed to be held together with little more than hope.

In some neighborhoods, engineers and laborers employed by the city were busy shuttling people across the water in large wheelbarrows. At the Quai de Passy on the city's western side, a local workman with a cart pulled up to a small ramp at the base of a staircase, where a throng of people, including women in large fashionable hats, waited their turn to be pulled through the ankle-deep water. This cart-puller splashed through the water day in and day out, far wetter than his passengers. City workers—perhaps men from a road-mending crew, gardeners from one of the parks, or Métro drivers—wove dozens of such carts through the streets to bring relief wherever they could. In Rue Félicien-David and the surrounding streets, the water had risen so high by January 26 that these workers and volunteers could no longer pull their carts loaded with human passengers. To compensate, many people from the neighborhood worked to raise the height of the *passerelles*. Fortunately, several boats arrived, and a flotilla of small craft piloted by marines and soldiers from the engineering section began to scour the neighborhood looking for people in need.

Back at the National Assembly on the night of Wednesday, January 26, the dark, cold corridors echoed with only a few footsteps. The small oil lamps on the walls cast such a low light that the deputies and staff could barely find their way through the building. Robert Capelle wrote in his journal that the people in the building that night "seemed like souls wandering through Hades," an ironic comparison given the icy temperatures inside the Palais Bourbon.[40] Staff members now living there lit stoves with scraps of wood they had been saving to try to keep warm. The mood inside the seat of government was growing anxious. Food was running short. Capelle watched as the water continued to rise. By the next morning, it would begin to engulf the statue representing the Law just outside the building.

Part Two

PARIS UNDER WATER

Chapter Four

RESCUING *a* DROWNED CITY

First responders and city workers lined the quay walls with sandbags and stones to hold back the water's force.

On Thursday, January 27, the Seine had reached the Zouave's shoulders, about eighteen feet above normal. Robert Capelle and his fellow staff members at the National Assembly were keeping track of the water level on a staircase inside the Palais Bourbon. Early that morning, Capelle noted that the water covered the two bottom steps. Five hours later, it had risen up to the sixth step.

On another trek through the waterlogged city, Guillaume Apollinaire looked up into the sky for a sign of hope, perhaps a rainbow to end what seemed to him this flood of biblical proportions. "Did God forget His promise?" he lamented in an article in *L'Intransigeant.* Then he found his answer: "The sun had disappeared."[1] A gray sky blanketed the city for another day, and large portions of the population grew increasingly fearful as they saw more homes and businesses being submerged. As the water continued to rise, the situation could only get worse. No one could be sure when the rain and flooding would cease.

On the Right Bank, the water was coming dangerously close to the top of the quay just outside the Louvre, the home to so many of France's national treasures. On January 27, reports began to circulate that the Seine had overrun the storage facility in the museum's basement and that the water-soaked quay walls were buckling and bending under the pressure of the mounting river. Alongside the former palace with its precious artifacts, the sagging roadway threatened to collapse.

As soon as police arrived on the scene that afternoon, they quickly shut off the streets on the side of the Louvre facing the Seine. Workmen began hauling hundreds of sandbags and dozens of shovels, the most basic tools of flood control, to the quay wall. The small group of onlookers that gathered behind the police cordon soon turned into a nervous crowd as more Parisians realized what was going on and stopped to watch. The sound of the rushing water grew closer over the wall as several dozen engineers, soldiers, and city workers piled up sandbags, packing them tightly to reinforce the barrier. Shouts rang out to keep them coming, and row after row of bags went up, thudding into place as wet burlap met wet burlap. Other workers mixed cement nearby, stuffing it into the crevices between the sandbags to bolster them. A few of the men grabbed their supplies and moved farther down the wall to close off the staircase that, in normal conditions, pedestrians used to descend to the riverside. The crowd stood quietly by for several hours, listening anxiously to the sound of shovels slicing into moist sand over and over again, then dumping it into the wet, brown sacks. Sweat, mingled with the rain, drenched the men who leaned their backs into the task throughout the day, grunting as they heaved the heavy bags into place.

Elsewhere, workers were less successful at fending off the flood's worst ravages. Crews moved swiftly to erect a wall in hopes of keeping water from invading the Place de la Concorde, the grand square at the eastern end of the Champs-Elysées, where the gilded obelisk of Luxor, given to the French by the Egyptians, had been installed in 1833. Water pushing up from the Métro had, in the words of one worker, "engorged the soil," threatening to spill into the square.[2] The water on the Champs-Elysées was already so deep in a few places that, according to press reports, at least one horse had drowned.

Workmen dispatched throughout Paris cemented over many of the manhole covers to stop the water's invasion, but there were too many points of entry to plug them all. One angry resident of Rue Félicien-David, in the western part of the city, argued that the sewers were at least partially to blame. A flyer he distributed to his neighbors on January 27 read: "The flood of which you are a victim is not a case of *force majeure*." In other words, this was not a so-called "act of God." "The City of Paris brought the flood to you with *its sewers*."[3] He claimed that the necessary protective structures around manhole openings that might have prevented the upward flow of water during a flood had not been installed.

Writing in the newspaper *Gil Blas* on January 27, journalist Gaston Lagrange remarked on the irony of a nation that had mastered the air—

France was a leader in developing aviation technology and by 1910 boasted the beginnings of a significant airplane industry—now losing its battle to control water. "It's the revenge of nature: the water has avenged the air. We leave this affair a bit wet and very humiliated." Despite having been bested by nature, however, Lagrange saw signs of hope. For him, "We are beaten-down to be sure, but we can defend ourselves. Above all, we help each other." Looking around the city, even as the river was rising, Lagrange argued that there was "a great movement of fraternal solidarity animating Parisians and France. Everywhere, in every corner where one passes ruins or the threat of death, brave people suddenly appear to fight with courage and helpful efforts."[4] From soldiers, sailors, and police to ordinary Parisians, according to Lagrange, everyone was working as one.

Editorialist Jules Claretie wrote of Paris's perseverance in *Le Temps* on January 27. Nature had humbled the city, he claimed, but people would triumph regardless. "Aren't people's hearts filled with pity, and aren't their hands tender and generous toward the suffering? Goodbye for at least one day to silly quarrels. Danger reunites people by something invisible which the ancients called Destiny." A common sense of humanity, Claretie argued, bound people together, especially in the midst of disaster. "The water is powerful, like a cyclone, devastating like a fire." Despite the obvious differences, Claretie compared Paris with Pompeii, "where the flood waters have like lava . . . chased the inhabitants out."[5] Whether the unity would last, Claretie did not know, but for the moment, it linked everyone in the city.

In the Javel neighborhood, however, people's sense of desperation intensified as the day wore on. Boats allowed people to travel cautiously through the area, but fear and hunger were growing rapidly. Law and order seemed on the verge of collapse. Anxious residents, hungry and unable to shop for food, began threatening to break into the few bakeries that had remained dry. The military ordered soldiers into the district to prevent pillaging and to reassure the local population that they and their property would remain safe.[6]

On January 27, President Fallières and Louis Lépine once again traveled to Javel, as they had done two days before, to reassure residents. Then the men joined Premier Aristide Briand on a visit to the temporary shelter at Saint-Sulpice, where refugees were taking their meals in the soup kitchen. Born in Brittany and trained as a lawyer, Briand had worked as a journalist for many years before entering politics. Despite his bourgeoisie background, Briand aligned himself with socialists and others on the left, and he saw himself as a man of the people, promoting reformist measures throughout his career. Briand had helped form French trade unions and was elected to the National Assembly in 1902. Renowned for his oratorical skills, Briand quickly became a seasoned politician and fought vigorously for the separation of church and state, a policy he helped to oversee. During the flood he was still new on the job. Briand, then age 47, became premier in July 1909, only six months before the flood, and he still had much to prove to the people of Paris.

Briand, Fallières, and Lépine moved through the crowd, shaking hands with first responders and flood victims alike. In a public show of solidarity with the shelter's residents, the president tasted the soup himself, much to the delight of onlookers. Briand offered a smile and a kind word to the refugees from underneath his wide handlebar mustache. France's leaders then traveled by car to Bercy, where city and military officials guided them through a school serving as a safe haven. As Fallières talked to the victims, he brought much good will and comfort in a moment of need, and people responded with a great fondness, greeting him with loud cheers. The Republic's leaders were showing that in a moment of crisis, they were unquestionably on the people's side.[7]

That day, President Fallières received a telegram from American president William Howard Taft, who also headed the American Red Cross, which could mobilize massive resources from around the United States. Taft cabled: "Is there any manner in which, through the National Red Cross or otherwise, appropriate expression could be made of the sympathetic distress with which the people and Government of the United States learn of the reported calamities which floods are causing in your beautiful and historic capital, as well as in the provinces of France? Meanwhile I offer you the sincerest sympathy and the most ardent wishes that the cause of these disasters may soon abate."[8]

Musicians also raised funds and showed their support for the Parisian victims by offering their own kind of solace as they sang in the streets. Songwriters told moving stories of the flood so that others would generously donate to the cause of flood relief. Louis Raynal, a popular songwriter of the day, composed "For the Flooded Ones," which promised on its cover that a portion of proceeds from the sale of lyrics sheets would go to flood relief. He called on the better angels of people's natures:

> Our Paris in tears
> Appeals to your wealth.
> It addresses your hearts.
> Comfort the distressed![9]

A song by Valentin Pannetier, "For the Flood Victims," offered a refrain that captured the increasingly somber mood:

> Ah! What a frightful misfortune.
> O! Paris, where the Seine has swelled.
> She creates horror,
> Ruin, sadness, pain!
> The river has overflowed
> And spreads bitter misery everywhere,
> So that children and their mothers
> Can do nothing but weep![10]

Poets also promoted giving through their verse. Roger de Talmont dedicated a poem, "A Call to Solidarity," to Louis Lépine, in honor of the prefect's devotion and leadership. The cover of the pamphlet in which the poem appeared said that it must not be sold for less than ten cents so that it would make enough to cover printing costs and still have some left over for the benefit of those he intended to help. De Talmont's poem created a melodrama in miniature, complete with heroic soldiers, grieving mothers who lost children, and Paris, "Queen of the World," ravaged by the waters but ultimately saved thanks to valiance, devotion, and patriotism. He even evoked a vision of complete social harmony in the face of disaster, in which political enemies gave up their differences to come together. And he ended with a call for further giving:

> Yes, let us give without regret, give, give again,
> Away with cruel egoism . . . ah! this dishonorable word—
> Our victimized Brothers claim their help,
> They wait for nothing, give, give again![11]

By January 27, much of the world was reaching out to Paris in its time of need. During the six days since the Seine had started its devastating rise, the flood had become dramatic worldwide news, with headlines splashed across papers that told of the city's drowning. As word of the flood spread, donations from foreign governments, individuals, and organizations around the world poured in to aid the flood victims, bringing millions of francs' worth of assistance to the relief effort. The Lord Mayor of London established a fund to which Britons could contribute; the city of Prague sent its condolences and money; Russian Czar Nicholas II sent 100,000 rubles; Pope Pius X sent 30,000 francs and his prayers. Donations came from Italy, Australia, Canada, and Switzerland. Milan's La Scala theater donated the proceeds of a performance of Saint-Saëns's *Samson and Delilah* to the victims.

While reporting on the worst of the flood, the *Chicago Daily Tribune* told the heartwarming story of a six-year-old girl who, upon hearing about the distress of French children, took all the money she had been saving in her piggy bank to buy herself a new doll and instead donated it to help the victims.[12] Groups in New Orleans, who celebrated their city's historic ties with France—such as the Society of July 14th, the French Union, and the French Benevolent Society—gave generously as well. Philanthropist William K. Vanderbilt gave 100,000 francs to the cause. The U.S. Chamber of Commerce provided a great deal of assistance, and Ambassador Robert Bacon met with American businessmen living in Paris to help coordinate their efforts. Bacon presented the French government with a check for 600,000 francs. At an exchange rate of about 5 francs to the dollar, that donation alone totaled around $120,000 in 1910 currency.

Even German Kaiser Wilhelm II sent a telegram of sympathy and a donation to flood victims. Apparently the German emperor was not sure whether his gift would be well received given the recent history of conflict between these two nations and the lingering resentment over the German annexation of Alsace-Lorraine. But a series of diplomatic inquiries cleared the way for this small expression of détente between the two former enemies. One German military officer was not equally generous with his view of the French relief efforts, however. On observing the French army's work on behalf of flood victims, he quipped sarcastically: "It seems that the character of our dear neighbors has not changed since 1870. I'm not surprised, for I never believed in the value of learning from disaster."[13]

If the German officer did not see much hope emerging from the situation, French citizens certainly did, and they proved to be the most generous of all. The Parisian newspapers that brought the bad news to so many had established funds to which readers were contributing millions of francs. On January 27, they again printed lists of donors, both large and small, to the accounts they had created as a public display of citywide solidarity. President Fallières himself, the press reported, gave 30,000 francs. The municipal government installed *troncs* (donation boxes similar to those at the doors of most churches) outside government buildings. People could place even a few coins into these boxes specifically for flood relief. One handwritten roster of gifts taken at the town hall of the 16th *arrondissement* records names, amounts, and the signatures of the donors: P. Vareillaud, five francs; A. Motté, three francs; G. Debessy, one franc. Under the circumstances, no gift was too small.[14] "Public generosity is real," wrote *Le Figaro* on January 27. "But to this charity, we must note, an anxiety which hardly any part of our city can escape."[15]

Industries, including automobile manufacturers and the Paris-Lyon-Mediterranée rail company, among many others, established funds for their unemployed workers. So did French labor unions, which wanted to make sure that the children of laborers in particular were being cared for. An association of businesses and industries in the 15th *arrondissement* collected money for victims in their neighborhood. Owners of a flooded telephone factory in Saint Cloud distributed bread and meat to their workers and even paid them for two days out of every four. Police headquarters regularly received large anonymous donations.

In addition to money, people throughout France made in-kind donations. The proprietor of Luna Park, an amusement park near the Bois de Boulogne, offered police the fleet of flat-bottomed boats featured in some of his water rides — they proved to be perfect for moving through the streets. Other boat owners donated their crafts to local officials or went through the flooded zone themselves rendering assistance. One Madame Dabernat wrote to the newspaper *Le Temps,* offering to house up to twelve women and children in her property in Saint-Rémy-les-Chevreuse outside Paris. Some food vendors donated fish, meat, and potatoes. The clothing manufacturer's association sold items at a discount to help people who had lost their belongings. Owners of stables in Maisons-Laffitte, downstream from the capital, allowed a flooded-out farmer to temporarily house his nine hundred sheep there. All kinds of gifts multiplied throughout Paris and beyond. On January 27, boatmen from the town of Dragnignan, in the southeast near the Mediterranean Sea, offered six men and three boats to assist in relief efforts.[16]

Even though the floodwaters spared many areas, the press coverage left readers with the impression of a shared experience of suffering throughout the entire city. *Le Matin* captured that sense of citywide solidarity on its front page on January 27: "Miserable neighborhoods and rich quarters, Bercy and Rue du Lille, Javel and Avenue Montaigne, are equally covered. The most beautiful furniture, the newest are as hard hit as the oldest prisons. . . . There is not a single Parisian at this

moment who can feel entirely safe in his home."[17] The newspaper imagined a Paris in which everyone, regardless of social status or wealth,
was suffering together through the same danger and suggested a sense
of common cause among all Parisians and a unity that many believed
was crucial to the survival of their city.

Residents of a multistory apartment building in a working-class neighborhood peered out from their windows all around the central courtyard to watch a small craft being pushed along by a boatman with a long
pole. On the windowsill of her apartment, a little girl looked down cu-
riously at the visitors in the boat below, especially Archbishop Léon-
Adolphe Amette, who stood quietly in the craft. Amette's stout body
was draped in clerical regalia, his bald head covered by a wide-brimmed
hat that he took off when the priest accompanying him offered a prayer
and made the sign of the cross. Amette gazed up compassionately to
the faces staring at him from the windows.[18]

The grandfatherly archbishop had studied philosophy and theology
in Paris as a young man at the seminary in Saint-Sulpice. He worked his
way up through the church hierarchy, serving in a variety of posts
throughout France, and he was appointed to his Paris office in 1906.
The sixty-year-old Amette had been keeping a busy personal schedule
since the flood began, venturing out into the flooded zone numerous
times, including January 27. As part of his pastoral duties as spiritual
leader of the Parisian flock, he visited flood victims in shelters and hospitals around the city and suburbs, often bringing food and clothes.

On a visit to the Saint-Antoine neighborhood near the Place des
Vosges in the 4th *arrondissement,* the archbishop met several older people who had refused to leave their homes. He brought these frightened
residents supplies, a smile from his round, friendly face, and a blessing.
The people crowded by their windows, cheering and shouting for their
pastor: *"Vive Monseigneur!"* The archbishop also called at the seminary
at Saint-Sulpice. Amette reached out to a group of victims there, telling
them to "Think of God, my good friends, say a little prayer to Him so

that your suffering will not be forgotten and so that you can be counted in heaven."[19]

Archbishop Amette oversaw the church's prodigious fundraising efforts, which brought in well over a million francs within the first few weeks, as well as in-kind donations. The church distributed clothing, linens, shoes, and bedding, along with bread and meat. It supplied heaters to many, purchased furnishings for ruined families, paid the rents for some, and loaned funds to businessmen.

Parishioners whose homes and possessions were destroyed wrote passionate letters directly to the archbishop, begging for monetary help. One correspondent told the archbishop the story of his son, whose new business was ruined during the flood. All the younger man had left, the letter writer told Amette, were the clothes on his back. "We live near a rich family," the man lamented in his note, "but their hearts are hard and completely closed to our suffering." In begging the archbishop for help, this man concluded, "My cross is heavy, but if assistance were granted to me . . . our situation could be improved and maybe even relieved."[20] When the church answered these kinds of prayers by providing money, people also penned grateful letters of thanks to the archbishop for generosity in a time of need. "I will never forget your kindness," wrote one person who received twenty francs, "and I pray every day for Monseigneur the Archbishop and for our good priest."[21]

Around the region, the clergy provided an important lifeline for many. The priest in Alfortville, just across the southeastern edge of Paris, became famous for his devotion. According to the *London Times,* he "has hardly quitted his boat . . . and continues to help the artillerists who are engaged in this district in removing the helpless, the aged and the sick from their menaced dwellings."[22] Nuns from the Order of Saint-Vincent-de-Paul scoured the area along the Quai de Tournelle in boats, bringing help and relief to people in the neighborhood who were relieved to see their white headdresses in the distance as they approached. The bishop of Versailles toured the towns in his diocese. The archbishop of Sens, upstream along the Yonne, opened the cathedral to the homeless. Yet clergy were not immune from the flood's ravages: One priest, upon returning from his rounds ministering to others, found all of the books and research he had stored in the church basement sitting in water.

The Javel parish newsletter, published after the flood was over, told the story of the local priest rushing out to comfort frightened parishioners. During one visit to a family trapped in their home, he saw a mother moaning with fear. "Have faith, I won't abandon you," he called out, eager to be of help in this moment of panic. In the following days, he visited the family, trying to rekindle their sense of hope. Each time he came, the woman "hugged me and put each of her children to my lips; this brought her such happiness, she claimed."[23]

*P*aris's few remaining electric lights flickered on January 27 as water invaded power plants and substations and short-circuited power lines throughout the city. In many places, pumps had proven reasonably effective in keeping much of the water out of these buildings. Over the course of the day, they were no longer sufficient, and most of the remaining generators shut down, plunging parts of the city that had previously been spared into darkness. Candles and oil lamps were now the city's main sources of light.

From across the nation, members of the military were arriving in Paris in large numbers. Soldiers stationed throughout France, including approximately ten additional infantry battalions and fifteen companies of engineers, had been mobilized and were being deployed throughout the city to reinforce rescue efforts already undertaken by the Paris garrison. General Jean-Baptiste Dalstein dispatched French soldiers and sailors, both individually and in teams, to patrol the streets of Paris, ready to ensure law and order with their weapons if necessary and to distribute relief and rescue citizens in danger. According to rough estimates in the press, the military was providing at least 3,500 horses, 200 boats, 300 cars, and 15,000 cots from the army base just outside the city plus whatever supplies the newly arrived soldiers brought with them.[24] In no time, troops became a familiar sight in the watery streets.

Sailors from port cities like Brest, Cherbourg, and Toulon brought hundreds of Berthon boats to the capital. These fourteen-foot collapsible dinghies made of waterproof canvas were widely used aboard ships as portable lifeboats. With these craft at their disposal, sailors and the city's river police rallied at the open square in the shadow of Notre-Dame cathedral on the Ile de la Cité on January 27. They unfolded the Berthon boats and set up support equipment in the battering rain. From this site, in the very heart of the city, they launched their vessels on rescue and recovery missions into the river, which still raged around both sides of the island. Just feet from their staging ground, the Seine broke into the basement and inner garden of the gothic masterpiece and seeped into the cathedral's crypt, the burial place of the city's archbishops.

A few hundred yards from this site of sacred authority, some of the city's secular power centers were challenged by the Seine as well. Floodwaters flowed into the law courts, throwing the Palais de Justice into chaos. Press accounts told of sewage backing up into the basement, destroying the heating system and thrusting the courtrooms into a winter chill. Throughout the day, guards began taking prisoners, including the mentally deranged, away from the rising water in their cells to other secure sites. Nearby, the water climbed to nearly eight feet deep underneath the gothic arches in the central hall of the old medieval prison, the Conciergerie.

On January 27, firefighters and police under Prefect Lépine's command and soldiers and sailors under General Dalstein's concentrated on human rescue. To do the job, these leaders requisitioned hundreds of boats and vehicles from private citizens, and Parisians freely donated many more. After visiting other suburban towns, the local police prefect from Versailles had reported to the minister of the interior that town laborers, mariners, and residents of various communities "rivaled one another with zeal to rescue, protect, and supply" their villages.[25]

Many of Paris's municipal workers, from every branch of the city's staff, came to people's aid. Among them were the agents of Métro Line

8, who, as the water rose on the Left Bank, fanned out across the area, diligently alerting and preparing residents for what was to come. These men were lauded for their valor by their supervisor, and he nominated them for a special commendation: "They immediately warned the inhabitants and businessmen of the Grenelle neighborhood and recommended that they protect their merchandise and furniture for the time being."[26] Several of the Line 8 agents spent hours at a time in water at least two feet deep, collecting scraps of wood to construct rafts and walkways that could be used to move stranded people out of harm's way.

City road crews also pitched in on jobs they normally did not do. A road worker named Charles Leconte spent each day until around midnight driving a cart to carry victims away from the flooded area. Another, Jean-Baptiste Moreau, worked day and night tending the manholes in the Javel area. Pierre Syrieux labored tirelessly for days, collecting and burning the garbage created by the flood. Eugène Jeangeot was put in charge of keeping pedestrians on walkways safe because he was a good swimmer. When helping people walk across the narrow *passerelles,* he often stood in water up to his waist. Jeangeot also took his turn piloting a rescue boat through the flooded streets. Other road workers built walkways, made repairs, and carried frightened residents to safety on their backs.[27]

Word of ongoing rescues circulated throughout the city on January 27, lifting the spirits of those who were still trapped. As the presence of troops, police, and firefighters grew in various neighborhoods, Parisians welcomed them warmly as a sign of order and safety in the midst of dangerous conditions. Many witnessed firsthand these men delivering supplies, constructing walkways, reinforcing levees and dams, providing basic security, and fighting fires. "The popularity of the troops is unbounded and has been increased by their invariable good humor, friendliness, and gaiety," reported the London *Times.* As throngs of curious Parisian sightseers continued to brave the cold, pressing against the quay walls or hanging over bridge railings to gaze at the spectacle of the rushing water, police and troops controlled the crowd to avoid accidents. "Sentries posted in flooded streets conversed freely with pedestrians and prevented adventurous sightseers by persuasion, rather than by force, from risking their lives in perilous places. . . . The gangs of soldiers who were engaged in damming back the flood on the quays with bags of cement and of sandbags sang cheerily at their work and were everywhere congratulated and thanked by the grateful inhabitants."[28] Lépine sent word that he would treat the soldiers and all the others working so hard to generous amounts of hot coffee and *vin chaud* (mulled wine) to provide a little comfort against the miserably wet and freezing January air during their around-the-clock efforts.

The flood created a strange kind of intimacy. Police and soldiers showed up unannounced. Occupants of a rescue boat or a shelter suddenly became neighbors and maybe great friends. Men carried women across a flooded stretch of water, bringing into contact bodies that would ordinarily never touch so directly: a soldier and a proper middle-class woman, a servant and his wealthy employer. Men carried other men on their backs. People handed their children off to complete

A little girl is steadied by police as she crosses a narrow walkway to be reunited with her father.

strangers, if only for a few minutes, so that they could reach safety. The desperate work of rescue required bending some of the social boundaries that normally kept many Parisians separated by status, sex, or occupation.

In addition to rescues, however, Louis Lépine's police forces also had to contend with the growing threat of thieves. Most Parisians rallied to one another's aid, working to save each other and their city, but others chose to take advantage of the situation for personal gain. Criminals roamed through the shadows of darkened neighborhoods and the chaos of the devastation, looking for empty houses to loot or abandoned goods to steal. Silent, evacuated districts were prime targets for thieves.

A police report on January 27 noted that in the town of Saint-Ouen, "all access points to the flooded areas are guarded by the military and by agents of the Gendarmerie . . . in order to prevent looting."[29] Despite the presence of police and troops, many Parisians were soon living in a state of panic, especially in areas where the lights had gone out. Even as additional troops arrived to help provide law and order, reports of looting spread across the region.

Crime had already been much on the minds of Parisians. Since the last years of the nineteenth century, growing numbers of criminals, most commonly young men under the age of 25 — sometimes as young as 14 — had generated worries about juvenile delinquency and urban safety. In many cases, their grandparents or parents had been forced out of the city center by Haussmannization and into poor and undeveloped outlying districts with little police presence, or to the suburban towns beyond the reach of the city's police force. They were no longer the young political rebels of earlier generations, who believed they could fight against a corrupt system and win. The failure of the Commune and the growing class divide had put an end to many of those idealistic dreams. These hooligans had given up on society altogether and had resorted to crime for the money.

The gangs had been dubbed the Apaches. Novelist Gustave Aimard had made the Native American Apache tribe famous among Parisians in the mid-nineteenth century by depicting them as brutal warriors in a series of exotic novels. Sensationalist newspapers picked up the term and applied it in 1902 to the men involved in the so-called golden helmet affair, when several gangs fought over a prostitute. This race-based slur applied the supposed characteristics of a "savage" group from the New World to another group of outlaws who threatened to undo the civilized city of Paris. The name helped to cement the criminals' reputation as fierce street fighters. [30] Certain neighborhoods, particularly working-class districts, such as Javel, Grenelle, Glacière, the areas around Les Halles, Belleville, Clichy, Rue Saint-Denis, Rue Montmartre, Canal Saint-Martin, and many suburban towns, were well known as the stomping grounds of these gangs. Photographs of Parisian Apaches from the years around 1900 show them with a host of weapons, many of them homemade, including spiked cuffs and wire used for striking and strangling a potential victim, in addition to pistols and clubs. When arrested, they were often paraded in front of press cameras to demonstrate that the police took the threat seriously. Lépine fought vigorously against these criminals, proclaiming to Parisians throughout his tenure as prefect that the streets were safe and that the danger was exaggerated. It was not enough to calm the fear, especially among the middle class, about the gangs' presence in the city.[31]

In the months leading up to the flood, French newspapers had printed articles about the ongoing threat that these criminals posed to the capital. In January 1910, one policeman had been killed and another wounded in a gunfight with an Apache that started in a local bar and moved to a nearby house. Later that month, just days before the river began rising, a group of young hooligans convicted for theft and weapons possession climbed over the dock in the courtroom and jumped into the gallery, screaming and making faces at the frightened spectators. In its January 22 issue, *La Vie Illustrée* magazine featured a report and dramatic photographs—unrelated to the flood that was bubbling up in the city—that reenacted Apache confrontations with the police. The January 23 cover of *Le Petit Journal Illustré* dramatized this case with the question: "How can Paris rid itself of the Apaches?" Even during the worst of the flood, numerous articles about the general horrors caused by the Apaches ran in the press alongside stories about the impact of the disaster. The focus on crime was part of a growing trend among mass-circulation newspapers to feature sensational tales that would help sell copies. Yet these stories also helped to generate a culture of fear in the city by magnifying the danger. When criminals took advantage of the situation during the high water, newspapers paid a great deal of attention to the crimes.[32]

When the first reports of looting and pillaging during the flood started circulating, it was hardly surprising that Parisians connected them to a broader set of anxieties about the city's dangers. Criminals personified the sense of chaos during the flood and gave people someone to blame. Thieves, however, did not do all the looting during the flood; some was surely the work of desperate and hungry but otherwise law-abiding people who were trying to survive in the midst of a crisis the likes of which they had never before experienced. In this atmosphere, however, events easily escalated to high drama, and many assumed that any stealing was the work of a hardened criminal. When the city's lights and the sense of safety they provided were extinguished, the fear of villains, especially among those who owned property that might be looted, cast even more darkness over Paris.

By January 27, the police had restricted people's movements within flooded zones and prohibited any kind of circulation among homes in many suburban towns, even by residents who were allowed to return home to retrieve items only if accompanied by a police officer or soldier. Police in some of the most devastated areas had orders to shoot looters on sight.

As the sun set in the afternoon of January 27 at the end of another brief winter day, the men shoring up the quay outside the Louvre were still hard at work. The museum staff, watching the workmen nervously and hopefully, prepared to stay throughout the long night. With the city becoming dark, the workers used flares to shine a bit of light onto the walls they were so desperately hoping would hold against the rushing river just on the other side. Sandbags began to run low, so the crew looked around for other material and found it in the paving stones beneath their feet. Now they drove their shovel tips into the street, the sound of metal on rock echoing through the air as they pried loose the pavers and pulled them up with their bare hands. They worked to stack one layer, then another, and then a third against the sandbags and the cement as quickly as they could.

Parisians had long used the paving stones in their streets during moments of desperation, most recently during the Commune of 1871. The rebellious Communards had pulled up stones to form barricades, blocking off neighborhoods from advancing troops. From behind these fortifications, they could fire their weapons or launch loose rocks into the air to fight off their enemy. Barricades made with the very stuff of the city—stones, trees and the metal grills that encircled them at the base, debris, wagons, sewer grates—were a time-honored tradition in Paris, from the French Revolution through uprisings in 1830 and 1848. Some of the most dramatic scenes in Victor Hugo's *Les Misérables* take place on the barricades where young men fought and died defending their vision of a France free from tyranny. Now, in 1910, the cobblestones became a new kind of barricade against a very different enemy.

With midnight approaching on January 27, the sandbag, cobblestone, and cement barrier continued to rise on one side of the thick quay wall outside the Louvre, but the river was still climbing on the other side. The men working to save the museum worried that their efforts to strengthen the wall would not be enough. Fearing the worst, the rescuers began to pile more sandbags on top of the wall to add additional height to their improvised levee. Their anxiety was real. Within a few more hours, the level of the water on the other side of this barrier reached over the height of the worker's heads—three feet over by some accounts—as the men still labored in the bitter cold of that January night. "There was need of haste," wrote British journalist H. Warner Allen,

> for the water that looked black and stagnant in the glare of the naph-
> tha flares was creeping up apace and licking the lowest tier of cobbles.
> Others were recklessly digging great holes in the footpath between
> the poplars, and ramming the earth into bags, or nailing together great
> pieces of driftwood, fished from the river, to form a screen behind the
> sandbags on the parapet and hold them against the pressure of the
> current, while carts kept rumbling in and unloading piles of stone and
> rubble against the wall and screen.

Very little stood between the men and the river. "A few hours later," Allen noted, "and the river would have won; all the basements of the Louvre would have been flooded, and the water would have carried ruin across the Rue de Rivoli and Palais Royal."[33] The men struggled into the early morning hours, endangering their own lives, conscious that the water had already breached the basement of the Louvre. When dawn broke the morning of January 28, they looked over their work and saw that they had won over the Seine; the barricade held fast.

As the barrier climbed outside the Louvre, across town another rescue effort was beginning at the waterlogged Hôpital Boucicaut. The hospital was one of the most modern in Paris, only open since 1897. Its location on Rue de la Convention, however, placed it squarely in the heavily flooded Javel neighborhood. During the dark early morning hours of January 28, the hospital's director contacted the police. He reported the increasingly dire situation, appealing to Louis Lépine for emergency help as he prepared several hundred patients for evacuation.

Muddy water was seeping into the wards and climbing the walls, both from the river and from the sewers backing up into the hospital. Muck now covered this once sterile space, filling it with a horrible stink. The staff, exhausted by the worsening situation, grew even more anxious when the telephones suddenly went out of order, cutting off the facility from any immediate assistance. Getting messages out to other parts of Paris and bringing in necessary supplies was now the sole work of their two motorized ambulances, which administrators repeatedly dispatched back and forth across the city. One nurse at the scene told a reporter that the rising water inside the wards had become filled with human excrement from the bedridden patients. She feared that the sick were now in danger of drowning in their own filth.[34]

At 8 AM on January 28, Lépine received word of the crisis at the Hôpital Boucicaut and immediately departed with a detachment of police and firemen.[35] When he arrived, the prefect found waist-high water blocking the main entrance. At Lépine's direction, police and hospital staff hastily constructed a wooden walkway to carry patients from a side door across the lagoon to where the water was relatively shallow. The hospital's horse-drawn ambulances began pulling up to the end of the walkway, one by one, followed by carts the army had supplied and numerous delivery wagons that private citizens donated to the evacuation effort. The icy water slapped against the horses' chests, sometimes sloshing onto their backs. By about 8:30 AM, doctors, nurses, and other rescuers were busy wrapping the sick and dying patients in blankets to shield them from the cold and moving them toward the wooden walkway. Many of the female patients openly sobbed.

A pair of rescuers shifted each bedridden patient to a cot with handles on both ends and then shuffled carefully across the *passerelle* to the rain-soaked wagons that in some cases were already taking on water. Very few of the vehicles had any form of covering to protect the sick on their journey to safety, nor were they particularly clean. Coal dust or plaster, left behind from their everyday uses, coated the interior of many of the improvised ambulances. An eyewitness told of the horses rearing with fright as they stood in the cold, swirling water, while their drivers struggled to restrain them. Under the great stress of the moment, one agitated horse threw its driver clear, knocking him unconscious. After lying down a few minutes to rest, the driver recovered, remounted, and guided his wagon full of patients to safety. Later in the morning, rescuers tried to operate some motorized ambulances, but the water was too high and their flooded engines would not work. Policemen on bicycles sped off to find additional vehicles that could assist in the effort. Once the wagons got underway, they pushed very slowly through the high water, sometimes taking as much as an hour to reach a shelter or another hospital already packed with frightened patients.

Throughout the morning, a gawking crowd gathered to watch the sick and injured, only a few of whom could still walk out of the hospital on their own. "Suddenly there was a cry," reported the *New York Times*. "A man, whose face was horribly eaten by disease, whose nose had partly vanished in an abominable ulcer, dropped the bandage that had hidden it. The hideous lesion was thus exposed to the cruel rain, which fell like pellets of lead from a black sky."[36]

Rescuers worked for hours in the downpour until all of the patients were safely removed from the hospital. The *New York Times* reporter remarked of the hectic scene: "It was like a disordered retreat after the butchery of a defeat." Parisians who watched the rescue would not have missed the familiar sight of one man overseeing the evacuation. "On the threshold of the entrance of the hospital," according to the *New York Times*, "stood the calm, always efficient, always sympathetic prefect of police, Monsieur Lépine, giving his orders, but in a voice that sometimes trembled with pity."[37]

Around Paris on January 28, doctors improvised some two thousand beds in hospital facilities to accommodate the refugees from Boucicaut as well as others injured in the flood, but water also had breached these places in the preceding days, making it difficult for victims to find help in their moment of need. Reaching another hospital was no guarantee of safety for the Boucicaut's patients or for anyone else. The city's ambulance service worked overtime during the flood. Nurses, many of whom endured 36-hour shifts, accompanied each ambulance to provide immediate care. The *New York Times* journalist interviewed one nurse who claimed that she did not sleep for 60 hours straight at the height of the disaster. Even if they were not directly plagued by water, many hospitals had to do without a regular supply of clean linens once the central laundry facility for the entire Parisian hospital system flooded. The city was so interconnected that most dry neighborhoods still suffered the consequences of the flood.

That same morning at the old people's home in Ivry, officials were beginning to evacuate those residents physically capable of moving. Aided by police and firefighters, the staff guided these elderly Parisians along a narrow wooden walkway, more than 130 feet long, that stretched from the building to dry land. Once safe, they could be taken to their families or to other locations. Despite the danger, more than 1,500 people crossed the makeshift bridge to escape from harm's way.[38]

Others weren't so lucky. In another part of the city, according to one press report, police had found a lonely elderly couple dead in their apartment. They were sick and knew that they couldn't move far or fast enough. To escape the rising water and their fear of it, they hanged themselves from a bedpost.[39]

By Friday, January 28, in less than a week the Seine had climbed higher than anyone alive had ever seen, turned yellow, and increased in velocity to speeds no one had anticipated. Northern France had experienced a "perfect storm" of events that led to the drowning not just of Paris, but of the entire region. As the Seine set new records, many people panicked, but others were able to keep their spirits up. Walking through the city, Guillaume Apollinaire encountered one youngster who talked about the arriving water "as though talking about guests coming to a party: 'We're waiting for the Yonne, the Loire, the Armaçon, and the Seraing.'" All of the rivers were flowing into one. An adult who overheard this remark had a curt answer: "The crazier you are, the more you laugh."[40]

When the sun climbed higher that day, Parisians could see that the Seine was almost twenty feet above its normal level. The Zouave was up to his neck.

Chapter Five

UP *to the* NECK

⊨ ⊨

The interior of the Gare d'Orsay became a favorite for photographers who focused on the light-filled archway inside the central hall. The electrified tracks sat under several feet of water.

*J*ournalist Henri Lavedan splashed along the quays on Friday, January 28, taking it all in: "It's the Seine, the Seine of Lutece . . . rolling like a silent chariot, galloping horizontally and furiously with a team of muddy horses which carry it rushing to the sea," he wrote in *L'Illustration.* Lavedan's use of Paris's Roman name, Lutece, reflected his feeling that the river's rampage was nothing less than the modern version of an ancient tragedy, on the order of Pompeii or other disasters that had left cities in ruin.

Over the previous few days, Lavedan had stood beside his fellow Parisians, lingering along the quays and peering over the edges of the six bridges—out of some two dozen—that still remained open. Like them, he had marveled at the swirling yellow river full of debris. Today, as Lavedan struggled against the wind and water along the riverbank, he was largely on his own. The extremely harsh weather kept most of the gawkers away from the river's edge: "The curious were not as numerous since the wind shot the rain on people's faces like cold little needles."[1] A visit to the bloated Seine had become too grueling for most.

After building for days, the river's full force now barreled down its channel at a speed of 25 miles per hour, according to one estimate in the press. On that rain-soaked Friday, it finally crested around 20 feet above normal, just shy of the all-time high water mark set in 1658 when water had also flowed freely throughout the Left and Right Banks. The stone Zouave still stood bravely with his three fellow soldiers on the pillars of the Pont de l'Alma with water up to their necks. When several flesh-and-blood soldiers struggled to tie up their boat along the Quai Debilly that morning, just a few dozen yards downriver from the Pont de l'Alma, the Seine's flow swept away one of the men as he disembarked. He survived, but authorities forbade any further attempt to dock small craft along the river's bank because of the grave danger caused by the powerful currents.

Steady rain pounded the streets and the surface of the Seine with a dull, deafening sound, adding more moisture to the pools of standing water throughout Paris. The river now spread out so far on both banks that it transformed a once-familiar landscape of streets, bridges, and monuments into a strange seascape. Colorful posters pasted to advertising columns announcing performances or department store sales were now faded and peeling from the prolonged soaking.

Balloons filled with sightseers and photographers departed the headquarters of the Aero Club in Saint-Cloud on the rare occasions when the rain ceased, floating through the gray sky for a bird's-eye view of the devastation.[2] Their craft passed below the clouds that had hovered over Paris for so long that some Parisians could not remember when they had last seen the sun.

American writer Helen Davenport Gibbons had been anxiously watching the Seine rise for days. On Friday, January 28, she and her family hailed a taxi and rode as close to Notre-Dame as they could get. They approached the city's Gothic cathedral in the freezing rain, hoping to go inside the tower and view the flood from above. Gibbons was shivering in the winter air: "I was cold enough to enjoy the climb." When she reached the top, she gazed over the parapet across the breadth of the city and was awed by the sight. "The view from the top of the tower was unique. The next day would have been too late. We caught the flood at its flood. Paris was swimming. On both sides the cathedral had become an angry menacing rush of water." In the distance, she could see debris floating downstream and catching on the bridges. The city that she was so accustomed to seeing, after living in France off and on for several years, now looked entirely different. "One realized that habit had given us a sense of proportion to the cityscape. The effect of diminished lampposts and trees was sinister."[3]

Even as the Seine was approaching its maximum height, with the roaring current striking against the decks of bridges and edging up the last few feet of the quay walls, it did not actually flow over the quay walls in the central part of the city.[4]

Instead of going over the top of the barriers in the historic center, the Seine coursed through the channels underneath Paris. As it had been doing all week, water continued pushing upward from the sewers,

the subway tunnels on both banks, and the saturated soil. Puzzled rescuers remained unsure about how to defend the city against the rising
tide from below the surface. One frustrated worker filed a report on
January 28 explaining that along the Cours la Reine, the beautiful green
space that borders the Seine just downriver from the Tuileries gardens,
he and his team "dammed the Seine nonstop, but the Cours was flooded
by water coming from the Avenue Montaigne; our efforts were in vain."[5]
Fighting the flood along the river's edge didn't necessarily have any effect. The water simply found other routes to the Cours la Reine by traveling through the soil and underground conduits, emerging above
ground from several dozen yards behind the quay walls. Streets, squares,
and roadways, soaked from their underside, were buckling and caving in.
The city was literally collapsing beneath the feet of Parisians. Helen
Davenport Gibbons remembered: "We saw wooden paving-blocks in a
messy jumble" in areas where water had dislodged the street surfaces
some of which were normally covered in wood to allow traffic to move
smoothly.[6] Any remaining electric lights now failed, enveloping the entire city in the cold winter darkness.

At the start of the flood on January 21, when Prefect Louis Lépine had
entered his small note in the police logs about the water that infiltrated
the construction of the Nord-Sud subway near the Orsay train station,
the event was clearly not an emergency. A week later, on January 28,
Lépine could see just where that breach had led.

The Gare d'Orsay—today one of Paris's most popular museums
housing hundreds of Impressionist works—was the first urban station
in the world featuring electrified lines and trains, a fitting addition to
the celebration of electricity's power when it opened for the *Exposition Universelle* on July 14, 1900. It was also the pride of the Paris-
Orléans Railroad Company, which acquired the land for the new
terminal alongside the Seine from the French government in the late
1890s. Architects crafted a beautiful station that blended into its historic surroundings on the Left Bank, near Saint-Germain-des-Prés and

just down the quay from the black-and-gold-domed Palais de L'Institut, home of the prestigious Académie Française, from which the nation's intellectual luminaries govern the French language.

On the outside of the station, high arched windows, a mansard-style roof with Beaux-Arts decorations, and enormous clocks faced the Seine. The façade proudly proclaimed the names of the line's destination points, advertising the places to which Parisians could travel. The letters "PO" reminded everyone that this was the Paris-Orléans company's prized possession. The station's sumptuousness fit the character of the wealthy neighborhood, and it also served as a model of modern, twentieth-century technology, complete with elevators, luggage conveyance machines, and sixteen underground electrified tracks.

The Orsay offered a more central location for its parent company, whose other terminal, the Gare d'Austerlitz, located on the river upstream across the river from the Bercy warehouse district, had previously served as its main Parisian destination. To link the two sister stations, an electrified rail line traced the edge of the Seine. But when engineers embedded the tracks into the soil running alongside the river, they laid the rails far below the lowest depth that Baron Haussmann's chief engineer for water services, Eugène Belgrand, had recommended due to the risk of flooding. Protective barriers that separated the tracks on one side from the quay and the water on the other were only high enough to hold back an ordinary flood.

On January 28, the walls barring the river from the electric rail lines proved to be nowhere near sufficient to stop the Seine. Waves of murky floodwater sloshed over the wall at various points between the Austerlitz and Orsay stations, a distance of more than two miles, filling the entire railway channel. The floodwaters had also begun to weaken the stones of the Quai des Augustins, along the river near the beautiful Saint-Michel fountain that had long served as a popular meeting spot for students in the Latin Quarter. When the walls gave way in places, thousands more gallons of water spilled onto the tracks below. The underground rails alongside the river became one of the primary conduits that allowed the flood to come inland onto the Left Bank.

Throughout the day of January 28, as the Seine flowed along the length of the entire track toward the Gare d'Orsay, it also pushed into the narrow streets of the surrounding neighborhood. Shopping districts like Rue Saint-André-des-Arts and the Carrefour de Buci, crowded with stores and cafés, sat nearly two feet underwater. So did the Rue Jacob, where wealthy patrons normally visited the dozens of galleries filled with paintings and drawings. Residents of the quiet residential buildings along Rue de Lille and Rue de Bellechasse, where the murky water was now more than four feet deep, found their basements flooded with several feet of water. Rue Mazarine, behind the Palais de l'Institut, was filled with more than two and a half feet of water. The sixth-century abbey and church of Saint-Germain-des-Prés, from which this neighborhood took its name, was one of the oldest in the city and was normally far enough from the river to avoid any flood damage. In 1910, priests probably looked down from the high bell tower and prayed for the ancient structure's safety.

Once water reached the Gare d'Orsay, it flowed up into the station's interior and moved through the building's drainage system, eventually exiting the building and falling back into the river in a giant circuit. The station's main hall became an indoor lake, with the platforms and tracks inside submerged under several feet of water. The flooded interior of the Gare d'Orsay became a favorite subject for photographers. Capturing images of the devastated city, they concentrated their lenses on the enormous arched window inside the central hall, which allowed light into the dark and empty space of what would normally have been the bustling platforms. In these photographs, the illuminated archway reflected in the still water creates a stunning symmetrical image. Although the water was stagnant and foul, the reflection made the Orsay look like a beautiful ancient temple in ruins. Its inundation cut Parisians off from other parts of the country and trapped people in the city since it was one of the major terminals serving points to the south.

As Lépine had noted in the police log the previous week, in addition to water flowing through the station, along the tracks, and into the subway, the Seine also found an entrance to the Nord-Sud subway line through the openings in the street left by the line's incomplete construction. The immense pressure and suction of the water and air inside the tunnel soon turned this unfinished subway tube into a siphon. It drew in the water in the street through the holes dug by workers building the subway line. That water then began gushing through the tunnel, running back underneath the river between the stations at National Assembly and Place de la Concorde.

In other words, water from the Seine was actually traveling from south to north, from the Left Bank to the Right Bank, through the subway line itself underneath the main river channel, which flows from east to west. The Nord-Sud Métro was designed to carry people, but now it was moving water into areas on the Right Bank where no one had expected it to go and where it could not have gone on its own.

That afternoon, water sucked into the tunnels spewed out onto the Right Bank, nearly a mile from the Gare d'Orsay, where its journey started. It gushed out through Métro stations and manhole covers, washing over dozens of streets and infiltrating hundreds of buildings that everyone had thought were safe. Floodwater reached up from the banks of the Seine into Right Bank neighborhoods in a great arc roughly following the Métro line, from the wide-open space of Place de la Concorde, where the cruel guillotine had operated during the Revolution, to portions of the Champs-Elysées, the neoclassical Church of the Madeleine, the Opéra Garnier, the Boulevard Haussmann, and the church of Notre-Dame-de-Lorette. Areas that sat a great distance from the Seine were now underwater, including the neighborhood around another of the city's important train stations, the Gare Saint-Lazare. The tracks underneath that structure were covered with water and muck. Workmen hastily erected a barricade of stone and cement to block the passage linking the Nord-Sud and the Gare Saint-Lazare, but the damage had been done. The normally busy square in front of the train station became a lake in the heart of the city, making the surrounding area impassible for days.[7]

From Saint-Lazare, the water quickly flowed to other areas nearby, filling the basements of the famous *grands magasins*—the magnificent multilevel department stores packed with the latest fashions and household goods. Two of Paris's most renowned shopping destinations—the Galeries Lafayette, with its beautifully colorful stained glass dome, and Printemps—were forced to close. Troops moved in to secure these business districts and to prevent chaos and looting.

In the nearby Place de l'Opéra, the unfinished Métro station filled with so much water that the sidewalks aboveground began to wobble and then cave in and collapse, leaving ornate lampposts tilted at wild angles. A cavern opened up in the broad square, revealing portions of the world below, including the half-constructed subway station. Given the instability of the street, police soon roped off the area to prevent anyone from falling in. One journalist at the scene feared the worst for the city's opera house: "The whole place might crumble in, and one pictured a great chasm opening up and Garnier's huge and flashy monument tumbling bodily into the hole."[8] Between the water, the police blockades, and vehicles trying to navigate the few dry streets, the entire area was now a mess, and what would have been a short, quarter-mile cab ride between the Church of the Madéleine and the Opéra now took, according to journalist H. Warner Allen, two hours.[9]

When water reached the Boulevard Haussmann from underground, it pushed up with incredible speed into buildings, many of which had only recently been built, and cascaded down the street. Rescuers dammed the boulevard with sandbags to try to prevent the water from spreading further, but they could not move rapidly enough, and the improvised levees simply sent the water in other directions to enter more houses. Reports circulated in the press that buildings appeared to be sinking around the Gare Saint-Lazare. Some observers noted that many structures were now sitting at strange angles. It was all a great shock to residents. A flood along the riverbank was, perhaps, to be expected, but not in these neighborhoods at some distance from the Seine.

Police and soldiers were continuing to rescue Parisians from the water, but not all were successful. Twenty-two-year-old Corporal

Eugène-Albert Tripier had already gone on many missions during the flood when, alongside two of his colleagues, he boarded a small boat to launch another rescue on January 28. Just before the boat pulled away from the dock, a telegraph operator asked to go with them so that he could make an important delivery. The four men huddled in the small, now overcrowded craft floating southward on the Right Bank's Rue Foucault, just across from the Eiffel Tower, heading toward the Seine. As they approached the river, a powerful eddy swirling below the water's surface swept their boat forward. The men held tight as the turbulence tossed them around. Within seconds, the water's pull thrust them over the top of the quay as if they were heading over a waterfall. When they landed in the main channel of the Seine, two of the men toppled into the churning water but were able to grab hold of tree branches nearby. Struggling to keep their heads above the icy water, they shouted for help.

The boat, now out of control, carried the remaining two men farther out into the Seine. Tripier stood up in the boat and dove into the yellow river to swim back to the bank, probably in hopes of rescuing his friends. He fought against the powerful current, straining all his muscles in hopes of reaching the quay. Within a matter of moments, he disappeared, exhausted, into the freezing Seine, drawn under by the force of the huge volume of water still flowing through the channel. The two men clinging to the trees and the soldier, who stayed in the boat because he could not swim, were all rescued.

Tripier's death immediately became the stuff of legend throughout the city. Newspapers lauded his sacrifice, and Louis Lépine proclaimed that if his body were found, the city of Paris would pay for the funeral as a show of thanks for his service.[10]

Although Parisians clearly welcomed the military, thanks in part to popular stories of heroism like Corporal Tripier's, anxious residents did not always make their work easy. Occasionally in Paris and the suburbs, soldiers had difficulty convincing reluctant individuals to evacuate when their buildings were in danger of collapsing. Some rescues turned into confrontations. Many residents merely wanted food and water but did not want to be transported to drier ground, fearing that their homes would be looted once they left. Others were simply distrustful of the authorities. Whatever their reasons, Parisians sometimes resisted the rescuers, preferring to take responsibility for themselves despite the potential danger of living in damaged buildings cut off by the flood. When soldiers were unable to remove flood victims from their homes, they often brought supplies in the following days. Occasionally, competing jurisdictions caused additional conflict. The mayor of the suburban town of Vitry refused to allow a military boat on its way to a nearby community to pass through his flooded streets. The prefect of the Seine had to write a memo specifically asking him to allow the military in.[11]

Not everyone was wary of the military, however, especially not City Council member Louis Dausset. According to some, perhaps his political enemies, during a private meeting of the City Council's budget committee on January 28, Dausset called for a "state of siege" in Paris to deal with the flood—in other words, to turn the city over to the military. Dausset, a former professor, was a founding member of the Ligue de la Patrie Française, a nationalist, pro-government group of intellectuals. Exactly what Dausset had in mind is unclear, but the idea of proclaiming a siege shocked and angered many. They believed that Dausset wanted to completely militarize the flood relief efforts. In the minds of his critics, especially those frightened by his right-wing leanings, that meant nothing less than establishing martial law in the city and thereby abolishing the democratically elected government. The response to Dausset's comment was a flurry of editorials in the next few days, fuming against the idea. Some politicians publicly denounced the idea, hoping to make clear that Dausset did not speak for everyone in power.[12]

Dausset insisted that he was merely calling for a greater degree of order by suggesting that a single, coordinated authority could make relief efforts more effective. He was not seeking to take over the city, he declared, nor calling for military or dictatorial rule. Perhaps unwittingly, Dausset had questioned the government's ability to handle the crisis at hand. That charge had potentially explosive political consequences.

Premier Aristide Briand hoped to weather the blunt criticisms of his government by declaring publicly that a measure as drastic as martial law was simply unwarranted. He assured Parisians that more forceful measures would be used, but only when appropriate. Briand knew something about the use of government authority. A few weeks earlier, despite his many years of hard work to promote French labor unions, he had broken a railway strike by drafting the protesting workers into the national guard and arresting their leaders. The people of Paris, however, had acted with such aplomb and calmness during the flood, Briand contended, that extreme measures were simply not necessary, and he hoped that the spirit of unity would defeat the call for more radical solutions. Many editorialists rallied to the premier and the government's side, denouncing Dausset's idea as clearly that of an extremist. One journalist writing in the newspaper *La Lanterne* likened Dausset's suggestion to Napoléon's coup d'état in 1799 and argued that "in every catastrophe, some people lose their heads," and placed Dausset in that category.[13] Meanwhile, the provincial and international press picked up the story, giving the impression to millions around the world that Paris was so damaged that its civilian leaders were on the brink of turning the city over to the army.

Dausset's January 28 remark launched a vigorous argument over how effectively the city was dealing with the crisis. As several papers reported, officials were not always distributing assistance in the most efficient way possible. One account told of residents of the 15th *arrondissement,* who hoped to receive monetary assistance, being turned away by government officials. Given the variety of complications emerging around the city, many could readily believe that having a central authority wasn't such a bad idea.

To conservatives in particular, the idea of using the military to control the city made perfect sense because it spoke to their desire for law and order. Dausset's remarks inspired vicious attacks against the Republican government and its business allies. Writing in the newspaper *L'Eclair* in response to the controversy, its conservative editor Ernest Judet raised the question of responsibility very bluntly, saying that "everyone is beginning to understand that the current catastrophes are not accidents without cause," because the city's numerous construction sites were not receiving sufficient oversight. Instead, the city had fallen for certain "seductive innovations" that were now creating chaos, including the Métro construction that was allowing water to seep up from below ground. For Judet, the fact that city services were divided into multiple jurisdictions was now hampering the rescue of Paris during the flood. That kind of diffuse responsibility led to flood victims getting the runaround instead of the help they needed. When an engineer and police officer argued over whether it was appropriate to fish driftwood out of the Seine, they couldn't reach a decision because each answered to a separate authority. Judet called openly for the kind of central authority that Dausset had, accidentally or not, suggested.[14]

Henry de Larègle, a member of an old aristocratic family, agreed with Judet, arguing in an editorial in *Le Soleil* that "it is incontestable that national and city officials are, in part, responsible, not for the flood itself but for the disastrous consequences." Construction was not regulated, he said, and "the engineers have weakened the subsoil of Paris without taking the most elementary precautions against the ever-present possibility of flooding of the river." Changes to the riverbanks, the quays, and construction of Métro lines had all elevated the water level, Larègle contended, and "the government was naive enough to say that it had exact maps of previous floods," without realizing that the urban space had changed. In the end, engineering, planning, and the government as a whole had failed to protect the city from what should have been an obvious danger.[15]

In the newspaper *Gil Blas,* critic Barthélemy Robaglia did not hesitate to call directly for martial law. Frustrated with the way the flood was being handled and by what he perceived as the lack of clear leadership, he shouted (using all capital letters) that, while every Parisian was doing his or her duty, "THERE IS NO DIRECTION, NO RESPONSIBILITY." He believed that the population of the city would not be thrown into panic by a state of siege, as some had suggested, but would actually be calmed by it because Parisians would understand the necessity. "A military chief is necessary," Robaglia stated, "under whose orders all the services, army, police, engineers, inspectors, etc., will be placed." In the end, he pleaded, "We can, we must proclaim a state of siege."[16]

It was not surprising that *L'Action Française,* the newspaper of the monarchist group with the same name, argued in favor of a powerful leader replacing multiple government agencies with unclear lines of authority. Attacking the democratic government as a sham and mocking Parisians' attachment to liberty, the paper called for a strong government—preferably, for this group, a new king—that could lead France. They were probably hoping that the catastrophe would rouse support for their cause.[17]

Right-wing journalist, novelist, and satirist Léon Daudet was one of the founders of *Action Française,* and he unabashedly denounced the Third Republic. Daudet ferociously attacked the government on a regular basis, regardless of whether a crisis was at hand. The venom he penned on occasion of the flood, first published as an article and then reissued in a handbill, called the government "A Criminal Regime." Daudet argued that the democratic system had put the city at risk by filling government with corrupt and ignorant civil servants. "At the peak of the administrative hierarchy, frantic men, swindlers, junk dealers, pimps," all robbed from the people and gave to themselves. Under such leadership, the city had ceased to be a functioning, civilized entity: "Paris, which was once a city, has become not just morally but materially an encampment, an assemblage of botched and sabotaged works of art destined to produce a brief illusion, something like a permanent universal exposition."[18]

For Daudet, the government was not only incompetent to deal with the emergency, but also was to blame for the severity of the flood because it had allowed engineers and greedy rail companies to build carelessly. In another critique, he blasted the Third Republic as "the regime of theft, of traffic, of usury, of chaos, of the liquidation of hierarchy" that had led to individualism and, therefore, to anarchy. Private self-interest, strengthened by the government, had run amok, he said, and

France was paying the price. "Since they have robbed glorious France, destroyed its natural defenses and used its land, their doctrine of death, de-mo-cra-cy [. . .] disaster and ruin will accumulate through their plans." Daudet believed that the engineers and scientists were "morons," and that the lesson of the flood was "Down with the Republic."[19]

In the midst of such nasty political charges, especially from the far right of the political spectrum, one unlikely source for volunteers was the Camelots du Roi. Founded in 1908 as part of a larger movement of anti-Republican, and thus antigovernment, right-wing nationalists, the Camelots du Roi was a group of young monarchists who engaged in populist organizing for their cause. As the youth wing of the larger L'Action Française organization, they promoted a vision of France based on connections to a royal and Catholic past, and they vehemently denounced Republicans, Communists, and Socialists, along with electoral politics generally, as completely corrupt. Sometimes, their disagreements with other young politically minded activists boiled over into brawls on the streets of Paris. The Camelots became notorious for attacking a Sorbonne professor in 1908 in retribution for his contempt toward Joan of Arc, a figure much revered by monarchist groups because she symbolized France's national tradition, rooted in the religious past the Camelots adored. They stormed into the professor's classes and engaged his supporters in street fights. Indeed, the Camelots saw themselves as men of action who were willing to use violence when defending their beliefs.

Nevertheless, when the floodwaters started rising, the Camelots began turning up at police headquarters—voluntarily, this time—to offer their services. Reports of their activities during the flood come only from right-wing newspapers. One author writing in the anti-Semitic newspaper *La Libre Parole* who came upon a group of Camelots in a boat referred to them as "chivalrous youth who since yesterday have worked day and night" on their rounds "to remove families imprisoned or ruined by the flood from their isolation and distress."[20] Other sympathetic accounts told of their offers to help the police or to go out on their own in boats. In order "to bring help to the victims, a good number of rescuers, all good swimmers, were chosen from among the Camelots du Roi."[21] Undoubtedly, people did welcome all the help they could get regardless of where it came from. In Charenton, to the southeast of Paris just where the Seine enters the city, as one story went, twenty Camelots reported to the mayor, "who gave them a warm welcome" and assisted with the ambulance service.[22] In Alfortville, they formed a nighttime patrol force to defend the town against looters. Léon Daudet described the Camelots in an editorial as "young and valiant friends who go into the cold shadows, snatch the old and the infirm from death, comfort the despairing young, symbolize our good news."[23]

A relatively new organization, the Camelots du Roi undoubtedly wanted to shape their public image and show themselves not as a rowdy group of troublemakers but as an organization of courageous soldiers devoted to a noble cause. They certainly saw themselves as partisans of the idea of France as a strong and proud nation with a rich heritage, which they believed was being attacked by liberals and Republicans. With France under attack by the Seine, the Camelots directed their actions toward saving Paris and its people. One of their leaders, Maurice Pujo, stated it directly: "The republic should be jealous because it was powerless against this kind of propaganda . . . a 'propaganda of the deed.'"[24] Only groups like the Camelots du Roi could save France, they believed, starting with their rescuing its people from the flood.

Edouard Drumont, the rabble-rousing anti-Semitic newspaper publisher, was no friend of the government. Although his words must be treated with caution given his ulterior motives, his account of the flood also offers a very different picture than those celebrating the city's unity. Writing in his paper *La Libre Parole,* Drumont reflected on the notion of heroism and solidarity and argued that "this is an inexhaustibly astonishing subject," since Paris was in fact "in the middle of a growing anarchy which gains ground each day like the water. . . . The leaders don't know which orders to give to the agents, moreover taking their time with the orders they do have. They have held onto their instinctive devotion, but they have confidence in nothing; they do their duty, but they do it while shrugging their shoulders."[25]

$\mathcal{I}$n this politically charged atmosphere—with heated antigovernment accusations being bandied about in the press, the ever-present potential for looting, and right-wing groups in the streets—the sight of a growing citywide military presence by January 28 undoubtedly raised questions about what actions soldiers might take in response to the crisis. Dausset's seeming call for martial law on that same day had given conservatives cause to hope for decisive action and possibly occupation.

For supporters of the Republic and those on the political left, Dausset's suggestion of martial law came as a horrible shock and betrayal. Memories of the Commune and its gory aftermath still haunted many Parisians. Especially for those who had supported the 1871 uprising, the idea of declaring martial law meant bringing to Paris the very same army that had executed their comrades in the city's streets and had occupied the city for years after the "bloody week" that crushed their hopes for Parisian independence. In *Le Matin,* one editorialist likened the city's engineering failures, which he believed had worsened the flood, to the French military's embarrassing loss in 1870, saying, "They have suffered a defeat which is due to their lack of prevision and their neglect of precautions."[26] "We lived through the flood just as in 1870, during the two sieges of Paris, we watched the bombs fall," wrote another editorialist.[27] To even raise the question of a siege was to resurrect one of the most divisive and horrific episodes in recent French history, still fresh in the minds of those who had lived through it only forty years earlier. This history of siege, occupation, and tension between city and nation was the nerve that Dausset had touched.

Memories of the Commune were not the only reason many Parisians distrusted the military. Much more recently, all of France had been deeply divided along ideological lines by the biggest scandal of the late nineteenth century, the Dreyfus Affair. At the time of the flood, the bitter memories of this notorious controversy were still very much alive in the minds of many Parisians. Thanks to that episode, the French army had lost much of its credibility as defender of the people and the nation.

In 1894, a series of top-secret French military documents were leaked to the German army, but no one was sure of the traitor's identity.

Still feeling the pain of defeat in the Franco–Prussian War and the humiliation at this new lapse in security, few in France could fathom that a member of their own military would willingly collaborate with the enemy. Yet some in the army had decided to lay the blame on a Jewish captain named Alfred Dreyfus. Edouard Drumont, founder of *La Libre Parole* and a virulent anti-Semite, played on popular fears and conspiracy theories of the day, calling for an investigation pointing to Dreyfus as the likely criminal. Hoping to save further embarrassment and restore its reputation, the military proceeded with a sham investigation that framed Dreyfus with false evidence and turned him into a scapegoat. Despite being innocent of any spying, military courts hurried the case toward prosecution and a pre-determined guilty verdict. Dreyfus was publicly stripped of his rank, condemned for treason, and sentenced by the French army to Devil's Island in French Guiana, all with the support of conservative politicians, anti-Semites, and many in the Catholic church.

Following repeated attempts by his family and other supporters to reopen the case, in 1898 the famous novelist Émile Zola published a scathing open letter titled "J'Accuse" in the newspaper *L'Aurore*. He publicly reproached the army for its treachery in denying justice to an innocent man and blasted the civilian government for letting the military get away with the travesty. Zola's critique went to the core values of the Third Republic and, in particular, to the question of the military's place in a democratic society. At stake was the status of the army as an institution and whether it could serve the values of a free society after having protected the privileged interests of monarchy, aristocracy, and church for so long. For many, it was the army, not Dreyfus, that had betrayed not only France, but also the nation's hard-won principles of individual liberty, religious freedom, fairness, and the rule of law. Nevertheless, many continued to believe in Dreyfus's guilt.

A full-blown intellectual civil war broke out between those who supported Dreyfus as a victim of military corruption and religious intolerance and those who saw him as a spy and traitor to France. By the time the struggle finally reached its conclusion in 1906 when the National

Assembly pardoned Dreyfus, many people in France had come to severely mistrust and openly detest the military because of its unfair treatment of an innocent man.

Only four years later, the very same army that had unjustly convicted Dreyfus was now in the streets of Paris, and many wondered whether its men could be trusted. These were the soldiers to whom Louis Dausset had seemingly suggested on January 28 that Parisians turn over their city at the very height of the flood. With the wounds of the Dreyfus Affair still open, many found the thought of surrendering their city to the army and declaring martial law both painful and frightening.

No state of siege was ever declared during the flood. Civilian authorities continued to direct the military's efforts, and despite the city's upsetting history with the armed forces, Parisians did welcome the soldiers and sailors in the midst of their crisis. The performance of the military during the flood went a long way toward healing some of the old wounds, especially as Parisians could see with their own eyes how hard the military worked to protect them and the city. On streets as well as in newspapers and magazines, Parisians could watch soldiers building walkways and keeping order to prevent looting. One photograph depicted uniformed soldiers gathered around a two-person hand-pump. Some waited behind it with their jackets off, while two—one on each end of the pump's lever arm—stood ready to extract water from a building's basement. French soldiers rolled up their sleeves and prepared to get dirty in order to rescue rather than occupy the city of Paris.

Chapter Six

a CITY *on the* BRINK

Shelters run by the Red Cross, the Catholic church, and the government housed thousands of Parisians forced out of their homes by high water.

A natural disaster of this magnitude inspired a range of spiritual explanations. Throughout January 28, Parisians were praying in Catholic churches all around the city at special masses that Archbishop Amette had ordered. One occult writer named Dr. F. Rozier had a slightly different interpretation of the inundation than most, seeing it not as God's punishment but as the result of another kind of supernatural force. He claimed to have had a vision of the flood in advance, and he said he was the only person to predict how powerful it would be. A student of prophecy, Rozier claimed that excessive deforestation had angered the fairies who lived in the forests of France. He believed that they had caused the flooding. Only replanting the forests would calm the spirits of both woods and water.[1]

By a bizarre coincidence, Halley's Comet was passing overhead during the week of the flood. Some speculated about a possible link between the cosmic visitor and the unusual weather. There was no connection, of course, but for some the comet's presence was a strange omen, harkening back to earlier epochs when signs and wonders in the sky were the way to explain unusual events. The floods were so extraordinary that only something as dramatic as an extraterrestrial occurrence could help make sense of what was happening.

As the water drew to its peak on January 28, journalist Laurence Jerrold, the Paris correspondent for the London *Daily Telegraph*, climbed down the stairs of his darkened apartment building to take stock of the city. Earlier, the lights had gone out, and, with no current, the elevator in the building had locked in place. Once he was in the street, the powerful smell of a burst drain knocked him back. Much of Paris and its environs were filled with a growing stench of sewage, garbage, and mildew. Undeterred, Jerrold began to walk through the waterlogged streets, gazing in disbelief at the scene of ruin.

Very few trains, soiled by mud and water, were still functioning, although they ran much more slowly than usual. Jerrold was able to board one heading for the Gare Saint-Lazare, whose steel shed covering the station's main tracks had been turned by Impressionist painters into a famous symbol of the modern city. When he stepped out the front door of the now dark, empty station, Jerrold looked at the familiar square. Instead of the Place de Rome, he was struck by an unbelievable sight: a lagoon hundreds of feet across.

The Gare Saint-Lazare and the neighborhood around it were usually bustling with shoppers, travelers, pedestrians, and traffic. The water had stolen the life from this part of Paris, and the silence of the neighborhood frightened Jerrold. The surface of the water was glassy and smooth, disturbed only by wind or by the boats rowing across this lagoon that had suddenly appeared on the Right Bank.

A powerful image came to Jerrold's mind as he contemplated the destruction that lay before him. Rather than thinking of Venice, as so many at the time did, Jerrold compared the unfolding scene to another recent devastating disaster. In December 1908 southern Italy had been rocked by a 7.5 magnitude earthquake in the Strait of Messina, which separates Sicily from the boot-tip of the peninsula. Immediately following the quake, 40-foot tidal waves washed onto cities and towns around the Mediterranean. The Messina earthquake was the most destructive in European history, with a death toll reaching at least 60,000 and, according to some estimates, as many as 200,000.

In Messina, which Jerrold had covered as a reporter, almost nothing remained standing in the aftermath of the quake, so Jerrold was over-reaching in his comparison. Yet as he stood surrounded by the flood's devastation in Paris, Messina was the only event that could help him comprehend the scene now before his eyes. "A lamppost or two awry, the pavement upheaved, railings twisted, a quiet sheet of water covering what had been streets, and everywhere dead silence; houses dark and empty, a crowd in the distance as silent, moving slowly," Jerrold wrote in *Contemporary Review* magazine in an article that constitutes one of the best and longest descriptions of the flood. "That was also what one first saw in Messina Harbour . . . St. Lazare looked as dead as the marina at Messina."[2]

Inside the station, water had done great damage. The agency that ran the facility reported that the water pressure had buckled a walkway leading from the Place de Rome to the Métro entrance, which was now threatening to collapse and bring other interior structures down with it. As a result, most entrances to the station were closed.

Jerrold joined a crowd of people exiting the Gare Saint-Lazare. "We shuffled along, looking blankly at what had been the Place de Rome and was now a sheet of filthy, brown, smelling water, in which an omnibus office, a newspaper kiosk all askew, and two or three drunken lampposts were islands, and which slimily washed the base of hotels, cafés, shops—all empty and dead." The crowd moved slowly and silently out of the station, searching for paths into the surrounding neighborhood. Some of the women whispered, "My God!" Policemen tried to keep people moving but could barely manage to mutter a few brief commands.

"Can the heart of Paris die like this in one night? It did seem dead. I have never seen a more complete image of death than was presented on that Friday by this once impossibly crowded station." The death Jerrold described was not human death, but the death of the city of Paris. "Would it not sink altogether? It very well might—all of it might crumble into a heap, not of dust, as at Messina, but of liquid mud, oozing over fallen stone and bricks." The streets around the nearby Opéra Garnier were like jelly, he observed, and the road buckled and moved underneath his feet. "Would whole pieces of Paris collapse? Would all Paris crumble in bit by bit? Perhaps the whole of Paris really was doomed; perhaps it really was to be the end of Paris, which means the end of the world for Parisians."[3]

After leaving the Gare Saint-Lazare, Jerrold headed to the Left Bank, across the river coming to Rue St. Dominique, a working-class area near the golden-domed Hôtel des Invalides, where ground-floor apartments had filled to the ceiling with water and the remnants of people's lives floated in the streets. Once-prized pieces of furniture that people had worked so hard to buy and had taken great care to polish were turned into muddy walkways that they used to climb into boats. One widow, evacuated from her small apartment, suddenly realized that she had left behind an old cardboard box filled with money. Jerrold watched the firemen row her back home so that she could retrieve her life savings. He also found a family of six near Saint Pierre du Gros Caillou, who had gone for three days without food, "forgotten by accident, too poor to have provisions put by, too cast down to make noise enough to bring help." An elderly concierge died when her building flooded; a sailor carried her body away in a boat. "Doctors could not get to their patients; babies were born in humble flats, and no help could reach the mothers for twenty-four hours."[4]

As Jerrold walked through the city on January 28, he would have noticed that the Esplanade des Invalides, the beautiful green space that connected the Hôtel des Invalides with the Pont Alexandre III and another key part of what had been the 1900 fairgrounds, was little more than a swamp. The entire stretch of riverbank between Invalides and the Orsay train station was nothing but water. In this area, a complex network of *passerelles* enabled foot traffic to continue. So many people had climbed onto the wooden walkway to cross the Esplanade that on this day, it gave way under the weight, plunging a crowd of Parisians into the icy, stagnant water. Quickly repaired, the walkway at Invalides was more carefully policed to limit the number of people on it at any one time.

The Paris correspondent for the London *Morning Post,* H. Warner Allen, recalled the potential for mishaps on many of the walkways. In his eyewitness account titled "The Seine in Flood," printed in magazines in the United States and England, he wrote: "Men left their homes dry-shod in the morning, and returning from business had to wade up to their knees through unlighted streets or creep perilously along a narrow plank gangway, only to find that it stopped short just where the water was deepest."[5]

Animals, as well as people, were trapped by the flood. Immediately to the north of the Gare d'Austerlitz on the Left Bank was the Jardin des

Plantes (the botanical garden) and home of the Paris zoo. On January 28, keepers had begun to fear for the safety of the animals since the Seine had entered many of the habitats, trapping the creatures in their pens without food or fresh water. The bears, helpless against the rising muddy Seine, climbed onto the elevated parts of their pit, which now formed an island. Zoo officials began to remove many animals, but doing so was not always easy. "The climbers were soon treed," noted American writer Helen Davenport Gibbons. "It was an engineering feat to rescue them with planks and prod them into portable cages. The non-climbers narrowly escaped drowning. We watched them lifted out by cranes, caught in sturdy nets."[6] When their tank flooded, the crocodiles tried to escape into the river. Zookeepers flailed about in the water, struggling to capture and secure them. As word got out about conditions at the zoo, rumors began circulating that the animals had in fact escaped and were on the loose in the streets of Paris. Cold, wet, and hungry animals roared and ran around in their cages, confused about what was going on. Despite the best efforts of zookeepers, at least one giraffe refused to move to safety onto a rescue platform that had been introduced into its habitat and eventually died. Two gazelles also perished, and one of the elephants contracted rheumatism.[7]

At the same time, employees inside City Hall were struggling to prevent thousands of important legal documents from being washed away. Sewermen and employees of the municipal bank made dozens of trips down to the basement to rescue securities worth some 250 million francs. For six hours during the day of January 28, while the water rose nearly five more feet in the basement, these city employees climbed up darkened flights of stairs carrying some 130,000 files. Men piled sandbags up against the walls to keep out as much water as possible.[8]

"Oh! The poor people, the poor little people," wrote journalist Henri Lavedan in *L'Illustration* of the situation at the height of the flood on January 28: "The housekeepers who, penny by penny, have worked so hard to save to have a room in which to eat, a bedroom . . . a clock . . . a few knick-knacks and souvenirs . . . and who have lost these modest riches so precious and dear, that will take them so long to replace."[9]

Despite their belief in *Système D*—the faith that they could overcome a tough situation—and the ingenuity they had shown in carrying on with life in their city, after a full week of flooding, many Parisians had become anxious or panicky. Feeding the population had been a significant challenge during the siege in 1870, when long lines of Parisians hoping to obtain a morsel or two formed outside shops. Meat had been strictly rationed, and butchers could only sell to Parisians who appeared on their list of assigned customers. Late in the siege, the government began rationing bread. Whether rationed or not, the prices for everything shot up so that staple items were out of reach for many, especially the poor. In the worst days of the 1870 siege, many Parisians—not only the poor—were reportedly forced to eat rats, dogs, and cats. According to legend, even animals at the zoo became a necessary supply of nourishment for the starving city. These memories of the not-too-distant past haunted Parisians and their leaders as the floodwaters engulfed the city in 1910.

The food supply was of particular concern since Les Halles, the city's central market, was close enough to the river to make people worry that its contents might spoil if flooded. This enormous pavilion, packed with stalls, was another of Haussmann's interventions and an attempt to modernize the buying and selling of food, one of the most basic functions of the city. Its high, arching iron trestles allowed for throngs of Parisians to move through the marketplace. The structure's enormous windows surrounded shoppers and vendors with light and air.

Water had been penetrating several of the market's spaces through various small openings for several days. Administrators had called in city road-mending crews, who sloshed through the rising water in the basements to plug the leaks with great success. On January 26, *Le Matin* had reported that "it does not seem that 'the belly of Paris,'" as Les Halles was famously known, "has suffered too much."[10]

The fear of further damage to Les Halles contributed to a temporary spike in the price of some food items, and many worried that store owners might engage in profiteering if food supplies ran short. On January 28, outside a grocery run by one Monsieur Lefevre at 88 Rue du Faubourg du Temple in the 11th *arrondissement,* a small crowd of angry Parisians began to grow as people told their neighbors that Lefevre was raising the price of potatoes. Indignant and hungry, the crowd grew violent, charging toward the shop and taking out their frustration by destroying it. The newspaper *L'Humanité* described the situation: "Potatoes rained down . . . on the head of the merchant until the police intervened." The title of the article captured the theme of the incident: "Popular Justice."[11]

Responding to anxieties and rumors about food supplies, Premier Briand announced on January 28 that the government would prosecute any bakers or other vendors who tried to take advantage of the flood by raising prices. Wholesalers suspected of hoarding or speculating on food, especially potatoes (the price had already risen some 30 percent by some estimates) would also be prosecuted.[12] The government ordered additional flour supplies from the east to try to offset any shortage in stores and gave priority to all trains carrying necessary provisions to the capital region. The military kept reserves of wheat in its granaries, but since flour mills in the region had been flooded, many wondered whether such stockpiles would be enough to feed a hungry population.

Charges of price gouging, whether brought by government officials or rumormongers in the streets, deeply angered the bakers' union. Its leadership promptly hung posters around the city titled "The Price of Bread" to rebut the accusations that bakers were taking advantage of a shortage for their personal gain. "These accusations are absolutely false," the poster sternly declared. The union attributed the scandal to troublemakers and rabble-rousers trying to stir up the city's population. Instead, the bakers of the city had been working overtime throughout the flood, the union claimed, to supply the city with necessary food in a time of crisis at the regular price. Despite the rise in flour prices, the union said, "The price of bread will not be changed."[13]

The more people feared going hungry, the more people turned against one another. The quest for food sometimes highlighted larger inequalities. Laurence Jerrold recalled that, at the height of the flood, when troops delivering bread destined for poorer quarters of the city were rowing past some very wealthy homes, they heard the inhabitants shouting down. The rich people inside were calling out the amount they were willing to give for the food the soldiers were carrying. They would pay any price, even if it meant taking food out of the mouths of those who couldn't afford to pay anything.

At Les Halles on January 28, the situation began to look like an emergency when one of the food vendors discovered water pouring into the basement of the salt warehouse. Maintenance crews hastily erected walls to try to keep it out, and for a while these dams did the trick. Just as the Seine was peaking, however, vendors with booths in pavilions 7, 8, 9, 11, and 12 flew into a panic when they witnessed water from cesspools on Rue Rambuteau flowing into their basements, one of which already had at least 16 inches of yellow water. Warehouse workers hurried to stack up sacks of cement to prevent any further infiltration, and they constructed temporary levees throughout the market complex as a precaution.[14]

Although some supplies of fish, butter, eggs, and game at Les Halles spoiled, the efforts of the workers on January 28 were ultimately successful in plugging the holes and building a barrier to keep the water out. Paris would not go hungry. Within days, the press reported that trains were bringing flour for bread, and prices returned to normal. More than 1,300 rail cars full of livestock began arriving from the east. The Red Cross and other relief groups continued to feed people across the city and in the suburbs. Butter and milk producers took up a collection of food items from their members and gave them to the Red Cross for distribution to the victims.

Bakeries in dry neighborhoods continued functioning, and hungry patrons lined up to buy bread from large baskets full of baguettes. Earlier in his life, American philanthropist Rodman Wanamaker, owner of the famous department store his father had founded in Philadelphia, had spent ten years in Paris, and he continued to feel a deep affection for the city. To help ensure the bread supply, he offered to buy a loaf of bread for every flood victim in the Paris region for thirty days.[15] Miraculously, no one starved to death during the flood, an amazing achievement in a region of some 4.5 million people. Keeping people fed allowed Parisians to press ahead under the arduous circumstances. It also built confidence in the government's ability to protect the city in the midst of crisis.

As the water peaked in Paris, the Seine continued to rise in suburban towns downriver from the capital. By January 28, Captain T. Vaux of the military engineers had already spent a full week directing the fight against the flood in the town of Colombes, northwest of Paris.

A few nights earlier, on January 22, the sewers had begun to overflow in Colombes. Vaux and twenty of his men sped to the site of the water's infiltration with shovels, picks, rope, and other tools to dig trenches to delay the Seine's rise until they could evacuate the area. The town hall ordered teams of six men to patrol the levees at key locations. Vaux began constructing makeshift rafts in preparation for what he feared would be a complete failure of the barriers. Vaux's fears were realized on the night of January 26 when water began to flow over the top and then breached the levees completely. Early the next morning, Vaux and town officials gave the order to evacuate and sounded the alarm. As the sun rose, Vaux's men boarded rafts and boats and began to carry the residents away, either in their craft or on their backs. "By nightfall," Vaux recorded, "around fifty people, old people, women and children, were transported to safety." The water continued to spread, and by January 28, the remaining residents went into "an indescribable panic." By this point, he and his men were clearly losing their battle against the rising water. Rafts could not float through the narrow spaces between homes, so rescuers had to struggle on foot through the water's strong current.[16]

Fiction writer Pierre Hamp captured the growing fear in the suburban towns in his short story "The Seine Rises."[17] Hamp, who had spent years working in kitchens and on the railroad before becoming a writer, infused his prose with a sense of sympathy for the common man and woman but also with a brutal realism about the lives of everyday people and the forces outside their control. He depicted events in the suburb of Choisy-le-Roi, south of Paris. In Hamp's story, as the waters rise, middle-class clerks in stiff, starched collars struggle to get into the city each day on trains that run more slowly and irregularly because of the flood. Gathering on the train platforms, they gossip and talk of what is happening throughout the region. Once on board, they either chat with other passengers from up the line who are crammed into the deeply delayed train or they devour the latest newspaper accounts while they ride. "One young fellow, with his eyes shining from sleeplessness, kept repeating in a tired voice: 'We've been rescuing people! We've been rescuing. . . .'"

Once the full force of the Seine hit the village, "panic took possession of those who were unable to escape," as Hamp describes it. One of the women in his story tries to rescue her bedding with the help of a barrel-maker and a mover. The men can only do so much before their boat is full. People begin fleeing their homes, carrying children through the streets. Police build a bonfire at the water's edge so that residents can warm themselves. Several guns are fired off in a fit of frustration. Residents struggle with each other over supplies. "If you want food you've got to get it yourself or starve," one hungry working man declares.

Neighbors turn to help one another, but there is already a feeling that it will not last. In Hamp's version of the flood, social divisions and the limits of human sympathy are clear from the start. Among the victims, the poor are hit much harder than the rich.

Law and order quickly break down in Hamp's tale. The soldiers who arrive don't know what to do and only add to the growing confusion. The barrel-maker knows that thieves are lurking and plots his revenge. When police and soldiers come to evacuate the residents of the town, tempers truly fray: "Boats, manned by policemen, called at every door, and the order 'Every one out!' was explained to the inhabitants good-humouredly, except to those who made a fuss, like Charlet, the mover, who told the policemen to run along and mind their business." When police suspect that Charlet's reluctance to evacuate is an excuse for him to stay behind and loot his neighbors, they promptly search him. The mayor tries to organize relief efforts but becomes the subject of rumor, ridicule, and anger. Monsieur Mécoeur, one of the commuting clerks, turns on the town's government and on the mayor in particular: "'What an administration! A hundred and fifty-eight francs in taxes, and I get thrown out of my house by the police!'"

Pierre Hamp's fictional account echoed the growing frustration and fear about conditions throughout the entire region that Parisian newspapers were reporting. One anonymous resident of the Saint-Germain neighborhood on the Left Bank near the river found a certain beauty in the flooded city for the first few days. By Friday, January 28, however, he told the newspaper *Journal des débats*, "Waking up became hard work. . . . We knew that the disaster was getting bigger everywhere. We saw the water rising. Little by little, we were losing hope." As boats came to evacuate people from their homes, the area became emptier and sadder. "No one in their windows or on the balconies. Just more and more frightened shouts. They would pay any price to leave. I wasn't sure if the danger was any greater than the day before. People were giving in to fear."[18] Many still remained trapped in their homes throughout flooded neighborhoods, screaming for help or food from their windows. Journalist Laurence Jerrold described the increasingly dire atmosphere of January 28 this way: "Coming down the Rue Royale that day I had the first feeling of something like tragedy. I think it was a feeling that all Paris shared . . . something approaching a panic fear lurked in us, through we would not let it out. It seemed genuinely clear to us that anything might happen."[19]

Parisians had been surviving, but by January 28, unsure about what was to come, many now seemed on the brink of a breakdown. "The help is insufficient," the newspaper *Le Journal* proclaimed that day. "In spite of their devotion, the harried, weary officials cannot provide sufficient help for the overwhelming task that faces them. The material needed for rescue is too little; there is disorder amidst the disaster." The Parisians gazing at the river were, in this writer's estimation, "pacing around tirelessly, telling each other terrible stories, although fortunately usually false. The noise and the gossip had made Parisians a bit nervous."[20] Most government bureaus, including Paris's public assistance agency, were working to distribute what they could. This office normally dealt with poor relief, so handling the requests of thousands of flood victims proved to be a daunting task.

One disgruntled flood victim wrote a letter to the Communist newspaper *L'Humanité,* claiming that when his family arrived at the shelter in Maisons-Alfort during the worst of the high water, representatives of the Union of French Women "closed the door on our noses and told us that we had no right to receive help at Maisons-Alfort because we were from Alfortville." A man from Billancourt also wrote to *L'Humanité,* stating that "the incompetence of the mayor was most noticeable in how he organized relief." He claimed that a ferryman employed by the town refused to rescue some twenty people from their homes because the current was too swift. Meanwhile, according to this author, the ferryman really was busy rescuing the rabbits and chickens of the rich people in the area. In other words, either he was trying to curry favor with the wealthy in town or he was busy robbing them by "rescuing" their animals for his own benefit.[21]

By January 28, Paris's much-vaunted solidarity was clearly cracking, and fraud was becoming a problem. Most posters hung throughout the 4th *arrondissement* on this day promoted giving, but some warned about imposters. These announcements cautioned neighbors to watch out for "the schemes of individuals who present themselves as charity collectors on behalf of the victims."[22] They were reminded that the actual charity funds were located at the town hall, at the newspapers, and at government offices. People should bring their contributions there since no one was going throughout the city collecting—except for the scam artists.

In one memo circulated to the town halls throughout Paris, the head administrators of the public assistance bureau complained that there were important gaps between the means and needs of certain districts. Many Parisians had been donating money directly to their own neighborhood relief, but this meant that wealthy areas were flush with funds while other *arrondissements* with poorer populations had much less. Administrators urged local officials to redistribute monies to avoid the "shocking inequalities" that resulted. "If this was known to the public or the press," the memo claimed, "it would doubtless raise a great deal of concern."[23]

All the charity flowing into the city did not always relieve the immediate suffering. Guillaume Apollinaire observed in his article for *L'Intransigeant* numerous scenes of the flood's human impact. "Near the Pont-Royal, a legless cripple seemed to meditate," and from time to time, "he asked passers-by 'Is the water still rising?' before falling back into his thoughts." Polish immigrants in Paris headed toward Gare du Nord: "Without doubt they were hurrying toward Antwerp to take the German steamer headed for America." Among them, Apollinaire reported, was an elderly Jew who was so disturbed by the dark, terrible mood in the city that he proclaimed his deepest fears aloud: "Soon there will be pogroms in Paris!"[24]

As the sun sank behind the drenched landscape and the gray day of January 28 turned to the cold of early evening, Robert Capelle, the stenographer still living inside the Palais Bourbon, stepped outside into the brisk air. After days of camping out in his waterlogged workplace, he wanted to go home and check on his belongings, but he faced a long, wet journey through flooded, pitch-dark streets. Before starting out, Capelle pondered the fate of the building now filled with the murky waters of the Seine. What would become of the Palais Bourbon, he wondered. "I loved it, in spite of the long hours and difficult moments. . . . It was where I had earned my bread for the last twenty-one years."[25] Taking a last look back, he and four friends launched themselves into the rainy night.

The men traced the edge of the riverbank in the dark by holding onto the ropes that police had strung alongside the Seine to cordon off dangerous sections of the quay to prevent people from falling in. When they arrived at Rue de Beaune a few blocks away from the Orsay, upriver from the Palais Bourbon, they still could not find dry land. They mounted "a *passerelle* established on platforms about two meters above the ground; 150 meters long; one meter wide; vision obscured or blinded by the acetylene lamps. I arrived at Rue du Pré-aux-Clercs; all five of us still had dry feet to take us home." Capelle was relieved that his day was finally over. "I had never heard anyone say with the same emphasis the simple words 'at home.' The challenge made being 'at home' feel like such a prize."[26]

Like Capelle, many throughout Paris tried to preserve as much of a normal existence as they could in order to keep their spirits up, even at the water's peak. That evening, American ambassador Robert Bacon and his wife decided to receive the guests they had invited weeks earlier to a dinner party. Bacon was a businessman who had worked for J.P. Morgan and U.S. Steel before being named assistant secretary of state by Theodore Roosevelt and then ambassador to Paris in December 1909. As the new chief representative in Paris, he kept a close check on American business interests and Americans living in the city during the flood and communicated the U.S. government's desire to provide any assistance possible. He also helped to coordinate relief funds arriving from the United States to aid Parisians. The embassy off the Champs-Elysées had remained relatively dry up to January 28, but because of the rising water, this would be Bacon's last night inside this building as he evacuated his family to higher ground the next day.

Performances continued at several of the city's theaters on January 28, as they had throughout the flood. Despite the need for distraction from the worsening conditions, fewer people ventured out into the wet winter chill to attend the shows. At the Comédie-Française, one of the most important state-run theaters, acetylene lamps installed in its performance space allowed the production to go on after the flooded basements had cut off power. The technical crews at both the Opéra-Comique, France's national comic theater company, and the Odéon theater on the Left Bank stood ready to activate generators if the electricity failed so that their shows could continue. Producers tried to keep their venues operating, but many decided to close their doors because the flood had made working conditions too difficult and the audiences too sparse. The Théâtre Sarah-Bernhardt sent its troupe to Brussels for the duration of the flood so that they could continue to work. When performances did go on in Paris, most theaters donated their receipts to flood relief.

Despite efforts to keep Paris as lively as possible, the city was now eerie. An American journalist writing in the *Los Angeles Times* described the unusual scene of the night of January 28 this way: "Tonight the city presents a weird spectacle, the soldiers, sailors, firemen, and police hastily constructing temporary walls by the light of camp fires and torches in an endeavor to keep out the invading floods, while pickets patrol those sections of the city which are plunged in darkness by the bursting of the gas mains and the stoppage of the electric lighting plants."[27]

*O*n January 28, the water was cresting in Paris, but downriver the river's force was still growing. Gennevilliers, home to some 7,500 people in 1910, sat in one of the horseshoe curves of the Seine several miles west of Paris. This suburban village had a special relationship with the capital and its water. Since 1868, the runoff from the city's sewers had been collected in the fields near Gennevilliers and was available as a free fertilizer to anyone who wanted it.

As the protective walls along the riverbank buckled under the weight of the rising Seine, an alarm sounded, warning the inhabitants of impending doom with only a few minutes to spare. *"Sauve qui peut!"* the cry rang out—"Save yourselves." A short time later, at about midnight on January 28, the levees at Gennevilliers burst with a terrifying explosion that boomed across the region. In an instant, thousands of gallons of water washed across the plain, flooding the entire town along with the neighboring low-lying village of Asnières and other nearby communities.

The force of rushing water ripped enormous holes in the walls of houses, reducing many to rubble. People literally ran for their lives through the darkness, but no one was sure where to go for safety. Not everyone who wanted to could escape. Fifty young girls were trapped, screaming for help, in the dormitory of their boarding school. Around 2 AM, rafts from neighboring towns arrived to help save those who were stranded in their homes. By dawn, French soldiers, sailors, and local firemen had to come to the rescue of the population, saving several hundred from danger and bringing food supplies, although these resources had to be carefully rationed by local officials to prevent them from running out.

During the night, the rushing water destroyed the five-year-old gas factory that provided heat and light to over eighty surrounding communities and with it went the jobs of some nine hundred laborers. The Fleury pharmaceutical factory was forced to close its doors, taking more jobs with it. The water that flowed through the breach in the Gennevilliers levee soon reached the electrical plant near Clichy, shutting it down and thrusting that area into darkness.

The river, which was normally not even a quarter mile across, was now reportedly three and three-quarter miles at Gennevilliers. The next day in the National Assembly, the deputy representing Gennevilliers would claim that eighty thousand people were without homes or food or both in that region and that unemployment would cause many of them additional harm.[28]

Yet even as the levee at Gennevilliers broke, the flood was beginning to fall almost imperceptibly through the early morning hours of January 29. Everyone in the Paris region was at the brink of exhaustion. Most were still working to save one another and their city, but the social fabric was beginning to tear. After a week of living under water, all people could do was hold their breath and wait.

Part Three

WATER FALLING

Chapter Seven

the CITY *of* MUD *and* FILTH

⊹⊟⊸ ⊸⊟⊹

Women begin the arduous process of disinfection in the Rue de la Convention in the 15th arrondissement.

As the sun rose on Saturday, January 29, Parisians looking up into the sky immediately saw the dramatic change overhead. The weather had finally cleared, and the sun was breaking through the clouds. The gray canopy was turning bright blue. Just at the point when Parisians thought they could take no more, the Seine had reached its peak. Now it was falling—slowly—back into its bed. As the river descended, inch by inch, it left behind a dark, muddy line on the quay walls to remind people just how far it had risen. Parisians had been hunkering down for days in the cold and damp. They had stayed in their own homes if they could or in the temporary shelters if they had to. As the sun returned, doors and windows across the flooded landscape opened wide, and Parisians came outside, some for the first time in days.

Unsure that the nightmare was really over, their first steps were tentative. Once they realized that the rain had stopped, huge crowds began pouring into the streets to celebrate their survival and the city's. Laughing, shouting, and clapping Parisians clustered at the quays, sharing the good feeling of relief with one another. Bundled up in winter clothes, groups gathered at the bridges, their "faces and eyes no longer with the same anxious expression," according to *L'Humanité*. Pointing at the Seine, they said to one another, "It's going down, it's going down. Ah! It's not soon enough." *Le Matin* described the city now united in its joy: "Men and women of every sort, bourgeois, artisan, wage-earners, manual laborers, rich, poor, everyone mingled, glowing with the same emotion, children, even the paralyzed who were brought in cars. It's unimaginable." The Parisian weekly *La Vie Illustrée* put it more succinctly: "The water didn't rise during the night. The sun is shining. Hope is reborn."[1] A visitor to Paris might have been excused for thinking that the city had just been liberated from a wartime siege. There was, literally, dancing in the streets.

British journalist Laurence Jerrold joined Parisians on January 29 to watch the water recede. "The Seine certainly fascinated us," Jerrold wrote in his memoir of the flood, "a people unaccustomed to the beauty of a great rush of water. Its angry play almost amused us." Despite that sense of wonder, however, as the water descended, Jerrold's great sense of relief was tempered by the dawning knowledge that, under the right circumstances, even a city as old and beautiful as Paris could actually cease to exist. "I do not think our fears were quite absurd," he mused, "and I think the escape of Paris was a 'close thing.'"[2]

As people met on bridges and quays to watch the falling water and warm themselves in the sun, the atmosphere sometimes seemed like a carnival. Food sellers set up stands and called out to the crowd, hawking hot chestnuts, apple turnovers, croissants, candy, lemonade, and beer.[3] Nearby, soldiers stationed on the bridges kept a watchful eye on the scene, rifles at the ready. The sound of engineers still hard at work hammering together wooden walkways continued to ring out in neighborhoods all along the Seine. City workers climbed over bridge railings, struggling to remove debris caught underneath the decks. It was a strange carnival, indeed.

Postcard sellers weaved through the happy crowds along the sidewalks by the river, holding up handfuls of images for all to see and buy. Despite the suffering, many people wanted to remember the flood, now that it seemed to be over, and postcards were a cheap and easy way to do so. Vendors offered these mementos either individually or in small booklets with perforated edges so that cards could be easily detached. On January 29, publisher A. Noyer ran an advertisement in *Le Matin* under the heading "Flooded Paris," offering groups of twenty postcards for two francs.

The postcards provided unfamiliar and exotic views of places that were normally familiar, serving as both a form of odd novelty images and a documentary record of the flood's impact. Postcards also told the story of how Parisians had responded to the flood. Action shots of rescues abounded, making the people of Paris look their best even in the midst of disaster. One journalist put it this way: "Soon there will be nothing left of the flood except memories . . . and postcards."[4] Newspapers, the Red Cross, and other charitable organizations printed booklets full of flood images that sold for a few francs, with the proceeds going to relief funds. Buying one of these fundraising collections gave Parisians another way of participating in the recovery effort.

Shortly after daybreak on January 29, neighbors found the body of cabinetmaker Georges Husson and called the police. During the night before, Husson had stepped out into the cold winter darkness for the last time. His final moments are lost—perhaps he strolled along the Avenue Ledru-Rollin near his house to take in the effects of the disaster that had begun one week earlier. Even though the water was not very deep in his neighborhood, the air was wet and frigid. Records do not indicate why he died, but drowning seems unlikely since his part of Paris was not heavily flooded. There were many ways to die under these conditions, however. That same day, police carried the body of an elderly man to the Hôtel-Dieu hospital. They had found him hiding in the closet under the stairs of his building, but he was beyond help. Doctors pronounced him dead; he had been so frightened by the flood that he had suffered a heart attack. Stories of death and near-death had been appearing in the newspapers all week, keeping a sense of imminent danger clearly in the forefront of Parisians' minds.[5]

Arriving at an exact figure of how many people died in the flood is impossible, but one fact is clear: When it came to loss of life, Paris was not Messina after the earthquake. The *Annuaire Statistique de la Ville de Paris* for 1910, the official government tabulation of hundreds of statistics for the calendar year, records only six deaths in January under the heading "Accidental Drownings." For February, with the waters still higher than normal, the government documented seven such deaths. Firefighters accounted for 643 live rescues during the flood but only five dead bodies.

The statistics don't tell the whole story. Mortality figures in the suburbs were most likely higher because these communities were both more vulnerable to the floodwaters and less prepared to respond to the catastrophe. Those numbers, however, are not reflected in the *Annuaire*

Statistique. These records tally only civilian deaths, not those of soldiers and sailors. More importantly, the statistics for drowning fail to account for deaths from other causes triggered by the flood—as was the case with the old man under the stairs and probably with Georges Husson as well. The combination of wet and cold could easily lead to mortal illnesses. A city machinist named Monsieur Disant, for example, worked throughout the day and night of January 27 and 28 and then returned to his post the next day. During that time, he caught a bad cold, and around midnight on the twenty-ninth, his congestion became so bad that he had to return home with the help of a colleague. As soon as he arrived home, he died.[6] There is no way of knowing how many others got sick and perished because of the damp conditions, exacerbated by shortages of heat, healthy food, or clean water. Nor do the statistics reveal how many, gripped by their fear of the flooding Seine, committed suicide.

As soon as the water started falling on January 29, Louis Lépine ordered city engineers and road crews to crank up the powerful, deafening motors of steam-driven pumps. These men snaked enormous hoses across the wet boulevards to carry water away from buildings and back into the falling river. Writing in the magazine *L'Illustration,* journalist Henri Lavedan described a machine he encountered near the river: "A red and copper steam pump making an enormous noise emerged from the Avenue de l'Alma. Quickly brought to a standstill, the horse-drawn pump wagon was loaded with a team of operators who jumped to the ground, while the two big, impatient dappled horses, it seemed, also doing their duty, had already entered the water, causing it to spray up to their harnesses."[7] The large number of pumps rolling through the city jammed some of the main thoroughfares. Journalist H. Warner Allen, the Paris correspondent for the London *Morning Post,* described Parisian roads busy with activity: "In almost every street between Montmartre and the river, pumps were hard at work; encouragement came from the news that the Seine was falling to resume what had been before the hopeless task of emptying cellars and basements; there were pumps of every kind, large and small, hand-pumps, smart electric pumps, steam pumps, and monstrous indescribable pieces of machinery that took up half the roadway, obscured the sunshine with clouds of filthy smoke and looked as if they had been rescued from the scrap-heap."[8] Ironically, pumping created new dangers. The integrity of many structures that had soaked in water for days was compromised. Once pumping began, engineers feared these buildings might collapse. Crews supervised the process carefully to watch for any signs that a building might crumble once the pressure from the water holding up its damaged walls was removed.

Meanwhile, all people could do was be patient. In the suburban town of Corbeil, people huddled around a tarp-covered pump, watching police and soldiers remove water from a bakery, eagerly awaiting the moment when it could reopen and supply them with bread. Sometimes their patience ran short, such as when shoppers accused a Paris store owner of raising the price of vegetables on January 29. An angry crowd then gave the vendor a serious beating. Wrestling free of his attackers, he climbed upstairs above his shop and in frustration fired several pistol shots into the air to scare them away. Unfortunately one of his bullets found a victim, and a woman in the crowd lay wounded. Her injury only stoked the rage of those besieging the store, and they broke in and tried to lynch him, but the police soon intervened.[9]

All along the edges of the retreating Seine on January 30, thousands of exhausted Parisians returned home from the shelters, winding their way through the wet streets. Some found the contents of their houses and businesses lodged alongside the river's banks, next to debris that had floated down the river. Once-treasured family items filled the sidewalks. Rotting mattresses, crumpled wads of personal papers, soggy coal and wood used for heating, rancid food, stained and torn clothing, and soiled toys were now mere rubbish. One photo from the village of Alfortville captured a close-up of the disaster: a family's collection of belongings—

two tables, a woman's portrait fallen from its frame, a boot—strewn on the mud with the river looming in the background.

On January 30, Lépine issued detailed cleaning instructions to the entire population, and posters that explained the procedures quickly went up throughout the city. All infected buildings would remain empty until decontaminated. Lépine's guidelines required Parisians to push and shovel tons of silt, mud, and refuse as far from any water as possible and then heap disinfectant on top. Once inspectors had vouched for the structural integrity of a building, residents could climb into the basement with pumps to drain any standing water. Cleaners at each location were instructed to douse their brushes and mops with water mixed with quicklime or with a combination of calcium hypochloride and calcium chloride. After scrubbing basement walls and floors, they should scatter a layer of quicklime mixed with powdered iron sulfate. Lépine forbade the sale of any food from locations not yet cleaned, so many restaurants, groceries, and bakeries would sit empty for weeks, adding to ongoing worries about the food supply. In some areas, men dragged animal carcasses outside, coating them with quicklime. Clothes, thoroughly washed in disinfectant, hung out to dry on clotheslines or from windowsills. Lépine stipulated that any garments too soiled should be burned. He also ordered that fires be built in the fireplaces or stoves in each flooded structure to warm and dry them out. People left their doors and windows open for days to circulate as much fresh air as possible. The normal winter odor of smoke increased dramatically, and a city under water at times now smelled like it was on fire.

On January 30, a wall collapsed inside one of the city's original generators near the Palais Royal on the Right Bank, enabling sewage to penetrate and drown the generator motors. Three men working in the building to restore some of the city's electricity barely escaped with their lives.

Archbishop Léon-Adolphe Amette presided over two masses on January 30, the first at the Cathedral of Notre-Dame, despite the high water in the church's basement. At 3 PM, he said a special afternoon mass at the brand-new Basilica of Sacré-Coeur in the working-class area of Montmartre on the northern edge of the city.

The gleaming white, beehive-domed church of Sacré-Coeur sat on one of the highest peaks in Paris, on top of the Montmartre hill, making it visible from much of the rest of the city and safe from the floodwaters. The basilica was a double-edged memorial to recent history. On one hand, it served a kind of national penance for the bloodshed during the French army's brutal recapturing of the city during the Commune of 1871. On the other, it attempted to restore a conservative moral order to a neighborhood that had been one of the most rebellious and tenacious in fighting for Parisian independence, as well as an area known for a freewheeling lifestyle. Dedicated to the cult of the Sacred Heart of Jesus, the ultra-Catholic devotion to the increasingly popular vision of a loving, sympathetic Christ, it symbolized the widespread yearning for spiritual renewal in France in the aftermath of the Franco–Prussian War. Sacré-Coeur quickly became a pilgrimage destination for the most devout, where they could adore the consecrated host always on display in an enormous golden monstrance above the high altar. This was the site of a Catholicism reinvigorated for the new century.

Inside this monument charged with powerful political and cultural meanings, on January 30, Amette gave thanks for the city's salvation and called on Parisians to assist the needy. "We must give material and spiritual help to the flood victims," he told the faithful in his homily, as he stood beneath the glowing ceiling mosaic of an enormous Christ with his arms spread wide. "I have seen the horrible ravages of the flood, entire families ruined and deprived of everything, with no shelter, no clothing, no bread. I call upon you, dear ones of this diocese, to show your charity, not only today, but tomorrow, and in the long days to come, because the disaster is frightful and the victims are numerous."[10]

He also talked about the need for repentance and for the recognition of a heavenly plan, even in the midst of another national catastrophe. Amette's homily addressed what he saw as France's pressing spiritual needs. "We must pray to God for the victims of the flood and do penance, offering to God our sincere prayers for the relief of the victims. There is a divine, providential lesson in this flood but we can only see it in particular cases. We are all sinners in the eyes of God; we must all admit our faults and pray to God in order to obtain His proven protection for our country and for us." He used the occasion to make the case that France should return to its faith. In doing so, the leader of Catholic Paris was invoking a bit of history.

For centuries, the Catholic church had enjoyed a privileged place in French society, legitimating the entire social order and playing a crucial role at every moment of a person's life, from cradle to grave. Since the eighteenth century, a strong current of anticlericalism had called the church's role into question. Influential Enlightenment philosophers, such as Voltaire, had attacked the church for promoting ignorance, superstition, and intolerance. During the French Revolution, those who wanted to overturn the old political and social structure had no better target than the church. Houses of worship were destroyed or converted into sites to celebrate a non-Christian "supreme being" that fit with many revolutionaries' belief in a more rational religion. What remained of the church was subordinated to the state.

Under Napoléon and the restored Bourbon dynasty, the Catholic church had regained its powerful place and its legal protection, and it retained them for decades. Over time, more and more French people began to live their daily lives without religion, and criticism of the church remained part of a powerful antiauthoritarian sentiment. Religion would become a consistent political wedge between parties, with conservatives holding onto the traditions of the church and liberals working to create a society free of religious strictures.

During the last decades of the nineteenth century—as the Basilica of Sacré-Coeur was under construction—this ongoing conflict between secular and sacred reached its climax. The Catholic church and the Third Republic struggled bitterly over which institution would shape France's future, a fight culminating in the legal separation of church and state in 1905. The church surrendered its special status and any funding for religious groups and acknowledged the principle of religious freedom. The state took over all religious buildings, leasing them back to the church and retaining the ability to make decisions about their use and upkeep.

In the aftermath of the flood, Archbishop Amette took the opportunity to remind Parisians of this deeply divisive historical conflict—which, only five years after the separation, was still unresolved in the minds of many—by linking it to the disaster. Large crowds had gathered in the city's churches to pray and repent, he noted in his homily, counseling that "God hears those prayers, little by little, calm comes again to the sky, the waters recede, and one puts oneself to work on what the disasters have caused." In a letter to the diocese, however, he struck a more ominous note, reminding the city that one must humble oneself before God, who "often serves His purposes by using the forces of nature to punish the sins of humans." God, not humanity, he declared, is "the sovereign Master of nature, whose power dominates all science and progress!"[11] Although he fell just short of saying so explicitly, he implied that the flood might have been retribution on a biblical scale for removing the church from its historical position of influence in France.

An anonymous man entered an abandoned house in the suburban town of Ivry on January 30, just after the flood's peak. He had gone there not to rescue, but to steal. Pulling out the drawers of a stranger's dressers and hurriedly rooting around in the closets of this working-class home, he found a few possessions and tucked them into his pockets or perhaps a cloth sack. Then, probably climbing out the window to avoid detection, he moved next door, repeating his crimes again, and then again at other houses in the area as he collected pieces of people's lives.

As stealthy as he tried to be, someone saw him enter or exit one of the houses. Then things got ugly. The witness told others, and soon a crowd of angry neighbors gathered around the site of his latest crime. When he appeared, someone in the mob grabbed him, and seconds later dozens of pairs of hands were all over him, searching for the loot. The thief tried to break away from the crowd, but the strength of the angry throng was too much for him, and they dragged him, kicking and screaming, to the bridge. Someone found a piece of rope, just long enough to do the job. As the mob cried out for justice, the rope became a noose, pulled tightly around the thief's neck, the other end tied to the bridge. In an instant, he went over the edge. Struggling desperately for breath, he grabbed at the tightening rope as his feet dangled.

All of a sudden, an upward yank on the rope reversed the downward pull of gravity, and the thief found himself back on the bridge deck at the feet of the crowd, gasping for air. The police had arrived on the scene just in time and barely saved his life. Instead of going to his death, he went to jail.[12]

Scenes like this one were repeated around Paris, especially in the suburbs, on January 30. As the water rose, so did crime—and, occasionally, efforts at vigilante justice. The Seine's fall created new opportunities for criminals to move through abandoned homes with less fear of the high water. The *London Times* reported that, on January 30, thieves were "being hunted down without mercy, and the police have been instructed to proceed with the utmost rigour against offenders of this class who attempt to pillage deserted tenements."[13]

Newspapers splashed across their pages lurid stories about crimes taking place around Paris and in the hard-hit working-class suburbs. The press told of dramatic chases, gunfights, and arrests of looters in dozens of areas. One eyewitness told the story of Louis Lépine himself directing a motorboat through areas that had been terrorized by criminals and taking the refugees he had collected to a shelter in the Cemetery of St.-Pierre in Montmartre.[14] The *New York Times* also reported tales of cops and robbers:

soldiers have been sent to the various outlying districts to prevent the wholesale pillage which is still going on. A boat patrol surprised a band of Apaches robbing a villa tonight at Boulogne-sur-Seine. After an exciting chase, in which a fusillade was exchanged, an infantry sergeant sank the robbers' boat with a blow of an oar. Two of the Apaches were killed and the others were captured. Last night a number were shot and four men and four women narrowly escaped lynching when they were found robbing deserted houses at Alfortville. They had constructed a raft from which they entered the still partially submerged homes.[15]

In the suburban town of Ivry, located to Paris's southeast, police apprehended a group of eleven looters, eight men and three women, pillaging houses whose owners had been forced out and were living in a nearby hotel. As police brought them out, the criminals faced an angry mob of citizens who beat them and wanted to drown them.

On January 30, the newspaper *L'Echo de Paris* offered readers a lengthy list of incidents demonstrating how Parisians, frustrated and terrified, were taking the law into their own hands.[16] Residents of Ivry threw one robber into the water and then fished him out and took him to the police station. Others began to hang a miscreant from a tree but cut him down when police hurried to the scene. In the suburban town of Vitry, to the southeast of Paris, police on horseback surprised two criminals and led them through town. Soon an angry crowd surrounded the thieves, wanting to lynch them. When soldiers approached a group of Apaches in a boat in Alfortville, a gunfight broke out between the two sides. Two criminals fell into the water and drowned while one escaped. Residents who witnessed the scene tied the remaining looter to a telegraph pole. In Charenton, bandits captured the town hall and had to be expelled. The flood was an extraordinary situation that allowed people to suspend their normal behavior and gave them a kind of license to take their revenge on the lawbreakers they had feared for so long.

One sensational postcard re-created an episode much like the ones described in the press. It depicted the reenactment of a real-life lynching of a looter by angry residents in Ivry. Obviously staged for the benefit of the camera, this image showed one man in a bowler hat who had tied a criminal to a post while another man aimed a gun at the looter. Behind the man wielding the gun, another thief appeared ready to attack. The photographer did not show the viewer real violence or its aftermath but a simulated tableau of violence "before" it occurred. The

PARIS. — LA GRANDE CRUE DE LA SEINE (Janvier 1910)
182   *Dans la Eanlieue de Paris. — Des habitants ayant surpris un pillard,*
dévaliseur de maisons inondées, l'attachent à un poteau et se disposent à le lyncher.   ND Phot.

Looters threatened lives and property, especially in the hard-hit suburban areas, but
some Parisians took matters into their own hands to fight back.

picture distanced viewers from both the looting and the lynching while
identifying both of them as part of the flood experience. Even a posed
picture such as this would surely have frightened anyone who saw it by
reminding them of the dangerous Apaches who lurked throughout the
city before, during, and after the flood.

On January 31 Louis Lépine recorded an incident in the police log
that demonstrated how dangerous and complicated many criminal situations could be. A resident of the Boulevard Diderot asked a police officer named Justin Fleuriet to help defend him against several attackers.
Agent Fleuriet arrested two of the men. En route to the station, five or
six more jumped on the officer, hammering him with a blunt instru-
ment, breaking his fingers and pounding his left knee. Although Fleuriet
escaped from their clutches, the thugs followed the officer to a shop on
Rue Charenton and tried to push him inside. Lépine described what
followed this way: "The shop owner said, 'I don't want a scandal, get out

of here, policeman.' The customers pushed Officer Fleuriet outside. No arrest could be made. An inquiry has been opened."[17] Lépine did not comment on the incident further, but this puzzling affair involving one of his own men must surely have made him wonder whether Parisians had started to give up their sense of civic participation after more than a week's worth of anxiety in a flood-ravaged city. In the face of a brutal crime, this shopkeeper and his customers were willing to let criminals go free just to avoid becoming entangled in the situation.

*P*arisians continued to rummage through what remained of their personal effects on January 31, dragging the soggy bits and pieces of their lives out of homes and basements and piling them on the sidewalk as garbage. Shops and warehouses added tons of additional refuse. Mountains of waste were already spilling into the street, obstructing traffic in many neighborhoods. Police officers waved and blew their whistles to direct vehicles around the heaps. Louis Lépine sent urgent messages ordering crews to clean up the growing mess along quays, but with garbage incinerators still flooded, there was nowhere to put the trash. The only sure method of disposal remained dumping the garbage back into the river. Doing so added to the misery of towns downriver from Paris, but these towns could do little but protest in vain. The police hung posters announcing that a reward that would be paid to anyone who returned barrels and other commercial property to their owners. This hunt for missing merchandise helped clean the city and assisted businesses in recovery, but it made only a small dent in the problem.

Throughout the flooded zone, the work was overwhelming. Men with shovels and other tools loaded wagon after wagon with refuse from parks, government buildings, churches, schools, and other public places. Doctors visited affected houses to look for signs of epidemic or disease, especially after any serious illnesses were reported. Veterinarians and food inspectors scoured the region examining meat and seafood shops and any other business selling food in order to seize and destroy contaminated products. Inspectors told bakers how to disinfect their ovens and kneading machines. The construction workers' union made plaster available, and architects and building inspectors fanned out to catalogue the physical damage done to the city.

Water had demolished many street surfaces. Paving stones or wood pavers buckled and broke loose in huge chunks, either because of the water's power as it pushed up from underground or simply because of the intense and prolonged soaking that weakened the materials. By January 31 they lay scattered about, their absence exposing the muddy substance beneath the roadways. Receding water was uncovering enormous chasms or depressions in the roads, and some stretches of Paris's streets had gashes resembling open wounds. These holes revealed miniature underground lakes filled with floodwater. Many buildings had their foundations exposed to the elements when part of a street had torn apart. The seemingly solid ground had literally given way underneath Parisian feet. Trees had fallen over when the soil around their roots was washed away. Engineers worried that the downward pull of the receding water would create a vacuum and take more of the already weakened streets with it.

After his short sojourn home three days earlier, by Monday, January 31, Robert Capelle was again camping out inside the Palais Bourbon and reported temperatures that day as "Siberian." However, the water was falling and so was his anxiety level: "During the course of the day we felt above all a lifting of everyone's spirits; we were calmer and no one whispered about death as we had on Thursday and Friday."[18] He and his colleagues had even thought about having a party.

High water had disrupted the city's regular postal service since blocked train lines disrupted the flow of mail from elsewhere in France. In the suburbs, delivery had stopped completely for the past few days. Delivering the mail was difficult and even dangerous, although it had continued in areas free of water. Many postal carriers were also victims of the flood and stayed home to take care of their families. Nevertheless, the post office was beginning to resume service as quickly as possible by January 31 in many areas. Even in waterlogged neighborhoods, mailmen often came by boat, sometimes hailing a passing craft to cross a flooded street.

The City Council met again on January 31, five days after its first session on the flood, in a much better mood than when it had last convened. Council President Ernest Caron stood before the members and lauded the fact that "everyone had played a role in the good work; every citizen, every association, every group, each part of the administration, civilian and military, everyone had fought with zeal and courage. Every social and political difference had disappeared and blended, in the same spirit, toward those who are cold, toward those who are hungry." The members in the chamber shouted back in agreement: *"Très bien! Très bien!"*[19]

Swept up in the excitement of the moment and calling particular attention to the women's organizations of the French Red Cross and other charitable organizations, Caron continued: "Gentlemen, in each town, the municipalities, the representatives, the citizens have gone beyond the limits of their duty: I must make a special note of the women from every background who, throughout Paris and the suburbs, have become dressmakers, nurses, linen washers, cooks, serving girls, supervisors, and who, by their amiable way of doing good, and by their good work, make babies laugh, comfort the men, and make the mothers cry with joy."

City Council members took turns reading letters of support from various places across the country, and the meeting evolved into a powerful celebration of national unity. From the leaders of the local government of the Bouches-du-Rhône region on the Mediterranean came this sentiment: "In the midst of the profound pain which grips every heart, it is with a true national pride that we record here the steady attitude of the victimized population which we greatly salute. The acts of courage, of devotion, of social solidarity achieved since the beginning of these disasters brought about by the flood of the Seine . . . merit every encouragement and have touched the hearts of the country." Numerous towns expressed similar feelings of solidarity with Parisians. Most of the soldiers and sailors whom the City Council was praising for their hard work were from the provinces, not Paris, but in the midst of the city's suffering, nearly everyone in France became a Parisian.

As the council chamber rang with declarations of good will and emotional tributes to the city's survival, Louis Lépine's mind was focused on the work ahead. When he rose to speak, Lépine reminded the council that he and everyone would still have to be creative in finding solutions to the growing problems the flood had left in its wake. "In any case, we must improvise solutions and find ways to execute them. Above all, we must act quickly."

There were good reasons for swift action. One worried council member noted that in Charenton between 2,000 and 3,000 pounds of contaminated meat were now rotting. Another distressed member reminded the council that many homes were still filled with water, not from the Seine, but from the sewer. "This is precisely the case with houses which are near the Bièvre," he proclaimed, "where stagnant and urine-filled water have already produced a nauseating odor."

The suburban towns were under the jurisdiction of the prefect of the Seine and the prefect of police. Both de Selves and Lépine had worked for days to provide relief and rescue to these areas, as well as to Paris proper. The capital still sheltered thousands of refugees from outlying villages. The city and its suburbs had suffered together through the same crisis and would begin to recover together.

Yet this solidarity was not without its tensions. In the City Council meeting on January 31, everyone agreed that the suburbs had been particularly hard hit, but that in some cases Paris's infrastructure had made the situation of surrounding towns worse. A fracas broke out on the floor when council member Trézel argued that Parisian sewers had been responsible for the flooding of towns downriver. Others tried to shout him down, asking him to please remember that the capital and its suburbs shared the same anguish. The more practical question was whether the outlying towns would now pay for their own cleanup or would the entire departmental government, in other words, primarily the city. For all the ways in which Paris benefited from its suburbs, now they posed an added cost.

Later in that meeting, a member named Henri Turot changed the tone dramatically. After much talk about those policies that seemed to divide Parisians from the suburbs, he brought the discussion back to the larger theme of unity, in particular national unity. For Turot, a national crisis deserved a national solution. "The current flood is similar to a war. Other than deaths, it has caused the same level of disaster. The flood is the invasion of a cruel and brutal enemy that ruins and pillages in its path." The implication was that an attack on any part of France, whether by an enemy army or by the ravaging floodwaters, was an attack on the nation itself. In this context, fights over who might have suffered more became not only useless, but also petty and even unpatriotic. *"Eh bien!"* he continued, "France paid five billion francs for the liberation of its territory after 1870, and today we can and must make a similar effort." Then Turot made a call for absolute unity between regions and classes. "When one region in France is devastated, all the others suffer; it is in the interest of all, I repeat, that the farmer, the artisan, the small manufacturer can quickly repair the damage caused by the devastating flood, that the factories are not out of work for too long—that the activity and life returns rapidly to the desolated regions." In other words, Turot declared, they were all in this together.

Even as the City Council was meeting, public assistance officials were still frantically trying to find additional temporary shelter for people who had been displaced by the flood and were inquiring about empty hotel rooms. A few days into the crisis, they had found five thousand rooms and were looking for more. However, the director of the office complained before the City Council on January 31 that some hotel owners in the very bourgeoisie 16th *arrondissement* were not cooperating. "There," he told the council, "certain hotel owners demanded higher prices or refused those we are trying to help."[20] Shortly after, the public assistance bureau filed a protest and the hotel owners' association agreed to cooperate.

*O*utside the council chamber, however, some Parisians were questioning just how much the city's leaders would be able to accomplish and how far national unity could extend. Once the initial feeling of exuberance at the water's descent had passed, Parisians realized that they were now threatened by the kind of urban chaos they had worked for decades to prevent, as the infrastructure that had made the city run so smoothly ceased to function. The growing mountains of garbage, collapsed sidewalks, clogged sewers, and dislodged paving stones transported the city backward in time to the era before Haussmann's renovations.

The below-ground pipes bursting above ground revealed the speed with which modern urban life could be undone. The river's infiltration into the city and the contamination it brought upset Parisians' sense of how the city should be arranged and left its residents feeling violated.[21] Even the city's dogs, many of whom were now abandoned and left to wander the streets, didn't know which way to turn, according to journalist Henri Lavedan writing in *L'Illustration*. He described them as "poor beasts, forgotten or meandering on their own in the frenzy of the catastrophe and who, in the middle of this Paris of water, mud, sand, automobiles, lakes, gaps, craters, and wagons, obsessively searched for home."[22]

For some, the destruction of the city's infrastructure raised larger questions and provoked a deep crisis of confidence in the power of science, technology, and engineering. The Parisian daily *Le Matin* editorialized on January 31: "We were taught to have faith in science; we learned that it contains goodness, morality, and peace. . . . But today everyone is asking the same question: How could science, so sure of itself, be defeated by primitive waters? Why was it incapable of protecting our most beautiful city against the capricious river?" Many Parisians shared this sense of betrayal, not only by officials, but also by their own belief that the future would always be better than the past. The flood challenged many of the era's most basic assumptions about the inevitable force of progress. Railroads, telegraphs, steam engines, electricity, sewers, and hundreds more inventions had promised a better life. That's what visitors had gone to the world's fair in 1900 to see. In one week, the flood made that promise seem false, and their faith in an ever-brighter future seem so fragile. The editors of *Le Matin* put it very bluntly, saying they were tempted to call 1910 "the 1870 of the engineers"—another humiliating defeat, this time of French technology rather than of the French army, wrought by nature rather than the Prussians.[23]

Another newspaper, *Le Gaulois,* made the case against technology in even more philosophical and moral terms in an essay, "Science without God." Humanity had aimed too high, the paper's conservative editor, Arthur Meyer, suggested. "At the very moment when science reached its apogee, at the moment when we have successfully conquered the air, after having subjugated the sea and enslaved the land, a meteorological phenomenon comes to embarrass the educated, to show them the vanity of their efforts, to prove to them that there is a higher force which most of them deny and who—in just a few days—humbled their pride and temporarily destroyed all their work."[24] For Meyer, a Jew who had converted to Catholicism and who had believed Dreyfus to be guilty of treason, the flood demonstrated the folly of believing that humankind and its inventions were more powerful than God. Maybe the flood would be a cleansing baptism, Meyer speculated, and a time of self-reflection when society would consider the implications of replacing God with a human belief in science.

Mohandas Gandhi, reading about the flood halfway across the world, seemed to share some aspects of Meyer's perspective. Always critical of the quickness with which people substituted modern technology for the more difficult but more moral path, Gandhi seemed to view the flood as an example of the Western world's ethical failures. In an essay in *Indian Opinion,* he remarked on Parisians' faith in science as the foundation of their city: "Nature has given a warning that even the whole of Paris may be destroyed. . . . Only those who forget God will engage in such ostentation."[25]

Attempts to moralize about natural disasters are always dangerous, especially in the midst of suffering, when reactions are less than rational and blame difficult to place justly. However, the fact that many saw the flood not simply as a failure of engineering, but also as an indictment of an entire value system spoke to the kind of anxiety that some in Paris—

and certainly some around the world—were feeling about the costs, as opposed to the benefits, of modern life.[26]

$\mathscr{T}$he damage to streets and buildings was only one of the city's serious problems by January 31. Just as pressing was the issue of disinfection, a task that fell squarely on the shoulders of Louis Lépine as the prefect of police. Public health and hygiene was an important part of his charge, and no house, Lépine declared, would be reoccupied without first being cleaned.

Rampant rumors of burst sewers made Parisians extremely anxious about filth and disease. Under normal conditions, most people trusted the city's sewers to help reduce contamination and the illnesses it caused. Under flood conditions, however, many feared that the very sewers that made the city cleaner would now actually worsen the risk. Believing that the sewers had all burst along the length of the river and were depositing human waste into the water supply and into people's basements, Doctor Emile Henriot, a physician and member of the French Academy of Medicine, publicly predicted a typhoid outbreak.[27] *Le Matin* called the Seine "a sinister torrent that carries the terrible menace of typhoid fever in its yellow and muddy waters."[28] Not only was the water potentially poisonous, the press warned, so were food-stuffs that had come into contact with contaminated water. Hoping to serve the city and make money at the same time, a Parisian company called Sanitas Ozone offered to help rid the city's water supply of dangerous diseases by sterilizing it with ozone. Numerous other companies offered their services to filter the water or sanitize it with chemicals.

News of the city's contamination had traveled across the Atlantic. Prominent New York lawyer John Quinn was an important art collector and a supporter of modernist writers such as James Joyce and T. S. Eliot. A second-generation Irish American, Quinn's fascination with Ireland led him to meet Maud Gonne, an Irish activist, actress, and poetic muse of William Butler Yeats. Gonne lived in Paris at the time, and on January 31, Quinn wrote a letter to his long-time friend expressing his fear for her safety: "Poor Paris! If the accounts we hear are true, let me urge you not to stay, for some months, in Paris. Sickness is certain to ensue and I should take no chances with typhoid or malaria or any other infection caused by germs that must breed by the myriad out of the sewers and sewer-invaded streets of Paris."[29]

Despite such fears, modern floods of the Seine had never spread typhoid, nor did this one. The volume of water that flowed underneath and through the city was so large that it diluted any potential contagion. Tests conducted by city officials in charge of sanitation revealed that the levels of disease-causing bacteria were much lower than people had feared. Most importantly, rather than bursting, as many believed, the sewers as a whole had remained intact. In other words, despite people's worries, the overflowing sewers actually succeeded in nearly eliminating the threat of disease. Some cracks did open up in a few lines as the result of construction or the collapse of land around the sewers, but widespread rupturing was not responsible for the flood. Had the sewers burst, the presence of disease-causing bacteria might well have been much greater.

Many sewers did leak, however, because Paris's nearly 750 miles of sewer lines were used for more than simply the removal of wastewater. As the city grew, the interior walls of the sewer tunnels had come to serve as a convenient place to run pipes for fresh water, as well as electric and telephone lines, gas pipes, and compressed air all across the city. Small holes where these services entered and exited both the sewer system and the basements of buildings provided openings through which water could flow. The sewers were not watertight.

In an article assessing what happened during the flood published in *La Revue générale des sciences pures et appliquées,* the head of maintenance for the potable water supply, F. Dienert, called these kinds of gaps accidental openings. "If the water from the river or the ground water level passes the level of the water in the sewer," he explained, "the latter receives additional water through these accidental openings and fills the drain collector." In this instance, the sewer would serve its function by taking excess water away. If the water level of the sewer rose faster than the other water, then disaster would strike and water would enter basements and flow into the street. Many concierges—people who looked after apartment buildings—inadvertently made the situation worse, Dienart noted, because when they saw water in the basement, the first logical response was to pull the drain plug to let the water evacuate. In the extraordinary flood circumstances, however, opening the drain actually allowed more water to bubble up into the building from the overflowing sewer.[30]

The sewers couldn't remove all the floodwater fast enough because the volume of runoff was simply too great. This was partly the result of the city's belief in the power of engineering to solve the problem. *Tout à l'égout*—everything into the sewer, including street runoff and household wastewater, the engineers claimed. Sending everything into the sewers placed a great deal of pressure on the system, especially in a time of crisis.[31]

Chapter Eight

AFTER *the* FLOOD

Government leaders were very visible during the flood, bringing comfort and assistance to the city's residents. Police prefect Louis Lépine points with his cane to show President Armand Fallières the damage.

During the first week of February, with supplies of disinfectant distributed around the city, cleaning was well underway. Every Parisian was responsible for sterilizing his own property, and city inspectors made sure that individual owners did the job. If an owner failed to disinfect a building, city workers would do the work and send the proprietor the bill. The Herculean task of disinfection was so overwhelming that many homeowners became frustrated. Some, beleaguered by the work or defeated by the water, simply could not complete the enormous job. In basements where water had not yet been drained or pumped and remained several feet deep, owners and city inspectors simply had to wait before cleaning could begin, stranding many residents in shelters. Unfortunately, the standing water could continue to seep into a building's walls and wick upward, creating dampness and mustiness, and filling homes with a horrible smell for those who continued to live on the upper floors.

When an inspector, notebook in hand, paid his first visit to a flood-ravaged building, he looked over the property thoroughly to see whether river water or backed-up sewage had entered the building. He then noted whether water was still present and if disinfection had begun. Writing down the name and address of the proprietor, he also determined whether the building had any kind of heating device that might aid the drying-out process. If the building was a site of food sales, he made a special note since those structures needed additional attention. The inspector then gave the building's owner a copy of the mandatory cleaning order issued by the prefect of the Seine and the instructions for disinfection.[1]

Still, cleaning efforts were uneven. On February 2, when one city inspector visited the neighborhood near the Jardin des Plantes in the 5th *arrondissement,* he remarked in his report that "many people are ignoring how and with what they should apply the disinfectant."[2] He recommended to his superiors that posters should be hung immediately throughout the area to make sure everyone understood exactly what they were supposed to do. Some people were moving back into homes that had not been properly cleaned, probably because they had nowhere else to go.

French writer Emile Chartier, known by his pen name Alain, saw how much the city had suffered. "Goods were destroyed. Clothes, furniture, houses now full of mud and waste . . . ," he noted in his journal. Yet, there was hope as he believed that a new city would rise from the ruins. On February 6, he remarked in his diary: "The good earth, watered and completely filled with dirty water, would give us a marvelous harvest of everything; if the bad things were not compensated for automatically on this planet, there would be neither beasts nor people. I also see that thousands of human works will carry from one place to another, shape them, organizing them, making another house, more furniture, putting everything back together. . . . So, poor people, sharpen the plane and the scythe, begin hammering, dust off your arms and legs."[3]

Despite such hopefulness, evidence of fraud was beginning to appear. "In certain *arrondissements*," one public assistance department memo in early February read, "we have not hesitated to take vigorous measures, and I think it useful to note that the tribunal has given a six-month sentence to two con-men caught red-handed in the 7th *arrondissement* filing false receipts about their rent," as they sought a reimbursement from the government. In a letter to the city's public assistance office, a Parisian reported that acquaintances confided to him that they had executed *une bonne blague* (a great joke) by inventing imaginary losses and boosting the amount of their indemnity from government relief funds.[4] To try to keep fraud to a minimum, administrators could choose at their discretion not to hand out money but clothes, sheets, food, or other items instead.

While it was not necessarily criminal, numerous salesmen wrote to the government throughout February, offering every sort of equipment and resource that might be useful to flooded Paris—for a price. Boat salesmen; chemical salesmen hawking cleaning products; sellers of steam pumps, motors, mechanical parts, and other equipment; cement and chalk sellers; even manufacturers of burlap sacks for making sand-bags—all sent brochures and letters to government officials in hopes of profiting from the flood. Just like war, disaster could be good for business.

By the end of the first week of February, the Seine had fallen dramatically, returning to roughly the level it had been when the flood started, around the ankles of the Zouave. Tuesday, February 8 was Mardi Gras, and Paris had a tradition of lively celebration. Many hoped that a citywide party might help lift spirits after the intense stress and strain of the past weeks, especially since the water continued to fall quickly. Those wishes were dampened, however, by Louis Lépine. He forbade anyone from throwing confetti to prevent any further blockage of the already clogged drains and overstressed sewers.

To make matters worse, on this last day before Lent, a rainy February 8, the Seine rose rapidly again. The water did not reach the same heights as before, but it did shoot several feet up the quay walls and led many to wonder whether a second devastating flood was imminent. In some places, the water pushed back into homes and businesses that had only recently been dried out, angering many Parisians and increasing their sense of desperation about when their ordeal would be finished.

Dr. Henry Thierry, head of Technical Services for the prefecture of the Seine, oversaw much of the day-to-day cleanup that Lépine had ordered and worked to maintain clean drinking water.[5] With a task so large and with resources already stretched thin given the amount of work that had to be done, Thierry had to improvise. He had soldiers at his disposal to help with cleaning, but most had no training in public health matters and, he feared, would not perform the work as well as was required by the emergency. So in early February, Thierry drafted many Parisian municipal employees into his temporarily expanded service. He chose employees of road crews, the men who cleaned the animal stalls at the meat market at La Villette, and the employees of the public baths, because he believed they had the necessary skills to make the city clean again. Members of his regular staff quickly trained these new deputies and put them to work.

Their work was welcome. A growing concern for public health throughout the nineteenth century meant that by the early twentieth century Parisians expected their municipal and national governments to keep them safe from illness. A Paris public health council dating back to the early 1800s employed consulting physicians to help determine the outbreak of disease in the city and find cures. Over the decades, changing medical knowledge and the overcrowding of cities led officials to pay increasing attention to promoting public health, and by 1889 Paris had established a routine disinfection service, overseen by the prefect of police.[6] Crews pulled horse-drawn tanks full of chemical disinfectant through the streets, especially to neighborhoods where people were sick with typhoid, smallpox, or measles. They methodically pumped their cleaning solution everywhere, liberally dousing the walls, furniture, ceilings, rugs, the backs of paintings, and the undersides of bed frames. During the first week of February 1910, similar now-routine procedures, under Lépine's direction and carried out by Thierry, were taking place throughout the flooded zone to the great relief of Parisians.[7]

Dr. Thierry divided his newly drafted army of cleaners into three teams. The first group moved quickly around the city throughout the first week of February as a rapid-response force, arriving at a new location as soon as the water had subsided from the street. They focused on the filthiest buildings in each neighborhood, especially places where sewers and cesspools had overflowed. The second group, a troubleshooting team, moved through flooded neighborhoods, responding to emergency calls from police and engineers already on the scene. The third group began working systematically throughout the city to clean and inspect, often making sure that homeowners had followed the established guidelines. When a homeowner could not financially afford to undertake the cleaning on his own, these men assisted or sometimes did the entire job themselves to make sure it met the standards Lépine had set out.

By the time of the 1910 flood, urban disinfection had become such a well-established and familiar procedure that Parisians welcomed the work of Thierry's men, even when their arrival often meant the further destruction of people's possessions. British medical journal *The Lancet* described the disinfection efforts during early February: "Wet bedding, inferior furniture, and anything that was not of sufficient value to be sent to the disinfection stoves were thrown out into the street to be destroyed. What was most urgent was the destruction in the shops and restaurants of soiled articles of food." Most people cooperated, although legal questions sometimes arose as to who could authorize the destruction of private property even for reasons of public health. "In the presence of so gigantic a disaster," the journal noted, "these tradesmen, generally of very careful and saving a disposition, seem to have sunk in a splendid manner the sense of their own individual ruin. They gladly gave up the whole of their stock-in-trade to destruction since by doing so they might help to prevent an epidemic following the flood."[8] In most cases, of course, the items to be destroyed were already damaged beyond repair or salvation, so the disinfection teams were simply finishing what the flood had started.

Thierry claimed that during the first weeks of February, he personally visited some five thousand homes and witnessed this willingness of Parisians to destroy their spoiled food stocks as well as the personal belongings stored in thousands of basements across the city. There may have even been a positive side to the destruction, according to *The Lancet*: "Some of this rubbish had been accumulating for more than half a century, and the Parisians are to be felicitated on the fact that it has now been cleared out. Indeed, the citizens are confessing to themselves that Paris has never been so clean before, though the cost of the cleanliness is terrific."[9]

Despite the cleaning throughout the first weeks of February, much of Paris began to stink from the acid burn of disinfection chemicals, the stench of rotting garbage, and the dirty smoke from the fires that dried out people's homes and kept them warm in the continued winter cold. Older homes often still used cesspools under the staircase, which had overflowed as water came into the basement and filled them, forcing the stench of fermenting human waste out into the open air. With almost ten feet of water in the basement and an open drain nearby, one man living at 53 Quai de la Gare wrote to Lépine's office on February 16 on behalf of himself and his neighbors, declaring: "It is impossible to describe to you the odor that we are breathing."[10]

As the cleaning efforts wore on into February, Lépine became increasingly worried about the cesspools that were not being repaired quickly enough. In addition to being an especially potent source of filth and odor, they posed an ongoing threat to public health. In a memo to the mayors of Paris and the surrounding region, Lépine charged them with making sure that these crucial elements of the urban infrastructure were restored quickly.[11] Posters in the suburban towns gave strict orders that cesspools should be fixed and provided instruction on how homes whose cesspools had ruptured should be cleaned.

By turning to public health officials for help in restoring their city, Parisians reinforced the idea that the government was responsible for taking charge of the situation in a time of emergency, and by extension, that it had a duty to provide for their most basic protections. The government's response to the devastation also strengthened the long-term trend toward a more activist public health system. Public hygiene went hand-in-hand with the Third Republic's belief in a modern, rational, reformist democracy that promised to make people's lives better. It showed that science, not religion, could heal people and communities in danger. People's expectation that their government would clean up the city and keep them safe from disease spoke to a growing—if not total—faith in the ability of that government to serve the interests of the entire city.[12]

For the most part, the rapid, visible success of the modern disinfection procedures in the weeks immediately following the water's fall overwhelmingly confirmed just how important these practices were and how everyone could benefit from them. It proved that public health mattered. The flood cleanup provided the first significant city-wide test of the Parisian disinfection system and the scientific principles on which it was based. Their effectiveness strengthened people's belief in the power of human science to tame at least one part of the often chaotic urban space at a time when the flood had undermined that faith.

In suburban towns like Issy-les-Moulineaux, the challenge was in many ways harder than in Paris. These communities had experienced equal or greater destruction but had fewer resources for cleanup and re-building. In his history of the flood in Issy, photographer and publisher J. Hubert noted that, at its height, "The water had entered basements and ground floors with a squalid mud, containing germs of the most contagious diseases, refuse of every sort, along with the bodies of do-mestic animals that had been surprised and drowned." Cesspools had overflowed, sewers had backed up, and rotting debris was everywhere, creating a "pestilent lake" in the midst of town once the water began to fall.[13] To prevent disease, in early February the town refused to let in-habitants return until everything had been disinfected with any one of a number of chemicals brought in to do the job. Town pharmacists even handed out free medicines to flood victims in hopes of preventing any disease during the course of disinfection.

The suburban cleanup did not always go as quickly or as smoothly as planned, and much remained undone for weeks. One journalist described a school in Villeneuve that reopened in February in an incredible state of filth and disarray: "Nothing at all had been scraped, washed, or sani-tized."[14] Enormous holes pockmarked the floors. Books were stained and scattered about the still-grimy classrooms, and in the courtyard lay all the school furniture, rotting after extended exposure to the elements. Fami-lies received aid money, but once it was gone, there was none left for the school. With less money to purchase cleaning supplies, less equipment to do the job, and less infrastructure to handle the waste, the suburban towns suffered with their filth much longer than people in the city.

Monsieur Henry, a resident of the suburb of Rueil, wrote on Febru-ary 10 to the minister of public works that the water remained at levels so high, basements remained partially filled. "The candles are always half burned, an old wagon half submerged. A horticulturalist near the

Gare du Rueil has all his equipment underwater and can't get near it," he noted ruefully. Other than the local mayor, no officials had come to assess the situation, including the health and hygiene conditions. The engineering service for that area produced a memo for the minister saying that inspections had been done and that Henry was exaggerating the severity of his situation. For all the work that the engineer described, Henry still believed that the government had abandoned him.[15]

With so much devastation before people's eyes, the generosity of donors to relief efforts continued to expand in early February. As an integral part of Paris life, the theaters became a natural place to hold fundraisers to benefit flood victims. On February 6 Alexandre Millerand, the minister of public works, hosted a music and drama presentation. For many Parisians, getting the theaters up and running again was a sign that the city could return to normal and continue to be a center of art and culture in spite of the disaster.

The opening of one production in particular marked a psychological turning point for many in the city. On Sunday, February 6, numerous distinguished and enthusiastic guests attended the dress rehearsal of Edmond Rostand's highly anticipated new play *Chantecler* at the Théâtre Porte-Saint-Martin after years of delay. The following day, it opened to the public. Its launch had been postponed several times by the author's last-minute changes and concerns about its quality. When the flood hit, the debut was delayed again. Written in verse and set in a barnyard, the play featured actors in enormous animal costumes. The rooster Chantecler falls in love with a hen but is forced to kill a rival for her affections. He loses faith in himself as the one whose song produces the sun each morning and reflects lyrically on life and love. The piece had a deeper resonance, since the rooster is a symbol of France. Reviews of this experimental piece were mixed at best. However, its opening signaled a return to normal as the theater world came together for what was an important cultural event of the day and a celebration of the city's recovery. Rostand, author of the much beloved *Cyrano de Bergerac,* offered to donate the receipts of the opening night's performance to benefit flood victims.[16]

Sports were another important aspect of Paris's daily life that the flood had disrupted. Many feared that the deluge would delay the opening of the Vélodrome d'Hiver, the new indoor bicycle track and sports arena that could hold some seventeen thousand spectators, which was scheduled for February 13. The "Vél d'Hiv" was located next to the river in the 15th *arrondissement* on the Boulevard de Grenelle, one of the hardest-hit areas on the Left Bank. Nevertheless, the initial competition went on as planned. Cheering the cyclists as they raced around the oval track was a heartening experience for the thousands of spectators who witnessed the race. A return to normal life in Paris meant not only functioning infrastructure and commerce, but also a restoration of the sense of energy, creativity, and fun for which the city was famous.

In 1910 most automobiles were still owned by the wealthy, but under the circumstances, they became a valuable resource for everyone. Police had called on local members of the Automobile Club of France, a national association of car owners headquartered in Paris, to put their vehicles at the disposal of rescuers. Cars whose engines had not been flooded out and were still in working order soon splashed through the streets, hauling people and supplies. The Federation of Automobile Clubs asked its wealthy members to contribute to a fund for the men who lost their jobs in the car manufacturing industry when their factories were inundated. By February, it collected a total of 10,000 francs.

Many people had played a role in ensuring the city's survival. To reward those who worked so hard during the days of the flood, the city created a special medal as a sign of its gratitude. Given to soldiers, sailors, police, firefighters, and civilians who had helped to save the city, the medal bore the motto of Paris, *Fluctuat nec Murgitur* ("She is tossed about by the waves, but does not sink"). The phrase was emblazoned on the city's seal, which showed a ship afloat on rough waters. Dating back to the medieval period, these symbols acknowledged the city's long reliance on the river. The Third Republic adopted the seal as its own to proclaim that although it was born in the aftermath of war and rebellion and beset by enemies and critics, the ship of state would survive the tumultuous political waves. In the aftermath of the flood, this honor also reinforced the belief that a widespread sense of fraternity had brought everyone together in the midst of crisis. Some even proposed awarding the rescuers the Legion of Honor. Of the police, Lépine told a reporter, "The population of Paris owes them an infinite debt of gratitude."[17]

As the coordinator of much of the city's rescue services, Louis Lépine's role in the city's salvation was larger than most. On February 12 the Academy of Moral and Political Sciences awarded Lépine the Prix Audiffred, an honor that acknowledged dedication to duty and self-sacrifice and carried a purse of 15,000 francs. The words of the nomination hailed Lépine's actions during the preceding weeks. "We saw him everywhere, taking no time off, at every hour night and day and night, wherever danger was the greatest, striving to dispel fears and animate courage."[18] The Academy gave him credit for nearly everything: the *passerelles,* the boats from faraway ports, the extinguishing of the fire in Ivry, the evacuation of the Boucicaut hospital. Lépine had wanted to be the police chief everyone loved. On this day, he was.

Throughout February there were signs of recovery across the city. Most telegraph lines were up and running again within several days of the water's fall. Teams of municipal repair crews took their time inspecting the quay walls, just as they had done before the flood, but now they identified places needing to be dramatically rebuilt, work that would take months to complete. Sewer workers shone bright lights along the insides of the tunnels to find and patch cracks. Men from the gas company inserted balloons into ruptured lines and inflated them at the point of a break to make temporary repairs. As the water receded, they dug up and replaced broken lines, often working slowly and carefully to prevent an explosion. Although most gas service was restored by February 22, still in the depths of the winter cold, some repair work was not completed until early March. Electrical workers installed new lines and circuit breakers as the water receded, but the patchwork of light and dark continued throughout Paris since some areas were repaired quickly while others took weeks. The electricity on the Champs-Elysées would not be fully repaired until mid-March, and many places remained dark even longer. The state-owned phone company labored painstak-ingly for three months, replacing switches and wires to restore Parisian service to normal. Road crews laid hundreds of thousands of new paving stones to replace the ones that the water had washed away. Rail com-panies sent hundreds of workers to inspect and repair countless miles of track in and around the city.[19]

For visual artists, the flood presented a dilemma. On one hand, the remarkably changed landscape provided a chance for them to study a fa-miliar subject in a new way. The prestigious national art academy, the Ecole des Beaux-Arts, which itself was heavily flooded, embraced the opportunity by making the waterlogged city the subject of an annual competition that year. Art students sat near the water's edge or set up their easels in the streets to paint and sketch what they were witnessing. At the same time, artists knew that the flood brought much suffering to the city. Many of their own homes and studios had been destroyed along with their personal collections. Art galleries in the Saint-Germain-des-Prés neighborhood were damaged as well. The Sennellier art supply store on the Quai Voltaire near the art school, famous for its handmade pigments, must certainly have succumbed to the rising water.

Many artists responded by displaying their flood-related artworks to sell for charity. An exhibition for the benefit of flood victims opened on March 19 and 20 at the Charles Brunner gallery on Rue Royale, show-ing more than one hundred paintings, watercolors, sketches, and pastels depicting flooded Paris. These works—in the earlier style of picturesque late-Impressionist landscapes, rather than the more cutting-edge cu-bism that Picasso and Braque were developing in Paris at that mo-ment—captured the eerie beauty of the flood experience. The paintings showed scenes of water, trees, and bridges, as well as streetscapes with *passerelles* and horse-drawn coaches. Their focus was the city rather than the human experience, and most of the people depicted in the paintings were distant and faceless.[20] Nevertheless, the artists' connec-tion with their fellow Parisians was evident in this fundraising show. A few weeks later, the Ecole des Beaux-Arts conducted a raffle of artworks benefiting the flood victims.

As the city dug out, Parisians could see just how much had been damaged or destroyed, but the level of material loss in Paris and its environs is ultimately impossible to tabulate. The quantity of goods that had to be discarded in the aftermath of the flood was undoubtedly enormous. Beds, tables, chairs, armoires, mattresses, clothing, food—nearly anything that had come into contact with the water was now just so much garbage, especially as people still feared the possibility of bacterial contamination.

Much of the damage to and destruction of personal items surely went unreported or underreported. Work went undone for weeks, and daily routines were interrupted. Very few homes were completely destroyed, but some of the damage the flood had caused went undetected for weeks or months. Small gardens in suburban homes, which contributed to the livelihood and daily nourishment of many residents, were washed away, unlikely to be counted in the official losses. Raw building materials such as timber, which might have been used in construction, had been damaged by the water and had to be replaced. Many shopkeepers lost their entire stocks. Hotel, restaurant, and cafe owners surely lost thousands of francs in business, especially with the drop in tourism.

The Seine, so central to creating much of Paris's wealth, had now demolished large portions of the economy. One press report in early February put the numbers of unemployed at 15,000 agricultural laborers, 12,000 river workers, 11,000 men in the metal trades, 10,000 railway, tramway, and steamboat laborers, and many more in hundreds of other trades, but these were only early and rough estimates.[21]

In the first days after the floodwaters started rising, city and national government leaders began writing legislation that would allocate money to flood victims. By the end of February, the government had budgeted 20 million francs in loan money devoted to flood victims to be administered by a commission in each *arrondissement* or by each town in the Paris region that assessed the needs of applicants. The national government began distributing 100 million francs in loans on top of money from public grants and indemnities, three-quarters of which would be reserved for businesses both large and small. Additional private funds assisted individuals and families, and help from the Paris Chamber of Commerce and commercial associations further aided small businesses. Posters went up around the city throughout February, announcing the procedures for loan applications, what documentation was necessary, and where to apply. Local commissions began to examine each request and make judgments on its merits. The government response generally was as good as could reasonably be expected under the circumstances, even if people on the ground didn't always see it that way.

By 1910 France had already developed a sophisticated welfare state system designed to help smooth out the inherently rough ride of an industrial capitalist economy. Based on what French social philosophers called the principal of solidarism, which sought to preserve individual freedoms but also to embrace a larger sense of social responsibility, the welfare system had expanded during the late nineteenth century to include unemployment insurance, poor relief, family allowances, pensions, free education, accident insurance, and regulations on working hours. By instituting these state programs, solidarists hoped, the government would strike the tricky balance between the French Revolution's promises of liberty and equality, which were always in tension with one another. They believed it would keep the social peace at a time when organized labor was fighting for better working and living conditions, and revolutionary groups hoped to overthrow the government and create an egalitarian society based on Communist principles. During the flood, government loans and emergency relief spread this already-broad safety net to try to catch as many people as possible, although plenty of people continued to fall through the gaps.

By late February and March, unemployed workers began filing for compensation. River workers were the most devastated. The Bâteaux-Parisiens, the boat service that transported people along the Seine, shut down on January 20, and its employees remained out of work for weeks. Some of them eventually filed for more than fifty days worth of unemployment relief. Boat owners who made their living hauling material on the river were also in dire straits.

Margueritte Delhomme lived and worked on board a boat she owned called *Le Centenaire*. A single mother of five children, one of whom was sick, she was thrown out of work by the flood and applied for unemployment relief. Delhomme declared her total losses of salary as 510 francs in addition to the damage to her boat totaling 3,700 francs, but the government only gave her 100 in addition to 50 francs in emergency aid. One barge owner wrote to officials that while he was rowing through the streets in his smaller boat, helping people in the 16th *arrondissement,* some wreckage damaged his craft, but now his insurance company refused to pay. He could only hope that the government might help defray his 2,000 francs' worth of expenses.[22]

The Renault car factory at Boulogne-Billancourt, just outside the city, was out of commission for some time, and its employees also filed for unemployment assistance. François Bourbis, a mechanic at the Renault plant, addressed his letter to the mayor of Vanves, where he lived. "I am the father of a family (I have three young children and my wife does not work) and in that capacity, permit me to beseech you on the subject of assistance voted by the government for the unemployed." Although he had lost approximately 160 francs in salary for twelve days of lost work, the public assistance bureau had only given him 10 francs and then charged him 1.20 francs for a certificate of unemployment. Paul Pareuil, also a mechanic, wrote to the prefect of the Seine saying, "I find myself in a very precarious position because of my unemployment due to the flood of the factory." His employer offered no help, and "being the father of a family," he appealed to the government for assistance.[23]

Thousands of other working-class men and women were without employment. Leon Né and Jean Nicco labored as metalworkers at a factory on Rue Pasquier near the Gare Saint-Lazare. When the water rose, it put them out of work for ten days, a hardship for both their families. Né was the father of three young children; Nicco's only child was in the Hôpital Cochin. Marie Lourdin, a divorcée with a thirteen-year-old daughter, went from market to market in the Parisian suburbs selling costume jewelry and postcards to earn a meager living, but the flood had put those markets out of commission, and along with them, her business. She received ten francs in emergency assistance. Across the bottom of her unemployment claim, one of the bureaucrats wrote *"Réfus"* (claim denied).[24]

Businesses of every sort closed their doors: a bakery in Issy-les-Moulineaux, an automobile body shop in Paris, an ink maker in Issy, a sculpture studio and an enamel manufacturer in Billancourt, an industrial leather factory in Ivry, an excavation firm in Levallois-Perret, a masonry firm in Paris, a grinder in Courbevoie. Left Bank *bouquinistes* (vendors who sold books, magazines, and postcards from wooden stalls lined up alongside the Seine) asked permission to move their books and posters temporarily to some less-damaged areas on the Right Bank in hopes of staying in business. The *bouquinistes* of the 5th *arrondissement* then applied to the government for special relief funds. Those deemed deserving received twenty francs from the city on top of what they had gotten from their union. The owner of a metal box factory that employed the deaf wrote to government officials saying that his employees were temporarily out of a job because the gas had been cut off. In the case of his employees, he suggested: "There is a question of humanity above all others."[25]

On December 4, 1909, less than two months before the flood, a couple named Davan had married. Once the flood waters fell, Madame Davan wrote to the government on behalf of herself and her husband, both of whom were unemployed. "As you can see, we have had a very sad beginning!" One desperate woman appealed for help to Madame Fallières, the wife of the president, in a letter in early February: "I have five young children, the youngest is eight months." The flood had thrown her husband out of work because his boss "has no cement or sand" to prevent the water rising into the building. "If Madame could send me a little help, it would help me so much," she begged the First Lady of France.[26]

Most people received only relatively modest sums—20, 30, 50, maybe 100 francs—either for unemployment or immediate needs.

Those unemployed for longer periods of time received more since officials usually calculated amounts based on the number of days out of
work. Government relief efforts favored businesses by granting them
greater sums, especially low-interest loans intended to help them rebuild and restock their store shelves or to replace equipment. These
were hardly sufficient to restore their livelihoods completely, however.

Small business owners were particularly vocal in asking for help from
the government, expressing their concerns in the numerous requests for
indemnities sent to city officials. Their correspondence points to the
very real potential for downward social mobility that some faced when
they lost their possessions. In one letter, a woman whose artist husband
had recently died from a lifelong malady had been trying to repay debts
by selling his works. The flood, she argued, had caused her to lose money
on valuable sales by delaying her business. A man in Alfortville who lost
his small business during the flood received a 2,500-franc loan from the
government, but it was not enough to help him keep his house while he
was also going through a messy divorce. A photographer on Rue Royale
wrote to the city government asking for money to replace some 28,000
photographic negatives that he had stored in the basement of his building, the loss of which had destroyed his livelihood. A hairdresser-per-
fumer had only been in business for fifteen months when the flood hit.
He had spent all his money on establishing his business and trying to
support a sick child in the hospital, and the flood, he wrote, had wiped
out all his resources and the jobs of his employees. A frustrated pharma-
cist wrote of his inability to receive the payment he thought he deserved:
"I don't understand anything anymore!" Sometimes government officials
could get frustrated as well. One person writing to city officials asked
for money "if it is not too late." Scrawled in a fat blue pencil across the
bottom of the letter is the hand of the official: "Yes, it's too late. Letter
received 11 August 1910!!"[27] The deadline had been back in March.

A sketch of the sweeping damage to neighborhoods emerges from
lists of the occupations of those who received flood relief from the government: hairdresser, grocer, baker, wine merchant, linen seller, laundress,

restaurant owner, fruit seller, coalman, sculptor, dairyman, and so many others. Once bustling parts of town were now silent. Fearing for the fate of their neighborhood, the businessmen of the 16th *arrondissement* on Rues Félicien-David, Gros, and Pâture wrote to the mayor begging for a commission to come visit their area to begin assessing the damage so that they could file for damages as soon as possible.[28]

The flood did not radically change social welfare in France, largely because everyone saw the flood as such an out-of-the-ordinary event. It did, however, point out both the strengths and weaknesses of the system. When people received their allotments, they often found themselves with very little. Confusion over where to apply for help meant that some people received nothing. Others had difficulty navigating a heavily bureaucratic system and missed the deadlines. Many felt cheated out of what they thought they were owed. The slowness of inspectors meant that many people languished for weeks without any kind of compensation. Despite the flaws in the system, the government's willingness to provide an expansive amount of relief reaffirmed much of the public's broad support for a welfare system that generally acted in people's interests. By the time of the flood, people in France had come to expect such a response because in a democratic society, the government is the only institution that answers to the entire population. In normal times, the French social welfare system was nearly always willing to help those who could not help themselves. During the flood, that group constituted a much larger percentage of the population. People may not have gotten as much as they hoped for, but the fact that they got something helped to blunt the harshest effects of the flood.

Still, many people expressed their outrage at how the government handed out assistance. One unhappy painter named Bertris from Levallois-Perret, just outside the city, wrote with deep frustration to City Council member Louis Dausset, who led the commission for relief to flood victims in Paris, despite his earlier controversial statements. The water, the painter said, had invaded his basement studio for more than two weeks, stopping his work and destroying his materials and numerous canvases. He had already written to the finance ministry, where his case was still pending. Unfortunately, the official assessment of his property was far too low or so he believed. "The *malicious* information supplied about my assets before the flood was *absolutely false,*" he claimed, underlining the key terms to make his point.[29] He had only received 1,000 francs, instead of the 10,000 he thought was his due. On top of that, his wife had recently given birth to their third child.

In the weeks and months following the flood, numerous disgruntled Parisians like Bertris penned letters to politicians and government officials, sometimes repeatedly, expressing their anguish over not receiving the relief they thought they deserved. When part of the Boulevard Haussmann flooded, an engraver named Lefèvre lost most of his business. His wife, brother, and child fled to Alfortville, but he stayed behind. Despite his application for assistance, he had heard nothing from the government by mid-April, when he again wrote, suggesting insensitivity on the part of officials. "This charge is extremely serious," he intoned, "which is why I insist that you compensate me for all my misfortune." The owners of Guérin, Delahalle, and Company, which sold hunting equipment and guns, wrote saying that they were still waiting for members of the flood commission to assess the damage to their property, even though their neighbors had already been reimbursed. They believed that "there must be some mistake."[30] There could also be confusion about where to receive one's aid. One frustrated man who worked as a sculptor in the suburb of Boulogne applied for assistance there, as his colleagues had. He was a resident of Paris, and the mayor of Boulogne wrote back telling him to apply to his town hall in Paris.

Others were more frightened than angry. A dairy operator named Prudon wrote the government to say that although the 1,000 francs he received would help him put a few things back on his store shelves, the sum might not be enough. Small stores like his "have a great difficulty surviving. For the most part, we are disappearing in the struggle with corporations with a great deal of money."[31] He asked how a small shop like his could compete with a foreign company like Maggi, the Swiss food conglomerate with more than 1,200 outlets in Paris and the

surrounding communities, which regularly undercut the local competition by setting up stores nearby and driving down prices. In the end,
he absurdly attributed this larger economic trend to a Jewish conspiracy to control the price of milk. Regardless of the true cause for his
troubles, now that the flood had wiped out his business, his fears of
losing his livelihood were greater than ever, and the government was
not offering the help he needed.

The Seine remained high during February, fluctuating throughout the
month, rising and falling by a few inches from day to day, increasing people's anxiety about what was to come next. It remained at flood stage
until early March, when the water finally began its definitive decline.
Parisians gave thanks for their salvation by Easter on March 27, but not
without a Lenten season of difficulty, reflection, and mourning. By
April, the Seine was back to normal.

MAKING SENSE *of the* FLOOD

The cover of Le Petit Journal Illustré offered a
stirring allegory blending Marianne, the symbol of
France, and Geneviève, the patron saint of Paris, to
show both urban and national solidarity in the midst
of disaster.

After steering the city through the flood, Louis Lépine became a key player in the next pressing task at hand: the effort to understand what had happened. The job of directing that process, however, fell to another man.

Even before the Seine had fully returned to its channel, Premier Aristide Briand turned to Alfred Picard in early February to guide an august group of leading politicians, renowned scientists, and esteemed engineers who would study the causes and aftermath of the deluge. Picard was well known and trusted by the government. A member of the cabinet and the Academy of Sciences, he had only recently served as minister of the navy. There was a taste of irony in the premier's choice, however. Only ten years earlier, Picard had been the commissioner general of the 1900 *Exposition Universelle* that had welcomed the new century. Then, France had asked Picard to showcase its brilliantly electrified city of the future to the whole world. Now Picard's job was very different. He had to uncover why that same modern city had fallen apart. Everything had been done to prevent the river from destroying the city, Briand claimed in his letter that charged Picard's commission with its task. "But the Government believes that regulating the present is not enough; we must predict the future," Briand declared.[1] Picard's mission was, at least in part, to look ahead and chart a new, improved course for Paris in the aftermath of disaster.

By June 1910 Picard's commission had produced a massive series of documents, complete with detailed maps, analyzing the technical reasons behind the failure of the city's infrastructure and offering extensive plans for how to prevent another flood. In his introduction to the commission's report, Picard highlighted the sense of public unity that bound people together during the experience. He lauded the "calm and stoic" people, "our brave soldiers, our valiant marines, our government workers who struggled with zeal, endurance, and courage," and many more who helped to save the city and its environs from an even greater disaster. "This marvelous rising of national solidarity, which reached far beyond the borders of France, created a touching manifestation of human solidarity that we must be careful not to forget."[2] That was as close as Picard's commission came to writing about the people in the city. Its authors described the destruction of Paris in purely technical language. The voices of the Parisians who lived through the experience are nowhere to be found in this study. Instead, the focus is on the future and what engineers should do to repair the damage and forestall another flood.

In the weeks and months that followed, Parisians continued working hard to return to normal life. Government loans and the efforts of the Chamber of Commerce to organize and distribute assistance to businesses helped restart the economy and put people back to work, but the task was enormous. According to the official police statistics, more than 24,000 homes in Paris and the immediate suburbs that lay along the banks of the river were flooded, which had led to the evacuation of nearly 14,000 people and the hospitalization of some 55,000. Thousands more had voluntarily fled their homes in horror, gone for weeks without electricity, railroads, and basic services, and were thrown out of work for months. The damage cost around 400 million francs (2 billion dollars) in 1910 currency plus 50 million francs more in aid and assistance.[3] Even these figures could not account for such things as irreplaceable personal belongings, missed business opportunities, and lost tourism revenue, not to mention the loss of the priceless feeling of security in one's own home and one's own city.

Although Paris was returning to normal, many problems persisted, especially for those who had to navigate the French bureaucracy to receive financial help. A group of residents in Vitry-sur-Seine, to the south of Paris, whose apartment building had been flooded for weeks, wrote to the minister of public works in early March, telling him that they planned to start digging a trench to funnel the water that surrounded their building into the sewers. They all signed the letter in a show of solidarity.[4]

Frustrated by their inability to work through the system, in August 1910 an organization representing flood victims from both Paris and the suburban towns mobilized its members to pour into the streets for a large protest. Their shouts attracted the attention of Louis Lépine, who received a small delegation in his office at police headquarters in the Palais de Justice to hear their demands. They wanted the government to reexamine the tax relief that had been granted to flood victims, reconsider the conditions of loans, and provide to their group a list of those who had received aid—an attempt to make sure that government officials were in fact doing what they said they would. Lépine listened to their concerns and agreed to make inquiries on their behalf. But when Justin de Selves, the prefect of the Seine, was unavailable to take Lépine's call, the protesters became openly upset and threatened to return to the streets in anger. In response, Lépine snapped impatiently: "You came to me to negotiate, and now you threaten me? . . . You will get your justice through legal means, not by revolution."[5] Eventually, they found the aid they needed.

A few months later, during the first three weeks of November 1910, the Seine rose again as part of its normal winter elevation, reigniting people's fear that another catastrophe was on the way. As the Seine receded in February, city engineers had carved marks into the stonework of the quays to show the river's peak. Parisians now gathered at the newly installed measuring gauge affixed to the Pont Neuf to watch the water's climb. At the top of the gauge was the high water mark for the great flood, only a few months in the past, with other floods in the city's recent history far below it. Parisians were nervous that the water would again reach devastating levels. At its peak on November 20, the Seine once again lapped around the ankles of the Zouave. But it went no higher and Parisians breathed a sigh of relief. Yet they lived with a newfound anxiety about what the Seine was capable of and with the knowledge that the river was not easily tamed.

By the time of the November flood, the debate among engineers about the Picard commission's report was only beginning. The study provided guidance about returning the city to normal, and it offered a sense of hope. The report would take some time to implement, however, and not everyone agreed with its findings. Engineers, journalists, and concerned Parisians critical of the commission's plans put forward dozens of alternative ideas in discussions in professional societies, in the press, and in published pamphlets to convince people of their particular schemes, which encompassed everything from new canals to higher quay walls to a better warning system. Many continued to worry about the state of the sewers, calling for the city to rethink how they were structured and where they came into contact with the Seine, or how bridges might be reengineered to prevent high water from becoming blocked.

Despite frequent criticism in the press that the city was not working quickly enough to prevent another flood, Paris did begin to shield key elements of the infrastructure, especially gas and electricity plants and telephone and telegraph lines, by reinforcing quay walls and shielding lines in new casings. Engineers began modifications on the large posts of older bridges that had trapped debris and prevented the free flow of water to ease the situation. The high water in November 1910 and then another moderate rise of the Seine in February 1911, of the sort the city normally saw each winter, added urgency to their efforts because the memory of the 1910 flood remained so fresh in everyone's minds.

The larger significance of the 1910 flood lies less in Paris's failure to prevent the river from overflowing than in how its people dealt with the realization that the Seine was not completely within their control. "A wide range of people," said Alfred Picard in his introduction to the commission report, "paid a unanimous homage to France's traditional virtues. I can think of nothing greater that will console and guide our faith in the future."[6] With that future clearly in mind, Parisians quickly began to forget the complicated lived experience of the flood, transforming it into a myth of unity and progress. The commission's report gave the weight of official authority to the idea that the flood was in the past and that its lessons were being learned. It reflected the government's desire to emphasize how effectively the nation's leaders and its people had responded to the crisis, and how they had pulled together as a city and nation united in a common cause. Picard and his colleagues, including Louis Lépine, used the flood to draw conclusions about how to improve the city's engineering and to boost national pride, but they chose not to explore the human dimension too deeply, touching on people's experiences only in a superficial, romanticized way.

Picard's proclamation of national unity was certainly not the only one describing the solidarity of the Parisian people. For all the fear, cold, wet, inconvenience, and threat of illness or death, numerous Parisians and foreign observers had commented on the lively spirit of unity that permeated the city throughout the worst days of the ordeal. The newspaper *Le Journal des débats* had also advanced this point of view at the highest point in the flood. "The mass of the population remains calm and resigned because it's better to be so in the face of the inevitable." This sense of resignation did not mean simply giving in to circumstance, the paper wrote. Instead, it meant struggling together to endure the flood. Each Parisian "puts up with the hardships that accumulate each day without childish tantrums. They go about their business as they can." And, the paper claimed, they invent new ways to do so. "Deprived of their regular means of transport, they use their prodigious ingenuity to get to their destination. . . . Each one puts on a pleasant face and any nervousness in their hearts only comes out as a redoubled effort to be helpful and sociable."[7]

Others had tried to bolster the spirits of their neighbors. American travel writer Lee Holt overheard two people lamenting the collapse of the Boulevard Haussmann during the flood and described the scene in his memoir *Paris in Shadow*. The man exclaimed in frustration, "If these *sacré* floods continue, it is probable that the whole of the quarter will disappear in the same manner." When the woman shouted that she would leave Paris should that happen, the man forgot his anxiety and offered her comforting words: "But mademoiselle, what are you saying? *Il faut suivre le mouvement.*" (You must go with the flow.) "This is of course very French," wrote Holt, adding his own take on the scene, "and typical of the delightful manner the nation has of seeing every misfortune through witty spectacles."[8]

Of all the images of unity created during these events, the February 13, 1910, front cover of the illustrated supplement to the cheap, popular Parisian newspaper *Le Petit Journal Illustré* stands out. By the time it was published, the worst of the flood was over, and the city was busy cleaning up. This drawing by an anonymous artist makes the boldest claim for the belief in the city's solidarity in the midst of disaster and extends that sentiment to the nation as a whole.

An allegorical female figure towers over the scene of ruin. A bit mysterious, she nevertheless appears to blend two powerful symbols that would have been familiar to Parisians in 1910. She is Marianne, the symbol of the French Republic and its revolutionary values of liberty, equality, fraternity. And she is Sainte Geneviève, the patron saint of Paris traditionally invoked to defend the city against floods. Her kind and confident face looks toward the flood victims stranded on the roofs of their homes.[9] One person hangs perilously from the rooftop, so she seems to have arrived in the nick of time. The seal of Paris, bearing a ship to symbolize the city's relationship with the Seine, hovers above the drowned houses. That seal is shrouded in a translucent black crepe to show how the city mourns the victims. The motto of Paris, *Fluctuat nec Murgitur* (She is tossed about by the waves, but does not sink) appears above her head. Surrounding this inspirational embodiment of the French nation and its capital is a swarm of men and women from a range of social backgrounds that has come to rescue the city. In the foreground, sailors arrive on a boat. In the background is the symbol of the Red Cross above the heads of a well-dressed bourgeoisie woman and a wealthy man in a top hat extending a bag, presumably of money, toward the flood victims in the picture's other half. Marianne/Geneviève's right arm reaches back to the crowd of rescuers as her left arm stretches forward to the victims, symbolically uniting the two groups through her own body. Such a depiction sends the powerful message of a city and nation unified by a cause in which they all have a stake and all fervently believe.[10]

The association with Marianne also intentionally broadened the sense of community to include the whole nation. The picture looks very much like an updated version of Eugène Delacroix's famous *Liberty Leading the People* (1830), an image depicting the July Revolution of 1830 in which the Bourbon monarchy was overthrown for good and replaced by another branch of the royal family with a somewhat more democratic outlook. In that painting, in the aftermath of revolution, Marianne leads a socially mixed crew of Parisians through the smoldering ruins of Paris and over the corpses of their compatriots toward a brighter future—implicitly, one in which the whole nation will be united in common cause. In 1910 Marianne, depicted this time as a fully clothed, maternal rescuer rather than Delacroix's seminude liberator, has similar goals but the weapons of battle have changed. For Delacroix, emerging from a literal battle, Marianne and her cohort are armed with pistols, rifles, and swords. In 1910 the battle was fought with money, boats, Red Cross relief, and good works, all in good bourgeoisie fashion. The illustration's link with Marianne and the entire nation is further reinforced by its similarity to François Rude's powerful sculpture *Departure of the Volunteers of 1792* (1833–36) on the Arc de Triomphe, where an even more militant Marianne leads the charge to battle in the headiest days of the French Revolution. Like Picard's report, it spins a story of triumph and progress out of the ruins of disaster.

A drawing similar to *Le Petit Journal*'s cover illustration, this one by well-known Montmartre artist and leftist political activist Adolphe Willette, tips the balance of the representation toward the city's traditional Catholic patroness and her association with floodwaters. His illustration appeared on the cover of a booklet published by a Parisian paper that was sold to raise money for the victims. Captioning his image "For the Flood Victims," Willette shows a burly, working-class Parisian man carrying Geneviève, crown on her head and sword in her hand, toward a boat in which three other men wait. With Notre-Dame in the distant background, she looks toward the sky expectantly. This is clearly an image of salvation, which also mirrors many real-life rescues in which a man carried a woman through a flooded zone to safety. But roles have been reversed. Geneviève was famous for protecting the city from invading armies as well as from rising floodwaters. In Willette's more populist view, she is passive, except perhaps for a prayer, and all the hard work is being done by the people of the city themselves, not by their patron saint or by the Republic.[11]

Despite the talk of Parisians working together during the flood of 1910, beneath the surface, the situation was much more complicated. On the back cover of the very same issue of *Le Petit Journal Illustré* that featured Marianne/Geneviève on its front cover, an illustration called "After the Disaster" showed a husband and wife who had returned to find their home in ruins. The couple has just entered the door but can proceed no farther since the floodwaters have piled all of their belongings—bed and linens, armoire, chairs, table, lamps—into one enormous mass a few feet inside the door. The wife holds a handkerchief over her nose to protect herself from the smell and has pulled up her skirt to prevent it from becoming wet. Her husband, face darkened by the shadows and pant legs rolled up to avoid the water, is somber and quiet as he stands with his hands folded in front of him. This image reminded the magazine's readers that while the city and the nation as a whole might, in a sense, have triumphed, thousands of individuals suffered personal losses from which they would not easily recover. In the background, another Parisian walks by with a tool slung over his shoulder. The sadness of this scene is tempered only slightly by the idea that recovery is beginning.

Other Parisians also had difficulty being hopeful. Cartoonist Henriot offered a biting satire of the belief in a citywide solidarity in a series of panels titled "Nos Intimes" ("Our Close Friends") published in the

February 19 issue of *L'Illustration*. He drew a little story of a man and his wife who discover that their very good friends are in danger. "I took a boat and, at my own peril, went to the Dubriscard home," Henriot's main character says. He rescues his friends from their roof and brings them to his home. They were understandably happy, and "Madame Dubriscard kissed me constantly." As the days went by, though, the narrator becomes increasingly tired of having others in his tiny apartment. His guests are sleeping throughout the house and even complain that they don't like the food. "Dubriscard invaded my desk, took my clothes, my slippers," absconded with the newspapers, and even talked his host out of tickets to *Chantecler*. The last panel in the cartoon reflected a deep ambivalence about what the narrator had done: "I should have donated 10,000 francs to the flood victims and left the Dubriscards on their roof."[12] Henriot's satire seemed to be directed at both the ungrateful victims of the flood who took advantage of their hosts' generosity and at the hosts themselves, who learned the limits of friendship and solidarity in the midst of trauma.

This wider variety of accounts demonstrates a much more complex picture of living during those dark and trying days, memories that were sometimes forgotten by the mythmakers. The successes of *Système D*—the faith that they could overcome difficult circumstances—and the feelings of fraternity reported by newspapers and hailed by politicians were genuine, and they helped hold the social fabric of Paris together. The stresses and strains of an extraordinary experience, however, were also genuine. The fact that Paris survived in spite of those stresses suggested that its social bonds were relatively strong, but in the moment of crisis, it was reasonable to wonder just how far those connections could stretch without breaking.

If the social fabric of Paris sometimes frayed badly during the flood, in most cases it did not completely fall apart. The legislative elections that many feared might be interrupted by the aftermath of the flood went ahead as planned, in two rounds, on April 24 and May 8, 1910. The leading Radical Party retained its plurality, and Premier Aristide Briand continued as head of government. Throughout the flood, Briand had proved himself to be a master politician, as he had in preceding years when he deftly guided the highly controversial legal separation of church and state. Briand, President Armand Fallières, and Louis Lépine had been particularly active during the days of the flood, visiting victims and making the work of good government visible to people throughout the region. The press widely reported their presence, both in descriptions of their visits to working-class districts like Bercy, Javel, Grenelle, Saint-Denis, and Auteuil, and in photographs of them floating through the streets in boats and climbing through the mud. In the end, the flood had made little difference in electoral politics. In the coming years, Briand would form nine more governments. His diplomatic skills earned him the Nobel Peace Prize in 1926 for his work on the Treaty of Locarno, which helped to ease tensions that lingered between the World War I belligerents in the years after the Versailles settlement.

The lack of a major political scandal after the flood reflected the fact that for Parisians, in spite of the difficulties, the system by and large worked. The Republic lived up to most of its promises, and in general people believed that their government was, in fact, acting on their behalf in the midst of the crisis. There were many pointed questions about government oversight of railroad companies and how quickly assistance was being distributed. Political enemies of the Republic used the flood as an occasion to air longstanding grievances. Despite the political and cultural turmoil through which French society passed during the turn-of-the-century era, most Parisians were still willing to come together. At least at this moment, Paris overcame most of its divisions.[13]

The bonds that held the city together in part came from the breadth of common experiences that most Parisians shared as part of modern city life. Continued class and political differences aside, Parisians walked the same streets in the fast-paced city, read about Paris's daily doings in the mass circulation newspapers, and absorbed the same colorful advertisements splashed on walls and advertising columns throughout the urban landscape. Nearly everyone inhabited a common cultural space across the entire city. This shared set of sights and sounds linked residents into a new and more democratic definition of what it meant to be Parisian and allowed residents to reimagine themselves as part of a larger whole. Parisians were participating in a new, more inclusive experience of the city.[14]

This sense of unity was very different from what critics of urban life believed around the turn of the century. Many thinkers were greatly concerned with how fragile social ties seemed because they feared that industrial development, greater mobility, and growing cities were dividing individuals from one another. French sociologist Emile Durkheim depicted the anomie of modern life, the sense of isolation and aimlessness that led to a decline of shared values and community. For him, the unraveling of social bonds led to confusion, alienation, and an increase in suicides. Even the inner, psychological world, some thinkers argued, was fundamentally changed by the experience of living in the city.[15]

By contrast, Paris in 1910 proved to be a viable network of neighborhoods full of people willing and able to reach out to one another, even across class lines in calamity. Such unity was somewhat surprising since Haussmann's rebuilding of the city had deepened the divide between rich and poor, enshrining class even more firmly than before into the geography of the city. Nonetheless, during the flood, posters hung up in wealthy districts like the 8th *arrondissement* spoke directly to a sense of duty and solidarity even between parts of the city otherwise divided by social class. Resources distributed by the Red Cross and government aid were used throughout Paris, not restricted to any particular area. Although each part of Paris had its own distinct social and cultural identity, those barriers became porous in the midst of disaster. The flood's destruction was not the human-made kind, such as Haussmann's urban redevelopment, that either favored or discriminated against people by birth or class—although the wealthy certainly weathered the storm better than the working class. However, the flood's accidental destruction seems to have created a greater degree of unity, not necessarily within the physical space of Paris but within its social and psychological space, even if only temporarily.

*B*y and large, most cities are rebuilt following a disaster. Only rarely does one completely disappear from the map. Yet when cities are restored after a calamity, some thrive while others are crippled for years or even decades to come. Clearly Paris did not suffer this latter fate. Instead, areas affected by the flood were cleaned and renewed, and the city's management of the Seine eventually improved. Residents of devastated cities that recover from disaster shape the aftermath to their own purposes, turning tragedy into triumph and charting a course toward the future. Like people in other resilient cities, Parisians recast the flood as a moment of opportunity to continue modernizing the city, in many ways extending the project Haussmann had launched in the 1860s, rather than seeing it as an insurmountable setback.[16]

Perhaps this was another reason why the official narrative that Picard and others offered was so alluring. The experience of a steely stubbornness was so strong that, in rebuilding, Parisians erased much of the evidence of the flood altogether. In the process, they continued to tell themselves a story about the power of engineering to confront the forces of nature, as well as the ability of the Parisian spirit to triumph over adversity.

How a community tells the story of a disaster is often crucial to the city's recovery. Just a few years before the flood, for instance, when San Francisco's city leaders discussed the 1906 earthquake, they claimed that the damage had been mostly caused by fire, not by a catastrophic seismic event. Fire was easier to prevent, and to admit that their city sat atop an active fault line might bankrupt the town as no one would want to rebuild or reinvest. So the story of San Francisco in the wake of the earthquake became the tale of how the great city would rise from the ashes, rather than how it would constantly be at risk of crumbling in years to come.[17]

Such a sense of optimism—part denial, part coping mechanism, part hope—certainly came through in the stories that Parisians told themselves during the flood itself, and it undoubtedly helped create the state of mind that would help Parisians work together in the recovery effort. Even if some admitted that they were at the mercy of their temperamental river, and even if they sometimes felt uncertain that either their government or modern technology could protect them, Parisians generally believed that they could still count on one another.[18]

In 1914 France would be unified by another shocking tragedy many orders of magnitude greater than the flood. The outbreak of World War I forced people to put aside any differences and come to the nation's defense. Survival once again required solidarity. That cohesion had already begun to take shape in response to other events on the world stage. Conflicts with other countries over colonial possessions, such as the near-outbreak of war with Britain over the town of Fashoda in the Sudan in 1898, had already rallied people in France to their flag. In addition, many in France still burned with the desire to take back Alsace and Lorraine, which were ceded after the Franco–Prussian War, and exact revenge on the Germans in the process. Although political and social divisions still remained, by 1914 many French citizens had joined in jingoistic calls for war. As the conflict began and Germany invaded France, the spirit of national unity seemed to become nearly absolute.[19]

With all of these factors in play, one cannot say that the flood of 1910 alone brought Parisians together and prepared them for the Great War. The flood was dramatic and important, but it did not change the course of history all by itself. What the flood provided was a moment in which Parisians, who were normally divided by class and politics, could act out a different kind of relationship. The solidarity they created out of necessity during the flood would again prove useful during World War I.

The flood also served as a kind of dress rehearsal for the war. It gave Red Cross administrators additional experience in coordinating relief efforts. It showed many Parisians that, despite the anger provoked by the Commune and the Dreyfus Affair, the military could actually be their protector. It reactivated memories of the city's unity in 1870 (although forgetting the divisive Commune of 1871), helping Parisians to overcome the divisions that could have crippled the home front when the Germans invaded in 1914. It taught a new generation of Parisians what it was like to survive through such devastating hardship as they would encounter a few years later. And it presented the Third Republic with the opportunity to govern effectively during exigent circumstances, proving itself in the process. In some strange way, the experience of the flood might even have helped feed the growing desire for war by showing Parisians that they were part of a larger nation with which they had more in common than they sometimes believed. They could, in fact, fight alongside one another for a cause.[20]

When the war started in 1914, Paris changed in ways that were strikingly similar to 1910. Anxious Parisians journeyed to the city's edges to watch the military enhance the fortifications in preparation for a German attack, defenses that proved crucial when German armies advanced to the outskirts of the capital. Authorities piled up sandbags and wood braces around the famous monuments throughout Paris to prevent them from being destroyed. In the months that followed, streets emptied out of their normal busyness as vehicles came to a halt, ordinary routines were suspended, and Parisians hunkered down in anticipation of an assault. Shops and theaters closed, giving the city a quiet, somber feeling. Fearful that the city's illuminations would allow German Zeppelins to target civilians, the City of Light became dark around 10 PM for much of the conflict.

As they had during the flood, residents again saw large numbers of soldiers moving through the capital, but now these men were on their way to the trenches. With regular garbage workers in the battlefield, the city began to stink as trash piled up and rotted throughout Paris. On sale throughout the city, patriotic postcards with inspiring images buoyed people's spirits. Powerful photographs of Paris during the war showed scenes that echoed the worst days of the flood: troops on the march, shelters and hospitals full of war wounded and refugees fleeing the fighting, craters in the streets where German bombs had fallen, buildings damaged or destroyed by enemy attacks, cars requisitioned for the war effort, politicians visiting the city's residents to shore up morale.

During the war years, all around Paris people came together in a re-newed sociability as they worked toward the common goal of survival, just as they had in 1910. Parisian Jane Michaux, writing in her memoir of the war, remarked on how much people spoke to one another on the trams: "You would think it was one single vast family vibrating with the same emotion in the face of the terrible drama being played out at the front."[21] Although that unity was severely tested and sometimes chal-lenged outright as the war progressed, Parisians generally stayed strong together. Crowds huddled in front of maps displayed around the city, pointing to the battles won and lost and hoping for the best. Perhaps it is no coincidence that French symbolist poet, critic, and novelist Rémy de Gourmont chose a flood metaphor as the title for the final chapter in his journal of the early war years: He called the chapter "The River Rises" and opened it with the words, "The river rises, the river of blood. . . ."[22]

As a test of Paris's strength and solidarity under duress, the flood helped to draw a line connecting the experience of 1870, when the city suffered together, and 1914, when the Germans threatened it once again. Those flood-ravaged days in the winter of 1910 allowed the Re-public to deepen a myth of national unity in the years leading up to the Great War, even though the reality of French society was much more tumultuous and fractured.

American journalist Herbert Adams Gibbons traveled around the world as a correspondent for a variety of magazines and newspapers. In his memoir published in 1915, as World War I was raging, he recalled discussing with a young Frenchwoman the preparations for the defense of Paris against the German army. During their conversation, both re-membered the flood of 1910 as a point of comparison. "We were both thinking of that awful flood five years ago, in some ways much more of a disaster to Paris than the German invasion of 1914. What a wonderful heroism was shown in the face of a calamity that no earthly power seemed able to stave off!"[23]

Gibbons's wife, American writer Helen Davenport Gibbons, had witnessed the flood and described it in her memoir *Paris Vistas,* published in 1919, just after the Great War. Gibbons could only know France from the outside looking in, and she was clearly a sympathetic Francophile. Yet she was no ordinary observer; Gibbons had spent many years in France, living alongside friends and neighbors and working with the Red Cross in their relief efforts. She saw both the flood and the war firsthand and witnessed how both had brought the French together in a time of crisis. Gibbons picked up on this theme, echoing her husband's comparison:

> But we had seen during the dark week of flood-fighting a prophetic revelation of the real character of the people among whom we lived. Little did we dream that the precious qualities shown in the flood crisis were to be brought out more than once again in future years. In 1914 we were not surprised at the courage, persistence, unflagging energy and solidarity with suffering of the Parisians. The flood, as I look back on it, did more damage to Paris than was done during the war by German bombs. It was a more formidable enemy than the Germans.[24]

Epilogue

In November 1910 when the river began to rise again, anxious Parisians watched the water level on a newly installed gauge.

*I*n 1993–1994, extreme weather all across Europe led to the rise of the Seine, its tributaries, and other rivers throughout France. "As swollen rivers fell gradually to the east and north of the capital," Agence France Presse reported on December 29, 1993, "the levels of the Seine and its tributaries the Marne and the Oise went up and more homes were evacuated. Electricity and gas supplies were cut off as a precaution."[1] Police patrolled the streets to prevent looting, and downstream from Paris, some five thousand people had already been evacuated with more to come.

In 2002–2003, as the Seine climbed again, officials moved some one hundred thousand works of art from the Musée d'Orsay (what had been the flooded train station in 1910), the Louvre, the Ecole des Beaux-Arts, the Centre Georges Pompidou, the Musée de l'Art Moderne, and other institutions to protect them from a possible infiltration of water. In 1910, several of these museums did not exist, and others have since begun storing their works in basements, making the threat greater now than it was a hundred years ago. The Louvre basement currently contains important laboratory facilities and archives. "An overflow of the Seine comparable to 1910 has gradually faded from our collective memory," Jean-Jacques Aillagon, the French minister of culture, told the *New York Times* in 2003 during the relocation of the masterpieces, "but we cannot ignore the reality of such a risk this winter or in future winters."[2] Unfortunately, when past memories fade, future dangers grow.

Comparing the 1910 flood to more recent catastrophes suggests that this specific historical incident is part of a much broader pattern of how societies respond to natural disasters. People tend to pull together to fend off an attack from an external enemy, whether that enemy is natural or human. In many ways, the story of Parisians coming together is not unique.

Many students of disasters speak of a kind of euphoria and utopian spirit that happens in the immediate aftermath of a shocking event.

Down but not out, members of the community unite to show others—
and themselves—just what they're made of. When a ship exploded in the
Halifax harbor in 1917, people rallied in what one scholar called a "city of
comrades." After the 1937 Louisville, Kentucky, flood, one sociologist described the emergence of a "democracy of distress." A study examining
the aftermath of a tornado in Vicksburg, Mississippi, in 1953 reported "the
increased intimacy and solidarity which characterizes populations in the
post-disaster period. There seems to be a general reaching out to others
and a readiness to share one's resources and experiences that lasts for a
considerable period of time after a disaster."[3] Looking back on the 1997
Red River flood in Grand Forks, North Dakota, a staff writer for the local
newspaper reported that "the water also took us to new levels—of
strength, of compassion, resolve, and caring—that we may not have
known we could reach. In that way, too, it changed us and our community
forever."[4] In the 2008 floods along the Mississippi River, University of
Iowa students, faculty, staff, and friends formed a human chain along the
stairwells of the library to save valuable books and manuscripts from the
building's ground floor. In all of these examples, ordinary people were acting out the idea of "convergence," a term used by disaster researchers to
describe the tendency for people and resources to come together at the
point of greatest need in an altruistic effort to alleviate suffering.[5]

Not every disaster produces such an outcome. In his classic study of
the 1972 flooding of Buffalo Creek, West Virginia, *Everything in Its
Path,* Kai T. Erikson shows how one community destroyed by a catastrophe was broken beyond recovery. Usually people join together because there are more nonvictims than victims. Traumatized by events,
the victims cannot help themselves, much less others. However, the
people who are not as directly affected by the disaster come to the rescue, creating a sense of togetherness in the midst of chaos. None of
these acts of social solidarity came into play in Buffalo Creek because,
Erikson argues, "the victims outnumbered the non-victims by so large
a margin that the community itself has to be counted as a casualty."[6]

In Paris, although the victims numbered into the thousands, there
were still plenty of people from within the city and from across France

able to come to their aid. During the Paris flood of 1910, enough of the community remained intact to soothe the wounds and rebuild.

$\mathcal{T}$he flood of 1910 also raises environmental questions, since it was aggravated in part by the human desire to control the natural world. A few people in France argued that the flood was the result of environmental degradation. Excessive deforestation upstream from Paris could have contributed to the high degree of runoff unable to be absorbed by the earth, they believed. "The calamity of floods," wrote the newspaper *Le Journal des débats,* "which presently brings ruin to the greatest part of France, cruelly attests to the necessity of restoring the forest covering to our mountains, the greatest regulator of the water system." Not surprisingly, *Fermes et Châteaux,* a journal devoted to rural issues, agreed: "The forests protect the slopes against the force of the water; thanks to the intricate network of roots, they retain water in the soil so that it becomes a sponge allowing the rain water to flow slowly rather than to form a torrent."[7] The focus on environmental causes was not a consensus view in 1910, however. Instead, most people in France saw the flood as a freak event that people had failed to manage but could control the next time around. They were reluctant to consider the possibility that they had contributed to their own misery.

That ambivalence toward considering environmental questions and embracing green solutions runs deep in France. The French have adopted many of the values of environmentalism but at the same time have held onto a firm belief in humankind's ability to control nature.[8] In France, people talk about saving nature through technology rather than giving up on the kind of urban industrial society that harms nature in the first place. That same tension runs throughout much of European and American thought.

Although it is impossible to say whether the flood of 1910 immediately made Paris any more ecologically aware, it did highlight the relationship between cities and the environment at a time when people's ecological consciousness was broadening. By the turn of the twentieth century, conservationist movements in France, throughout Europe, and in the United States were beginning to reimagine resource management. At the same time as industrial development sped up, an enhanced appreciation for the beauty of nature captivated imaginations, leading to the creation of national parks, nature preserves, and the protection of certain species.[9]

In many ways, Paris has become a greener city in more recent years, and residents have tried to strike a greater balance between nature and the demands of urban life. In 2001 the city adopted a green neighborhood plan that included better traffic management, replanting vegetation and establishing more green space throughout the city, and encouraging "soft" transportation like biking, walking, and roller skating. The success of the city's recent Vélib bicycle rental program shows how greener urban living can be both viable and popular. In 2007 the Paris City Council passed a "climate action plan" that aims to reduce greenhouse gas emissions by 75 percent over 2004 levels by renovating buildings and making them more efficient. Recently, officials announced plans for the development of a sustainable office building that will produce a greater amount of energy than it uses, thanks to solar panels, high-tech insulation, and natural air conditioning. The building will be located in Gennevilliers, one of the most heavily flooded suburbs in 1910. Several groups have even proposed plans to resurrect the Bièvre river in portions of the city, creating new parks, bike paths, and recreational spaces along the route of this ancient stream. The Bièvre had become so dangerously polluted with industrial waste that the city buried it, but soon it might once again serve as a natural respite within Paris.

Undoubtedly there will always be limits to how well cities can protect their inhabitants from the forces of nature, regardless of the sophistication of the engineering or how much nature and urban space are integrated. The closest parallels to the 1910 flood are found in the stories of cities overwhelmed by an event—a flood, a hurricane, an earthquake—when the structures of urban life not only failed to protect people but actually made the danger worse. In the 1989 Loma Prieta earthquake in San Francisco, a collapsing interstate bridge killed dozens. In New Orleans after hurricane Katrina, the main cause of destruction and death was not the storm itself but the failure of the man-made levees that had promised to hold back water surging through the city's network of canals and from Lake Pontchartrain. In 1910 Paris, the Métro tunnels and sewers carried water much farther than it could have gone on its own. Unlimited faith in urban engineering can sometimes create a false sense of security about our ability to withstand natural disasters.

In such moments of crisis, when people cannot rely on the physical infrastructures of cities, they can only turn to one another, as Parisians generally did in 1910. The question then becomes: How does this human infrastructure stay strong? Even if there were episodes of rescue and neighborliness during Katrina, the divisions of race and class in New Orleans were still so severe that they added greatly to the suffering. In the 1995 Chicago heat wave, people died at a much higher rate in parts of town notorious for violence and crime where citizens were afraid to check on their neighbors. Critics of Los Angeles have argued that it has completely broken down along class and racial lines and that those divisions are deeply embedded in the city's laws, economic development, and real estate; should disaster strike, the social fragmentation would become clear.[10] Many Americans, especially outside densely populated pedestrian-oriented cities, have given up much of the face-to-face social contact that for centuries made cities lively centers of thought and culture and prefer to associate only with those most like themselves. The street is the place where one meets those who are less familiar, but who are no less a part of the city and society. Most of the rewards for more closely linked urban environments are not found in larger living spaces, but in closer and more humane communities that can help to survive a disaster.[11]

As a city, Paris has certain advantages should catastrophe strike again. Tightly knit neighborhoods with common spaces in markets and parks encourage human connections that can be activated in the event of an emergency. Thanks in part to the 1910 flood, Paris has prepared detailed plans for evacuation on the highly developed rail system, supplying food and water, maintaining a communications network, and guaranteeing the health and safety of the city's population.

Yet just as in 1910, the City of Light continues to struggle with its own dark side, particularly in the kind of racial and class divisions that have led to the creation of violent and impoverished suburbs. This process began during the nineteenth century, especially with Hauss-mann's reordering of the social and urban landscapes. Today, Paris still has a slum on its own doorstep.

Recent angry outbursts from immigrants and the French-born children of immigrants, denied a full place within society, show just how frayed the urban community in the greater Paris region has be-come. As the physical and cultural distance grows between people who consider themselves French and a new group of citizens—who are equally French by birth, language, and education, but who look dif-ferent and practice a set of customs unfamiliar to others—the social fabric stretches dangerously thin. The Parisian suburbs were once the site of radical political groups and consistently voted Communist throughout much of the twentieth century. Some of those very same suburbs, where many French people of color have been ghettoized to the point of feeling imprisoned, have become prime recruiting grounds for twenty-first-century radicals, the religious fundamental-ists who seek to wage a war against the West. As those populations are turned away from full inclusion within French society, they pur-sue other allegiances.

Today, France is again trying to understand itself, and this time its identity must expand to include people of color whose origins are in other parts of the world. Until it does, should the Paris region undergo a similar kind of catastrophe as in 1910, the same level of social unity might simply not exist, or it would perhaps be fragmented, with each unique group taking care of its own at the expense of others. It might look much more like Katrina's New Orleans.

More recent disasters have already tested the strengths and limits of Parisian society. In 2003 all of Europe suffered through a devastating heat wave, but it hit particularly hard in Paris, where nearly fifteen thousand people died. Heat waves are often silent killers, because the high temperatures affect people much more slowly and unexpectedly than a spectacular disaster such as a flood. In such situations, the most vulnerable and isolated members of society may suffer without anyone noticing. The 2003 crisis highlighted problems within the social network and the health care system, and in particular the way the elderly were treated. Despite efforts in France at creating a national social obligation to care for the old and the sick, the system ultimately broke down.

Paris in 1910 was certainly not an ideal community. It was already torn by political, religious, and class divisions before the flood. For all the ways that the city pulled together, it also pulled apart. During the disaster, looters, uncooperative hotel owners, a bureaucratic public assistance system, and price gougers all tested the resolve of Parisian social ties, even while numerous acts of rescue and kindness reinforced the city's determination to survive. Yet Parisian society functioned well enough to propel the city and its inhabitants through some deeply trying days. Maybe Paris can serve as a beginning point for thinking about how urban residents can reconnect with one another, since it is impossible to know when nature may present an unexpected challenge and when depending on one's neighbors may determine one's survival.

Timeline of Events

Summer 1909

Rainfall across northern France is much higher than usual and fully saturates the soil, including the entire 48,000-square-mile Seine basin.

Late November–early December 1909

The Seine experiences ordinary winter high water.

January 1, 1910

Unusually warm weather brings Parisians into the streets on New Year's Day, but also creates unstable atmospheric conditions. Off the Atlantic coast, a low-pressure system begins to move eastward, eventually settling across northern France and bringing heavy rainfall throughout the entire region.

January 1–January 15, 1910

Higher than average temperatures in the mountains in central France cause snow and ice to thaw, adding to the growing levels of the Seine's tributaries. The Seine rises slowly as more water pours into its channel.

January 21, 1910

The waters of the Seine begin to overflow in towns upriver from Paris. In Paris, the water is high but still resembles an ordinary flood. At 10:53 PM, when water invades the compressed air system, many of the city's clocks stop.

January 22, 1910

Parisians wake to feet of water in their basements after the Seine pushes up overnight through sewers, underground channels, and the saturated soil. Some Métro lines come to a halt as power plants fill with water and short-circuit. Many lights go out across the city.

January 23, 1910

Hundreds of Parisians flee their homes for higher ground. Police, firefighters, and soldiers move through the streets in boats, rescuing those in need. Engineers quickly build wooden walkways allowing people to move through the streets.

January 24, 1910

With three of the city's garbage processing plants out of service, city workers dump tons of refuse into the Seine. The National Assembly meets to vote on the provision of emergency assistance to flood victims. Electricity flickers and fails throughout the city.

January 25, 1910

A vinegar factory explodes in the suburb of Ivry after water invades the structure and mixes volatile chemicals. Red Cross shelters receive thousands of displaced Parisians.

January 26, 1910	The City Council discusses the flood, but many members are angry that officials did not respond to their neighborhoods quickly enough once the flood started.
January 27, 1910	Soldiers arrive from port cities with boats to help in the rescues. The city is in near-total darkness.
January 28, 1910	The Seine reaches its peak, approximately twenty feet above normal, its highest level in more than 250 years.
January 29, 1910	The Seine begins to fall, and the sun finally reappears after days of gray, rainy skies. Crowds pour into the streets to celebrate the river's decline.
January 30, 1910	Some Parisians return home from shelters and begin the cleanup process.
January 31, 1910	The cleanup continues as Parisians haul tons of waste from their homes into the streets. Many continue to fear that an outbreak of disease is imminent.
February 8, 1910	On this Mardi Gras, Paris does not celebrate despite the city's tradition of a lively party. The Seine rises somewhat, raising fears of further damage.
March 1910	After weeks at extraordinary levels, the Seine finally falls back to normal.

A Note on the History of the Flood

I discovered the story of the flood during the summer of 2005 while on a tour of the Paris sewers. In the historical display, dozens of feet below ground, I saw a dramatic photograph of the city's inundated streets. Despite ten years' worth of Parisian archival research and college-level teaching as a professional historian of France, I had never heard of the 1910 flood. That fall, hurricane Katrina struck New Orleans, and I remembered seeing that picture of Paris struggling through its disaster. As I watched the Crescent City suffer so profoundly and as my own institution temporarily took in university students displaced by the storm, I wondered how the City of Light had fared nearly a hundred years earlier.

Researching the flood opened up a new window onto the cultural, social, and political history of a particularly tumultuous moment in France immediately following the Dreyfus Affair and just four years before the outbreak of World War I. Historians tend to see this era as one of deep crisis in French society, but as Parisians pulled together during the flood, they defied some of the familiar stories I knew about the first years of the twentieth century. As my study progressed in the aftermath of Katrina, the story of Paris emerging from the floodwaters stronger than ever revealed a powerful, though complicated, tale of hope for people rebuilding their lives in the wake of nature's fury. As cities think about how to confront ecological disasters that may occur due to global warming, this research provided me with new insights about how people and governments could respond during times of crisis.

I found a wealth of information on the 1910 flood at archives and libraries around Paris, particularly the Archives de Paris, the Bibliothèque Historique de la Ville de Paris, the Bibliothèque Administrative de la Ville de Paris, the Archives de la Prefecture de Police de Paris, the Archives Historiques de la Diocèse de Paris, the Archives de l'Assistance Publique-Hôpitaux de Paris, the Archives Nationales, and the Bibliothèque Nationale. Back in the United States, the European Reading Room and Periodical Reading Room at the Library of Congress gave me access to additional material. The W. T. Bandy Center at the Jean and Alexander Heard Library of Vanderbilt University holds the largest collection of imagery on the flood that I have been able to locate in the United States.

The French archives house numerous boxes of engineering reports, official memoranda, informal notes taken during the events, telegrams, lists of streets underwater or darkened by the failure of electricity or gas, correspondence, lists of donors to charities, posters pasted up around the city, and personal observations by government officials, along with lots of photographs and some rare film footage. I found some of the best descriptions of the flood in the press, both French and foreign, including a wide range of periodicals, because the reports provided by correspondents who moved through the streets came the closest to capturing the devastation. The press accounts were often quite consistent, but they had their limits, too. Sometimes they contradicted one another, and at other times the journalists clearly became too caught up in the moment, thus requiring me to filter out the more obviously sensationalist accounts by focusing where possible on the kinds of descriptions corroborated by more than one source. But even the sensational storytelling and exaggeration are important because they reveal the kinds of fears, anxieties, and rumors circulating in the midst of the flood, and they shaped how people thought and acted during those days.

Firsthand, personal accounts, memoirs, and descriptions (other than those in the press), especially by "ordinary" Parisians, were among the hardest things to find. Some turned up in the archives and libraries, and others appeared in printed works of well-known authors. Parisians did not write as much about the flood as I had expected, perhaps because the events were too surprising and they were too busy surviving or because the seemingly innumerable photographs seemed to suffice in telling the story. The wide range of visual sources, whether photographs, paintings, or illustrations, helped to flesh out the written documents. Reading these photographs, along with some Gaumont film footage held in the Bibliothèque Nationale, has added texture to the story by revealing actions and scenarios not discussed in written accounts. For those interested in a more scholarly treatment of the photographs, see my article "Envisioning Disaster in the 1910 Paris Flood" in the *Journal of Urban History*.

For all the documentation, this story necessarily remains somewhat impressionistic since no one could ever fully recapture the day-to-day lived experience of so many people throughout a flooded zone that stretched the length of the city and beyond. Every historian imposes a narrative on the sources with which he or she works, and I have tried to stay largely true to the chronology of the story where possible. In a few places, I have had to go a bit further, imagining myself in the moment, a hundred years after the fact, in hopes of pulling out the "feel" of the experience of living in a flooded Paris. I did so by being grounded in thousands of pieces of archival evidence. Nothing here is fictitious, but sometimes it has required an extra helping of my historian's ability to sympathize with the subjects about whom I am writing.

$\mathcal{D}$espite the rich archival record and the powerful drama of the events, the story of the 1910 flood is largely forgotten. Except where mentioned by a few authors in passing, it is oddly absent from the written history of the city. Somehow Parisians have erased much of this moment from their past.

Yet it has survived in the unofficial oral history of the city as tales of Parisians working to keep the water at bay. Someone told me an urban legend about an office in the Paris City Hall where bureaucrats are supposedly still tabulating the losses and dealing with the paperwork generated by the flood. During the river's normal wintertime rise, newspapers occasionally remind their readers of 1910, though most don't delve into the history. Postcard collectors treasure the hundred-year-old scenes of their neighborhood under water. The stories are there, but they are scattered and fleeting, existing more as a kind of myth or lore than as formal history.

The process of forgetting began during the flood itself. The archival sources only tell a portion of the story and are something of a paradox, at once wonderfully exhaustive and surprisingly spotty. Not every piece of paper was conserved, and much was surely not recorded in the chaos of the moment. Many of the hastily handwritten documents are difficult to decipher. Certain parts of the city are overrepresented in the archives, but others much less. One of the most important sources on the flood remains the government flood commission's official report, written under the direction of Alfred Picard. Yet government documents also only tell us what government officials cared about, not necessarily how people lived life at ground level.

Forgetting intensified in the decades after 1910 through the work of rebuilding the city and with the passage of time. Beginning in 1911, the city installed plaques and markers along the river and on various buildings that show the level of the water during the flood, most of which survive today. But there were no other lasting attempts to indicate how high the river had gone, and most Parisians and visitors either ignore these rather inconspicuous marks or simply have no idea what they mean. In 1914 the Great War put a halt to most of the work along the Seine, and by the following year, the flood's fifth anniversary, all of Europe was engaged in the increasingly bitter and bloody struggle. In 1920, the flood's tenth anniversary, Parisians focused on rebuilding their society after the end of a destruction far worse than any natural disaster, and subsequent efforts at flood protection proceeded haltingly. Still, this generation of Parisians who had experienced the flood understood the importance of defending their city from the Seine. In continuing to fortify the city against high water, they were also erasing the damage and the record of what the river had done in 1910. Motivated by another inundation in 1924, city officials gradually accelerated the pace of renovations. By the twentieth anniversary in 1930, Europe and the United States were descending into depression, although in that decade, the government built a few small reservoirs upstream from Paris to control the level of the water and to generate electricity. But war once again intervened in 1939, and further upgrades were delayed indefinitely. By the flood's thirtieth anniversary in 1940, France was in the grip of World War II, which would far outdo the Great War in its brutality. When it came to memories of suffering, the largest flood in modern times could not begin to rival years of Nazi occupation in the minds of Parisians.

Once the war was over, the city turned its attention once again to the river. In 1949 several advocates—including future president François Mitterrand, then a local politician—took up the cause of flood control. Expanding the reservoirs built before the war, Mitterrand and others believed, would not only regulate the Seine's level, but also provide further electricity, assist with river navigation, and create opportunities for fishing and tourism. In 1969, the newly established regional government created the Grands Lacs de Seine (the Great Lakes of the Seine) along the Marne, Aube, Seine, and Yonne rivers. Six large reservoirs with dams upstream from Paris put more than 28 billion cubic feet of water under human control, holding back the Seine in winter and releasing it downstream during the dryer summer months. In the mid-1970s, engineers rebuilt the Pont de l'Alma so that its wide posts would no longer obstruct the Seine's flow. The four soldiers Parisians used to measure the flood waters were removed, but the Zouave was reinstalled, and his body continues to mark the levels of the Seine today. With these changes that helped to control the Seine's water levels in winter, the 1910 flood became an even more distant memory. During the floods of 1993–1994, some estimated that the Grands Lacs lowered the level of the river nearly twenty inches.

Not everyone remains optimistic about the prospects of completely taming the Seine. In his 1997 book on the flood—the only one on the subject—historian and journalist Marc Ambroise-Rendu interviewed Henry Wolf, the administrator in charge of the Grands Lacs. "In spite of the absence of flooding for the past few years," Wolf said, "the Paris region is still very vulnerable to large floods of the Seine and Marne." Although the water can be regulated, Wolf noted, such control has its limits. "Our organization does everything it can with dams to reduce damage, but we cannot eliminate it."[1] The system of reservoirs and dams can only hold back about one quarter of the water of a 1910-sized flood, Ambroise-Rendu concluded. Paris is less vulnerable than it was in 1910, but the risk of serious flooding remains.

*E*ven today, the complex history of the 1910 flood remains largely hidden. The Prefecture of Police's current emergency flood plan, like all Parisian government flood preparation, is heavily influenced by the events of 1910. However, those technical plans do not shape how people remember the flood.

The 2006 "docu-fiction" movie *Paris 2011: La Grande Inondation* imagines what might happen if the Seine were to flood disastrously today and depicts a catastrophe far worse than in 1910. With its population of approximately twelve million, the entire capital region is much greater than it was at the turn of the twentieth century. As the amount of pavement has grown substantially, the runoff from a prolonged rainfall would increase the amount of moisture that sewers and the Seine would have to carry away. In 1910 people still widely used candles, oil lamps, and coal stoves for light and heat, but if the electricity went out in 2011, millions would be in the dark with very few alternatives.

Yet *Paris 2011* offers a best-case scenario that recalls only the best stories of the 1910 flood. Dedicated first responders—police, firefighters, military personnel—worked around the clock. Although authorities use computers, television, weather satellites, and cell phones, many of the resources the filmmakers imagine are the same as they were in 1910: boats float through the streets, emergency shelters welcome the victims, and neighbors lend a helping hand. The city's flood plan succeeds tremendously as a spontaneous feeling of solidarity inspires Parisians to help one another. The filmmakers do not show any looting, and in their version no one refuses to house refugees or hoards food. Despite plenty of suspense and nearly tragic events, the film ultimately leaves viewers with a sense of relief by suggesting that the situation can be managed from a high-tech control room.

Today, thousands of photographs survive as postcards that collectors seek out in shops and on the Internet. Yet these mementos have also contributed to forgetting the flood. In 1910 photographers almost always made a conscious choice to depict Parisians as unified neighbors fighting a common foe rather than as rivals, enemies, or classes divided. They wanted viewers to see rescue, food distribution, and rebuilding, not injury or looting. The images taken in 1910 largely ignored the bad parts of the story in favor of the good.

In the process, they have transformed the flood from a dramatic and significant *fin-de-siècle* historical episode into a nostalgic moment when Parisians looked their best even in the midst of a crisis. At a time more commonly thought of as the "century's end," and the crumbling of the French political and social order before the whole continent was consumed in the fiery rage of World War I, these pictures are beautiful to behold because they portray Paris triumphant in the midst of tragedy.

Notes

PROLOGUE

1. Gautry's story as told here is based on what he related to his colleague and fellow stenographer, Robert Capelle, who recorded it in his memoir, *La Crue au Palais-Bourbon (janvier 1910): émotions d'un sténographe* (Paris: L'Emancipatrice, 1910), 17–18. I have fleshed out the bare-bones story that Capelle tells by imagining what Gautry may have thought and felt based on the facts of the event in Capelle's memoir and on dozens of descriptions of people in similar situations contained in accounts in the daily press, archival sources, and hundreds of photographs. My sketch of the condition of the city through which Gautry moved is also drawn from the numerous portrayals that relate the state of Paris at this point during the flood.

INTRODUCTION

1. Discussions of the Seine's history throughout this book draw on Colin Jones, *Paris: Biography of a City* (New York: Viking, 2005); François Beaudoin, *Paris/Seine: ville fluviale, son histoire des origines à nos jours* (Paris: Nathan, 1993); and Isabelle Backouche, *La Trace du fleuve: la Seine et Paris, 1750–1850* (Paris: Editions de L'EHESS, 2000).
2. Charlotte Lacour-Veyranne, *Les Colères de la Seine* (Paris: Musée Carnavalet, 1994), 14–15. This book also informed my discussion of the history of Seine's floods and flood control.
3. Moshe Sluhovsky, *Patroness of Paris: Rituals of Devotion in Early Modern France* (Leiden: Brill, 1998), 32–33.
4. Quoted in Harvey Levenstein, *Seductive Journey: American Tourists in Paris from Jefferson to the Jazz Age* (Chicago: University of Chicago Press, 1998), 88.
5. On the relationship between Paris and its suburbs, see Lenard R. Berlanstein, *The Working People of Paris, 1871–1914* (Baltimore: Johns Hopkins University Press, 1984); and Tyler Stovall, *The Rise of the Paris Red Belt* (Berkeley: University of California Press, 1990).
6. F. Voisin, "Avis au public," March 23, 1876, Archives de la Préfecture de Police, DB 159. For a discussion of evolving understandings of urban health in Paris, see David S. Barnes, *The Great Stink of Paris and the Nineteenth Century Struggle Against Filth and Germs* (Baltimore: Johns Hopkins University Press, 2006).
7. David Jordan, *Transforming Paris: The Life and Labors of Baron Haussmann* (New York: Free Press, 1995), 274. My discussion of Haussmannization and urban water control comes from several sources, including Jordan's work but also David Pinkney, *Napoleon III and the Rebuilding of Paris* (Princeton: Princeton University Press, 1958); Philip G. Nord, *Paris Shopkeepers and the Politics of Resentment* (Princeton: Princeton University Press, 1986); Matthew Gandy, "The Paris Sewers and the Rationalization of Urban Space," *Transactions of the Institute of British Geographers* 24 (1999), 23–44; and Roger V. Gould, *Insurgent Identities: Class, Community, and Protest in Paris from 1848 to the Commune* (Chicago: University of Chicago Press, 1995).

8. See Margaret Cohen, "Modernity on the Waterfront: The Case of Haussmann's Paris," in Alev Cinar and Thomas Bender, eds., *Urban Imaginaries: Locating the Modern City* (Minneapolis: University of Minnesota Press, 2007).

9. "Paris Exposition's Beautiful Fetes," *Philadelphia Inquirer,* October 26, 1900. Of the extensive literature on the 1900 *Exposition Universelle,* I have relied on *Exposition universelle de 1900: les plaisirs et les curiosités de l'exposition* (Paris: Librarie Chaix, 1900); John E. Findling, ed., *Historical Dictionary of World's Fairs and Expositions, 1851–1988* (New York: Greenwood, 1990); Paul Greenhalgh, *Ephemeral Vistas: The Expositions Universelles, Great Exhibitions, and World's Fairs, 1851–1939* (Manchester, UK: Manchester University Press, 1988); Richard Mandell, *Paris 1900: The Great World's Fair* (Toronto: University of Toronto Press, 1967); Jonathan Meyer, *Great Exhibitions: London, New York, Paris, Philadelphia, 1851–1900* (Woodbridge, UK: Antique Collector's Club, 2006); and Rosalind Williams, *Dream Worlds: Mass Consumption in Late Nineteenth Century France* (Berkeley: University of California Press, 1982).

10. "Child Born on the Trottoir Roulant," *New York Times,* October 14, 1900.

11. "Paris Exposition's Beautiful Fetes," *Philadelphia Inquirer,* October 26, 1900.

12. http://www.expo2000.de/expo2000/geschichte/detail.php? wa_id=8&lang=1&s_typ=21.

13. "Paris Exposition Formally Opened," *New York Times,* April 15, 1910.

CHAPTER ONE: *the* SURPRISING RISE *of the* SEINE

1. "La Température," *Le Temps,* January 2, 1910.

2. *L'Illustration,* January 29, 1910, 70. This journal provides an excellent account of the events in Lorroy. The daily Parisian press also covered the story.

3. See Elisabeth Hausser, *Paris au jour le jour: les événements vus par la presse, 1900–1919* (Paris: Editions de Minuit, 1968).

4. *L'Illustration: journal universelle 1910* (Paris: Dubochet, 1910), 75. This is the year-in-review issue of the magazine.

5. "Rapport du 20 janvier 1910," Archives Nationale, F7 12559.

6. "Saw Start of Paris Flood," *New York Times,* February 1, 1910.

7. "L'Eau monte partout," *Le Matin,* January 21, 1910.

8. Louis Lépine, *Mes souvenirs* (Paris: Payot, 1929), 195.

9. Jean-Marc Berlière, *Le Préfet Lépine: vers la naissance de la police moderne* (Paris: Denoël, 1993), 164–66. See also Jacques Porot, *Louis Lépine: préfet de Police, témoin de son temps, 1846–1933* (Paris: Editions Frison-Roche, 1994).

10. "Lépine, Famous Paris Chief of Police to Retire," *New York Times,* February 23, 1913.

11. "Rapport du 21 janvier 1910," Archives Nationales, F7 12559.

12. Commission des Inondations, *Rapports et documents divers* (Paris: Imprimerie Nationale, 1910), 85. This report describes the general practices and procedures of the Hydrometric Service.

13. L. Gallois, "Sur la crue de la Seine de janvier 1910," *Annales de géographie* 109 (January 15, 1911), 114.

14. Service Technique de la Voie Publique, "Etat des voies de la 4e circonscription," report from Quartier d'Auteuil, Archives de Paris, D3 S4 25.

15. H. Warner Allen, "The Seine in Flood," *The Living Age* 47 (April–June 1910), 33.

16. "La Moitié de la France est inondée," *Le Matin,* January 22, 1910.

17. "La Seine monte toujours," *Le Matin,* January 23, 1910.

18. "Death in the Paris Floods," *Washington Post,* January 23, 1910.

19. "La Moitié de la France est inondée," *Le Matin,* January 22, 1910.

20. Auguste Pawlowski and Albert Radoux, *Les Crues de Paris: causes, méchanisme, histoire* (Paris: Berger-Levrault, 1910).

21. "Les Inondations dans le bassin de la Seine en janvier-février 1910," *Comptes rendus hebdomadaires des séances de l'Academie des Sciences* (July–December 1910), 425.

22. "La Seine monte toujour," *Le Matin,* January 23, 1910.

23. Colin Jones, *Paris: Biography of a City* (New York: Viking, 2005), 109.
24. "La Seine contre Paris," *L'Eclair,* January 29, 1910.
25. L. Pech, "Les Inondations de Paris," *La Nature* (1921), 24.

CHAPTER TWO: *the* RIVER ATTACKS

1. "Rapport du Sous-Ingénieur de l'Eclairage," June 22, 1910, Archives de Paris, D3 S4 24. Archival material relating to the Société du Gas du Paris during the flood and the ongoing struggle over lighting can be found in Archives de Paris, D3 S4 26.
2. "Le Trottoir roulant," *L'Echo de Paris,* February 1, 1910.
3. Quoted in Hollis Clayson, *Paris in Despair: Art and Everyday Life under Siege, 1870–71* (Chicago: University of Chicago Press, 2002), 54. Information on the experience of the Franco–Prussian War in Paris comes from Clayson's work.
4. Robert de Sars, "Le Général Dalstein, Gouverneur Militaire de Paris," *Revue Illustrée* (c. 1906), in New York Public Library Digital Gallery, Print Collection Portrait File.
5. Helen Davenport Gibbons, *Paris Vistas* (New York: Century Company, 1919), 155.
6. Letter from M. Brez to M. le Préfet, Archives de Paris, D3 S4 21.
7. "Rapport du Conducteur," January 24, 1910, Archives de Paris, D3 S4 26, and "Note pour Monsieur l'Inspecteur chargé de la 2e section," February 1, 1910, Archives de Paris, D3 S4 26.
8. H. Warner Allen, "The Seine in Flood," *The Living Age* 47 (April–June 1910), 32–33.
9. "Rapport du 23 janvier 1910," Archives Nationales, F7 12559.
10. Theodore Zeldin, *The French* (New York: Vintage, 1984), 187.
11. "La Moitié de la France est inondé," *Le Matin,* January 22, 1910.
12. Conseil Général, *Etat des Communes: Issy-les-Moulineaux* (Montévrain: Imprimerie Typographque de l'Ecole d'Alembert, 1903).
13. J. Hubert, *L'Inondation d'Issy-les-Moulineaux* (Paris: J. Hubert, 1910), 4.
14. H. Warner Allen, "The Seine in Flood," 32.
15. L'Homme qui passe, "La vie qui passe: inondations et inondes," *La Vie Illustrée,* February 5, 1910, 166.
16. Conseil Général, *Etat des Communes: Alfortville* (Montévrain: Imprimerie Typographque de l'Ecole d'Alembert, 1901).
17. "La Disparition d'Alfortville," *L'Autorité,* January 28, 1910.
18. Memo from Maire [d']Alfortville to Préfet [de] Police à Paris, January 24, 1910, Archives Nationales, F7 12649.
19. G. Barrier, *Les Inondations de janvier 1910 et l'école d'Alfort* (Paris: L'Imprimerie Chaix, 1910), 6–7.
20. Guillaume Apollinaire, *Oeuvres en prose complète,* vol. 3 (Paris: Gallimard, 1993), 407–9. This essay originally appeared in *L'Intransigeant* on January 25, 1910.
21. "Un Fléau s'étend sur Paris et sa banlieue," *Le Matin,* January 25, 1910.
22. See David S. Barnes, *The Great Stink of Paris and the Nineteenth Century Struggle against Filth and Germs* (Baltimore: Johns Hopkins University Press, 2006).
23. "Extrait de Rapport de Monsieur le Docteur Heller," February 11, 1910, Archives de Paris, D3 S4 21.
24. *Le Javelot Illustré: bulletin paroissial de l'Eglise Saint-Alexandre de Javel,* Numero Exceptionnel, 1910, 9.
25. Report from Le Commissaire Central de Troyes à Monsieur le Président du Conseil, Ministre de l'Interieur, January 24, 1910, Archives Nationales, F7 12649.
26. Robert Capelle, *La Crue au Palais-Bourbon (janvier 1910): émotions d'un sténographe* (Paris: L'Emancipatrice, 1910), 4.

CHAPTER THREE: PARIS UNDER SIEGE

1. "Une Vinaigrerie saute à Ivry," *Le Journal,* January 26, 1910.
2. *Bulletin Municipal Officiel,* February 7, 1910, 581.

3. "Trois villes cernées," *L'Humanité,* January 26, 1910.

4. Archives de Paris, VD6 2101.

5. G. Barrier, *Les Inondations de janvier 1910 et l'école d'Alfort* (Paris: L'Imprimerie Chaix, 1910), 11.

6. Ibid., 14.

7. Robert Capelle, *La Crue au Palais-Bourbon (janvier 1910): émotions d'un sténographe* (Paris: L'Emancipatrice, 1910), 5.

8. Quoted in "The Great Flood of Paris," *Current Literature* 48 (March 1910), 266 (their translation).

9. Helen Davenport Gibbons, *Paris Vistas* (New York: Century Company, 1919), 164.

10. "The Great Flood of Paris," *Current Literature* 48 (March 1910), 261.

11. Gibbons, *Paris Vistas,* 164.

12. Memo from Commissaire spécial Gare [de] Lyon to Préfet [de] Police," January 25, 1910, Archives Nationales, F7 12649.

13. "Une Victime de la crue," *Le Matin,* January 25, 1910.

14. As the Union of French Women put it, their work allowed them to be "an active part of the greater family which unites all the French together with one heart but different actions." Union des Femmes de France, *Cinquantenaire, 1881–1931* (Paris: Croix-Rouge Française, 1931), 5.

15. "Sur les ruines," *Le Matin,* February 5, 1910.

16. "Les Inondations," *Le Temps,* February 6, 1910.

17. Comte de Sabran-Pontevès, "Sonnet," Bibliothèque Historique de la Ville de Paris, Flood Collection.

18. "Appel à la population," January 24, 1910, Archives de Paris, D1 8Z 1.

19. "Aux habitants du VIIIe arrondissement," January 26, 1910, Archives de Paris, D3 S4 27.

20. "The Floods in Paris," *Times* (London), January 28, 1910.

21. "M. Fallières visite la banlieue," *Le Gaulois,* January 26, 1910.

22. "Lights and Shadows of the Paris Flood," *New York Times,* February 13, 1910.

23. Martin Gale, "Le Carnet des Heures," *L'Intransigeant,* January 29, 1910.

24. Laurence Jerrold, "Paris After the Flood," *Contemporary Review* 97 (March 1910), 284.

25. Quoted in "The Great Flood of Paris," *Current Literature* 48 (March 1910), 266.

26. Ibid.

27. "Saw Start of Paris Flood," *New York Times,* February 1, 1910.

28. Alain [Emile Chartier], *Les Propos d'un Normand de 1910* (Paris: Institut Alain, 1995), 34.

29. *Bulletin Municipal Officiel,* February 5, 1910, 559.

30. Ibid.

31. Ibid.

32. "Désastre incalculable," *Le Matin,* January 27, 1910.

33. *Bulletin Municipal Officiel,* February 5, 1910, 560.

34. Ibid., 563–64.

35. Ibid., 562.

36. Ibid.

37. Guillaume Apollinaire, *Oeuvres en prose complète,* vol. 3 (Paris: Gallimard, 1993), 411.

38. Apollinaire, *Oeuvres,* 410–12.

39. "Trois villes cernées," *L'Humanité,* January 26, 1910.

40. Capelle, *La Crue,* 6.

CHAPTER FOUR: RESCUING *a* DROWNED CITY

1. Guillaume Apollinaire, *Oeuvres en prose complète,* vol. 3 (Paris: Gallimard, 1993), 408.

2. Report of Service de la Voie Publique, January 28, 1910, Archives de Paris, VO NC 834.

3. "Aux sinistrés de la Rue Félicien-David," January 27, 1910, Archives de Paris, D3 S4 25.

4. Gaston Lagrange, "La Revanche de l'eau," *Gil Blas,* January 27, 1910.

5. Jules Claretie, "Paris assiégé par l'eau," *Le Temps,* January 27, 1910.

6. "Buildings Fall in Paris Flood," *New York Times,* January 27, 1910; "Killed on Sight," *Los Angeles Times,* January 31, 1910.

7. "The Floods in Paris," *London Times,* January 28, 1910.

8. "The Paris Floods," *The Outlook,* February 5, 1910; *Papers Relating to the Foreign Relations of the United States* (Washington, D.C.: Government Printing Office, 1915), 508.

9. Louis Raynal, "Pour les inondés!" Bibliotheque Historique de la Ville de Paris, Flood Collection.

10. Valentin Pannetier, "Aux victimes de l'inondation," Bibliothèque Historique de la Ville de Paris, Flood Collection.

11. Roger de Talmont, "L'Inondation!" Bibliothèque Historique de la Ville de Paris, Flood Collection.

12. "Quick Chicago Aid to Paris," *Chicago Daily Tribune,* January 30, 1910.

13. Quoted in Roger Chickering, *Great War, Total War: Combat and Mobilization on the Western Front* (Cambridge, UK: Cambridge University Press, 2000), 116.

14. Mairie du XVIe Arrondissement, "Liste du souscription en faveur des victimes de l'inondation dans l'arrondissement," Archives de Paris, D3 S4 28.

15. "L'Inondation à travers Paris," *Le Figaro,* January 27, 1910.

16. Memo from Préfet [de Draguignan] à [Ministre de] l'Intérieur, January 27, 1910, Archives Nationales, F7 12649.

17. "Désastre incalculable," *Le Matin,* January 27, 1910.

18. This photograph is held in the collection of documents about the flood in the Archives Historiques de la Diocèse de Paris.

19. *La Semaine religieuse de Paris* 63 (January 1–June 30, 1910): 207; "Mgr. Amette visite les hospitalisés," *Echo de Paris,* February 1, 1910.

20. Letter from M. de Boisse to Archbishop, November 13, 1911, Archives of the Archdiocese of Paris.

21. Letter from Maric Bonafc(?) to Archbishop, March 19, 1910. Archives of the Archdiocese of Paris.

22. "The Floods in France," *London Times,* January 31, 1910.

23. *Javelot illustré,* 20.

24. "Les Suites de l'inondation," *Le Petit journal,* February 1, 1910.

25. Memo from Préfet [de Versailles] to [Minister de l'] Intérieur Paris, January 24, 1910, Archives Nationales, F7 12649.

26. Memo from Directeur des Travaux Publiques Service Technique du Métropolitain to M. le Conseiller, September 14, 1911, Archives de Paris, D3 S4 24.

27. "Rapport du Sous-Ingénieur chargé du Quartier de Javel," June 13, 1911, Archives de Paris, D3 S4 24; "Rapport du Conducteur," July 8, 1911, Archives de Paris, D3 S4 24.

28. "The Floods in France," *London Times,* February 1, 1910.

29. Memo from Maire [de] St. Ouen to Préfet [de] Police Paris, January 27, 1910, Archives Nationales, F7 12649.

30. On Apaches, see Anne-Claude Ambroise-Rendu, *Peurs privées, angoisse publique: un siècle de violence en France* (Paris: Larousse, 1999); and Dominique Kalifa, "Crime Scenes: Criminal Topography and Social Imaginary in Nineteenth-Century Paris," *French Historical Studies* 27 (Winter 2004), 175–94. The flashy entertainment district of Montmartre was also vulnerable to attacks. The possibility of being robbed by an Apache made a tourist's trip to that area more risky and, for some, more thrilling. Parisians had a romantic fascination with the Apaches, much as Americans would later glamorize gangsters like Al Capone. But most in the city took a more pragmatic view, worrying about late-night assaults by the Apaches.

31. Newspapers abounded with descriptions of the activities of these young men (boys, really, and sometimes girls as well) who wreaked havoc on Paris. The October 20, 1907, cover of *Le Petit Journal Illustré* created a visual metaphor that said it all: An enormously oversized and powerful young Apache—knife in hand, fists clenched, a look of rage in his eyes—towers over a tiny police officer who tries to defend himself with outstretched but empty hands and

an expression of fear and impending doom. In the background, the rest of the gang has shot a policeman and a dead civilian lies on bloody pavement. The caption reads: "The Apache plague of Paris: More than 80,000 criminals versus 8,000 police officers." Although the number of Apaches was undoubtedly inflated, it demonstrated the level of fear in the city.

32. Newspapers were particularly captivated by the story a shoemaker named Liabeuf. Following a drunken rant against the law in a Parisian bar, he killed a policeman and was accused of being part of a criminal gang. The papers continued reporting this story throughout the days of the flood. The press also covered the story of a soldier who had murdered two of his superiors and was referred to as the "Apache soldier." In reality, neither of these two men was an Apache.

33. H. Warner Allen, "The Seine in Flood," *The Living Age* 47 (April–June 1910), 35. Descriptions of the events at the Louvre abound in the Parisian and foreign press and include: "La Crue de la Seine, de janvier 1910," *Le Génie civil,* February 5, 1910, 258; "Documents et informations," *L'Illustration,* February 26, 1910, 221; "Les Sept jours de la semaine," *La Vie Illustrée,* February 5, 1910; "The Floods in Paris," *London Times,* January 28, 1910; "The Floods in Paris," *London Times,* January 29, 1910; "Panic Near in Paris," *Washington Post,* January 28, 1910.

34. "Lights and Shadows of the Paris Flood," *New York Times,* February 13, 1910.

35. Numerous accounts in the Parisian and foreign press cover the evacuation of the Boucicault Hospital, including: "Le Désastre dans Paris s'étend d'heure en heure," *Le Journal,* January 29, 1910; "Le XVe inondé—misère et dévouement," *Vaugirard Grenelle,* February 6, 1910; "Lights and Shadows of the Paris Flood," *New York Times,* February 13, 1910; "The Floods in Paris," *London Times,* January 29, 1910; "The Public Health and the Paris Floods," *The Lancet,* March 12, 1910, 754–56. Lépine tells his own version in *Bulletin Municipal Officiel,* February 7, 1910, 581.

36. "Lights and Shadows of the Paris Flood," *New York Times,* February 13, 1910.

37. Ibid.

38. "The Floods in Paris," *London Times,* January 29, 1910.

39. "Paris Floods Worse; Other Rivers Rage," *New York Times,* January 26, 1910.

40. Apollinaire, *Oeuvres,* 409.

CHAPTER FIVE: UP *to the* NECK

1. Henri Lavedan, "Courrier de Paris," *L'Illustration,* February 5, 1910, 90.

2. "Seine is expected to recede in Paris flood crisis today," *Christian Science Monitor,* January 28, 1910.

3. Helen Davenport Gibbons, *Paris Vistas* (New York: Century Company, 1919), 163.

4. Along the banks today one can see the large vertical measuring rods used to indicate the river's depth during high water. Above those indicators, in many cases just a few inches from the top of the wall, are lines with the caption "1910" above them.

5. Report of Service de la Voie Publique, January 28, 1910, Archives de Paris, VO NC 834.

6. Gibbons, *Paris Vistas,* 165.

7. Numerous sources describe the flooding of the Right Bank in this manner include H. Warner Allen, "The Seine in Flood," *The Living Age* 47 (April–June 1910); "L'Inondation de 1910," *L'Illustration,* February 5, 1910, 92–93; "La Crue de la Seine de janvier 1910," *Le Génie civil,* February 5, 1910, 259–60; Commission, *Rapports et documents,* 257, 261. Commission des Inondations, *Rapports et documents divers* (Paris: Imprimerie Nationale, 1910), 257, 261.

8. Laurence Jerrold, "Paris After the Flood," *Contemporary Review* 97 (March 1910), 285.

9. Allen, "The Seine in Flood," 36.

10. Publications with the story of Corporal Tripier include "La Première victime," *L'Eclair,* January 29, 1910; "Un Caporal noyé," *L'Intransigeant,* January 29, 1910. Tripier's funeral program is in the flood collection at the Bibliothèque Historique de la Ville de Paris.

11. Memo from Préfet [de la] Seine to Mairie [de] Vitry, Archives Nationales, F7 12649.

12. Files on the flood in the Archives de Paris contain a large collection of press clippings on the Dausset controversy, which suggests that someone in the city government found it an extremely meaningful episode. Archives de Paris, D3 S4 21.

13. "Semeurs de panique," *Lanterne,* January 31, 1910.

14. Ernest Judet, "Les Cinq pouvoirs," *L'Eclair,* January 29, 1910.

15. Henry de Larègle, "Les Résponsabilités," *Le Soleil,* February 14, 1910.

16. Barthélemy Robaglia, "Pas d'affolement, NON! Mais l'état de siège, OUI!" *Gil Blas,* January 29, 1910.

17. "L'Unité de commandement," *L'Action française,* January 30, 1910.

18. Léon Daudet, "Un Régime criminel," *L'Action Française,* January 28, 1910; flyer in Archives de Paris, D3 S4 25.

19. Léon Daudet, "La leçon de l'eau: A bas la république," *L'Action Française,* January 30, 1910.

20. Oscar Havard, "L'Inondation, Impressions d'un passager," *La Libre Parole,* February 1, 1910.

21. "Le Desastre," *L'Action Française,* January 27, 1910.

22. "Les Camelots du Roi a l'ouvrage," *L'Action Française,* January 28, 1910.

23. Daudet, "La leçon de l'eau."

24. Mario Pugo, "Le sauvetage et le ravitaillement," http://camelotsduroi.canalblog.com/archives/1a___les_camelots_lors_des_inondations_de_paris_en_1910/index.html.

25. Edouard Drumont, "Après le déluge," *La Libre Parole,* February 3, 1910.

26. Henry de Jouvenal from *Le Matin,* as quoted in "The Floods in France," *London Times,* February 1, 1910.

27. Arthur Meyer, "Catastrophe nationale," *Le Gaulois,* January 26, 1910.

CHAPTER SIX: *a* CITY *on the* BRINK

1. Dr. F. Rozier, *Les Inondations en 1910 et les prophéties: Théorie et prophéties* (Paris: Chacornac, 1910).

2. Laurence Jerrold, "Paris After the Flood," *Contemporary Review* 97 (March 1910), 281.

3. Ibid., 282, 283.

4. Ibid., 287.

5. H. Warner Allen, "The Seine in Flood," *The Living Age* 47 (April–June 1910), 36.

6. Helen Davenport Gibbons, *Paris Vistas* (New York: Century Company, 1919), 161.

7. "Flooded Paris," *London Sunday Times,* January 30, 1910; "The Floods in France," *London Times,* January 31, 1910; "The Floods in Paris," *London Times,* February 5, 1910.

8. *Bulletin Municipal Officiel,* February 11, 1910, 640.

9. Henri Lavedan, "Courrier de Paris," *L'Illustration,* February 5, 1910.

10. "Le Ventre de Paris," *Le Matin,* January 26, 1910.

11. "Justice Populaire," *L'Humanité,* January 29, 1910.

12. "The Floods in Paris," *London Times,* January 29, 1910.

13. Syndicat Patronal de la Boulangerie de Paris, "Le Prix du Pain," Bibliothèque Historique de la Ville de Paris, Flood Collection.

14. "Seine is expected to recede in Paris flood crisis today," *Christian Science Monitor,* January 28, 1910; "The Floods in France," *London Times,* February 2, 1910.

15. "Flood Victims Hurl Looters into River," *Los Angeles Times,* February 3, 1910.

16. Reprinted in G. Massault, *Colombes: L'Inondation de Janvier 1910* (G. Massault: Colombes, 1994), 14.

17. Pierre Hamp, "The Seine Rises," in *People,* trans. James Whitall (New York: Harcourt Brace, 1921), 71–88.

18. L. D., "Les Inondations," *Journal des Debats,* February 1, 1910.

19. Jerrold, "Paris after the Flood," 285.

20. "La Journée d'hier," *Le Journal,* January 29, 1910.

21. "A Travers Paris," *L'Humanité,* February 5, 1910.

22. Ville de Paris, "Avis," January 28, 1910, Archives de Paris, D1 8Z 1.

23. *Recueil des arrêtes, instructions, et circulaires réglementaires concernant l'administration générale de l'assistance publique à Paris, année 1910* (Paris, 1910), February 7, 1910, 22–23. Archives de l'Assistance Publique-Hôpitaux de Paris, 1J13.

24. Guillaume Apollinaire, *Oeuvres en prose complète,* vol. 3 (Paris: Gallimard, 1993), 414.

25. Robert Capelle, *La Crue au Palais-Bourbon (janvier 1910): émotions d'un sténographe* (Paris: L'Emancipatrice, 1910), 11.

26. Ibid., 12.

27. "Paris Flood Status Grows Worse Hourly," *Los Angeles Times,* January 28, 1910.

28. "A Gennevilliers, les digues se rompent," *L'Eclair,* January 29, 1910.

CHAPTER SEVEN: *the* CITY *of* MUD *and* FILTH

1. "La Baisse de la Seine a commencé," *L'Humanité,* January 30, 1910; "Un peu de joie après le danger," *Le Matin,* January 31, 1910; "Les Sept jours de la semaine," *La Vie Illustrée,* February 5, 1910.

2. Laurence Jerrold, "Paris After the Flood," *Contemporary Review* 97 (March 1910), 285.

3. "La Foule sur les quais," *Le Gaulois,* January 31, 1910.

4. A. D., "La Grande crue de la Seine," *Construction Moderne,* February 12, 1910, 236.

5. "La Seine diminue, mais l'eau monte sous Paris," *Le Journal,* January 30, 1910.

6. "Victime du devoir," *Journal des Piqueurs des Travaux de Paris,* February 15, 1910, 11.

7. Henry Lavedan, "Courrier de Paris," *L'Illustration,* February 5, 1910, 90.

8. H. Warner Allen, "The Seine in Flood," *The Living Age* 47 (April–June 1910), 37.

9. "Souvenez-vous marchands, de l'épicier saccage," *L'Eclair,* January 30, 1910.

10. All quotations from Amette's homily are found in "La baisse s'accentue rapidement de tous cotes les secours affluent," *Le Soleil,* January 31, 1910.

11. Archevêché de Paris, "Lettre de Monseigneur l'Archevêque de Paris au clergé et aux fidèles de son diocèse au sujet des récentes inondations et à l'occasion des prochaines élections législatives," no. 26, 4, Archives of the Archdiocese of Paris.

12. This account is based on a description that appeared in "The Floods in France," *London Times,* January 31, 1910. I have elaborated upon it to capture the widespread sense of desperation and urgency recorded in many of the press accounts of Parisians' battles with criminals.

13. Ibid.

14. Archives Nationales F7 12649.

15. "Paris Is Resuming Its Normal Aspect," *New York Times,* February 2, 1910.

16. "La Chasse aux pillards," *L'Echo de Paris,* January 31, 1910.

17. "Rapport du 31 janvier 1910," Archives Nationales, F7 12559.

18. Robert Capelle, *La Crue au Palais-Bourbon (janvier 1910): émotions d'un sténographe* (Paris: L'Emancipatrice, 1910), 16.

19. Narrative record and quotations from the City Council meeting on January 31, 1910, are in *Bulletin Municipal Officiel,* February 7, 1910, especially pp. 579, 581, 584, 596, 599.

20. *Bulletin Municipal Officiel,* February 6, 1910, 565.

21. For centuries, concerns about disorder in the city had gone hand-in-hand with larger fears about social disarray. Until Haussmann and Belgrand renovated the sewers, both criminals and revolutionaries had used them as meeting places, fixing in many minds the association between filth and social chaos. In the years following their renovation, the sewers became a tourist attraction, and well-heeled Parisians went underground to tour them in boats so that they could appreciate the power of science to control a space for so long viewed as unwieldy and treacherous. See William Cohen and Ryan Johnson, eds., *Filth: Dirt, Disgust, and Modern Life* (Minneapolis: University of Minnesota Press, 2005); Alain Corbin, *The Foul and the Fragrant: Odor and the French Social Imagination* (Cambridge: Harvard University Press, 1986); Donald Reid, *Paris Sewers and Sewermen: Realities and Representations* (Cambridge: Harvard University Press, 1991); Louis Chevalier, *Laboring Classes and*

Dangerous Classes in Paris During the First Half of the Nineteenth Century (New York: Howard Fertig, 1973 [1958]); David Jordan, *Transforming Paris: The Life and Labors of Baron Haussmann* (New York: Free Press, 1995); David S. Barnes, *The Great Stink of Paris and the Nineteenth Century Struggle Against Filth and Germs* (Baltimore: Johns Hopkins University Press, 2006); David L. Pike, *Subterranean Cities: The World Beneath Paris and London, 1800–1945* (Ithaca: Cornell University Press, 2005); and Matthew Gandy, "The Paris Sewers and the Rationalization of Urban Space," *Transactions of the Institute of British Geographers* 24 (1999), 23–44.

22. Lavedan, "Courrier de Paris," 90.

23. "Maintenant, l'Avenir," *Le Matin,* January 31, 1910.

24. Arthur Meyer, "La Science sans Dieu," *Le Gaulois,* January 29, 1910.

25. Mohandas Gandhi, "Paris Havoc," *Indian Opinion,* February 5, 1910, in *The Collected Works of Mahatma Gandhi,* vol. 10 (New Delhi: Government of India, 1969), 409; see also David Hardiman, *Gandhi in His Time and Ours: The Global Legacy of His Ideas* (New York: Columbia University Press, 2004), 75.

26. In fact, the flood was not the only event that shook Parisians' faith in a technological future in the first years of the new century. In 1903 a deadly fire on the new Métro had shocked and horrified the entire city. An electrical short circuit ignited trains on the underground rail line, killing more than eighty riders. Few could escape the darkened tunnels that quickly filled with smoke. Lacking ventilation and emergency exits, the Métro quickly became a death trap. The Métropolitain became known by critics as the "Nécropolitain"—the death train. The accident merely reinforced many people's fears about the new engineering wonders that had invaded their lives, making some wonder whether such inventions as the subway truly represented the progress they had been promised. In the wake of the flood, that same ambivalence toward technology that had been fueled by fire was now strengthened by water. See Peter Soppelsa, "Métro-Nécro: The 1903 Métro Accident and Its Impact on Infrastructure and Practice, 1903–1914," paper presented at the Society for French Historical Studies Conference, New Brunswick, NJ, March 2008; Peter Soppelsa, "The Fragility of Modernity: Infrastructure and Everyday Life in Paris, 1870–1914," Ph.D. diss., Univ. of Michigan, 2009. See also Pike, *Subterranean Cities.* Other concerns about technology more broadly are discussed in Anson Rabinbach, *The Human Motor: Energy, Fatigue, and the Origins of Modernity* (New York: Basic Books, 1990).

27. "The Floods in Paris," *London Times,* January 27, 1910.

28. "Voici venir la crue de la misère," *Le Matin,* February 3, 1910.

29. Janis and Richard Londraville, eds., *Too Long a Sacrifice: The Letters of Maud Gonne and John Quinn* (Selingsgrove, Pa.: Susquehanna University Press, 1999), 54.

30. F. Dienert, "Les Egouts de Paris pendant l'inondation de 1910," *Revue générale des sciences pures et appliquées,* January 15, 1910, 935. The government's flood commission later came to the same conclusion.

31. Despite the strong actions of those in power, by the end of January, officials in Paris had nonetheless debated the limits of their authority. A 1902 law, which created a national standard for public health codes, allowed the prefect of the Seine to declare a public health emergency and to take whatever measures he deemed necessary. It was not clear, however, that the flood qualified as a public health emergency, especially when no signs of disease had emerged. The fear of what might happen if leaders took no action spurred a decision. Despite the questions and some voices who urged caution, the prefect of the Seine did issue the emergency decree by the end of January and made cleaning legally mandatory. Parisians would have to chip in to cleanse their city. Much of the confusion focused on how to deal with the suburban communities. While the emergency decree required everyone to clean, the order only applied to Paris, leaving the outlying towns largely on their own. Most suburban towns, many in the City Council argued, could not afford to pay for cleaning supplies, even though their neighboring villages were beginning to help. For many, Paris had a clear responsibility to assist.

CHAPTER EIGHT: AFTER *the* FLOOD

1. This description of cleaning procedures and inspections is based on the extensive documentation in Archives de Paris, D3 S4 29.
2. "Rapport de l'Architecte-Voyer adjoint (5th arrondissement)," February 2, 1910, Archives de Paris, D3 S4 29.
3. Alain [Emile Chartier], *Les Propos d'un Normand de 1910* (Paris: Institut Alain, 1995), 51.
4. *Recueil des arrêtes, instructions, et circulaires réglementaires concernant l'administration générale de l'assistance publique à Paris, année 1910* (Paris, 1910), February 2, 1910, 18, Archives de l'Assistance Publique-Hôpitaux de Paris, 1J13; letter dated April 4, 1910, Archives de Paris, D3 S4 28.
5. "The Public Health and the Paris Floods," *The Lancet*, March 12, 1910, 754–56.
6. David S. Barnes, *The Great Stink of Paris and the Nineteenth Century Struggle against Filth and Germs* (Baltimore: Johns Hopkins University Press, 2006), 144. My discussion of the history of public hygiene in Paris and descriptions of decontamination are based on Barnes's excellent account. Underlying the concern was the powerful idea of "civilization," the notion of an increasingly rational, organized, safe, and orderly society able to master its own fate rather than being subject to forces outside of its control. Haussmann had tried to civilize the city, in this sense, by rearranging its infrastructure. Public health officials did the same when searching out the causes of disease and trying to eliminate them. Just as the French believed they were carrying civilization to so-called lesser people of the world in Africa and Asia by expanding their empire, so physicians hoped to civilize France itself by ridding it of illness.
7. As Barnes notes, when they were first introduced in the late nineteenth century, Parisians had taken some time getting used to these strangely dressed crews invading their privacy and filling their homes with unknown substances. Shopkeepers feared that the practice would ruin their businesses. Many people simply refused to cooperate, believing that washing with water would be enough to fight illness. Public education campaigns, lessons on hygiene in the schools, and the regular presence of disinfection teams in the streets helped show Parisians that these efforts yielded real results. By the late 1890s, the city added three dozen men to the cleaning crews as more people actually began to ask for their homes to be disinfected. And at the 1900 World's Fair, proud public health officials displayed the portable chemical disinfection tanks for everyone to see, touting the modern techniques and proclaiming to everyone that Paris was one of the world's cleanest cities. Louis Lépine was a reformer in the city's public health policy, as he had been in other areas of the police prefect's duties, helping to establish new procedures for cleaning the city during times of flood and institutionalizing the growing medical consensus about disease. Previous prefects, believing in the miasma theory, had advocated for primarily fresh air and sunlight after floods. Lépine called for a greater application of the now widely accepted germ theory and recommended using chemical disinfectants. Light and air were still important "to clear up the miasmas dangerous to public health," he noted in an 1897 circular to mayors on the subject of cleaning to prevent epidemics. Lépine also argued that "iron sulfate and lime are very inexpensive products, and I'm sure you will agree that it would be very useful to the city to purchase a certain quantity." He bolstered his case by noting that in other places where these techniques had been used "not a single case of contagious illness has been recorded." (Louis Lépine, "Epidémies," Circulaire no. 1, February 23, 1897, Archives de la Préfecture de Police, DB 159.) Over the next few decades, the germ and miasma explanations intermingled, but by 1910 germ theory was clearly the predominant way of understanding what caused disease.
8. "The Public Health and the Paris Floods," 754–56.
9. Ibid., 755.
10. Letter to Monsieur le Préfet de Police Paris, February 16, 1910, Archives de Paris, D3 S4 29.
11. *Mésures d'assainissement dans les communes inondées du département de la Seine*, no. 2 (February–April 1910), 3.

12. See Barnes, *The Great Stink.*

13. J. Hubert, *L'Inondation d'Issy-les-Moulineaux* (Paris: J. Hubert, 1910), 13.

14. Lucien Descaves, "Comment on a secouru les victimes de l'inondation," press clipping (possibly *Le Figaro* or *Le Journal),* Archives de Paris, D3 S4 24.

15. Letter from M. Henry to M. le Ministre, February 10, 1910, Archives Nationales, F14 16584.

16. "Floods Are Still Growing," *New York Times,* January 26, 1910.

17. "M. Lépine glorifie les sauveteurs," *L'Eclair,* January 30, 1910.

18. Quoted in Jacques Porot, *Louis Lépine: préfet de Police, témoin de son temps (1846–1933)* (Paris: Editions Frison-Roche, 1994), 390.

19. Commission des Inondations, *Rapports et documents divers* (Paris: Imprimerie Nationale, 1910).

20. Albert Vuaflart, "Les Peintres de l'inondation janvier 1910," *Societe d'Iconographie Parisienne* (1911), 81–84.

21. "The Floods in Paris," *London Times,* February 5, 1910.

22. Bâteaux-Parisiens unemployment claims, Archives de Paris, D3 S4 28.

23. Letter from François Bourbis to M. le Maire, April 15, 1910, and letter from Paul Pereuil to M. le Maire, April 13, 1910, Archives de Paris, VD6 2101.

24. Archives de Paris, VD6 2101.

25. Letters asking for government assistance provide a sense of the range of businesses affected by the flood; see Archives de Paris, VD6 2101; "A Travers Paris," *Le Figaro,* January 31, 1910; letter from P. Williame et Cie. to M. le Préfet de la Seine, February 1, 1910, Archives de Paris, D3 S4 22.

26. Letter from Léonie (?) and Gaston Davan to M. le Maire, April 7, 1910, and letter from Mme. Jacques to Mme. Fallières, February 9, 1910, Archives de Paris, VD6 2101.

27. Archives de Paris, D3 S4 24 and D3 S4 27; letter from L. Lingrande to l'Adjunt de la Maire du VIII arrondissement, May 7, 1910, Archives de Paris D3 S4 27; letter from M. Bouillot to M. le Maire du 16ème arrondissement, n.d., Archives de Paris, D3 S4 28.

28. Letter from Les Habitants de la rue Félicien-David et des Pâtures to Monsieur le Maire, February 17, 1910, Archives de Paris, D3 S4 28.

29. Letter from M. Bertris to Louis Dausset, November 30, 1910, Archives de Paris, D3 S4 24.

30. Letter from M. Lefèvre to M. le Maire, April 16, 1910, Archives de Paris, D3 S4 27; letter from M. Delahalle to M. le Maire, May 4, 1910, Archives de Paris, D3 S4 27.

31. Letter from M. Prudon to Louis Dausset, November 29, 1910, Archives de Paris, D3 S4 24.

CHAPTER NINE: MAKING SENSE *of the* FLOOD

1. Commission des Inondations, *Rapports et documents divers* (Paris: Imprimerie Nationale, 1910), v.

2. Ibid., xiv.

3. Statistics from Conseil Municipal de Paris, *Rapport géneral au nom de la commission municipale et départementale des inondations* (Paris: Conseil Municipal, 1910), 8; and Marc Ambroise-Rendu, *1910 Paris inondé* (Paris: Hervas, 1997), 6.

4. Letter to Monsieur le Ministre, March 3, 1910, Archives Nationales, F14 16578.

5. "La Protestation des inondés," *Le Petit Journal,* August 26, 1910.

6. Commission, *Rapports et documents,* xiv.

7. "L'Attitude du public," *Le Journal des débats politiques et littéraires,* January 29, 1910.

8. Lee Holt, *Paris in Shadow* (London: John Lane, 1920), 75.

9. Given their depiction in the image, these are most likely suburban homes.

10. This depiction of Marianne/Geneviève saving her people during the flood is also strikingly similar to the bronze statue by Ernest Barrias titled *The Defense of Paris* (1883), cast to commemorate the city's heroic resistance against the invading Prussian army during the Franco–Prussian War. Created as the result of a competition sponsored by the municipal government, it was installed in the plaza at Courbevoie, just outside Paris to the west (the area now known as La Défense), facing the direction of the former Prussian camps and

taking the place of an earlier statue of Napoléon. Barrias envisions the city as a woman standing straight and strong against the invasion. Wearing the coat of the National Guard troops, she looms over a cannon at the ready and a soldier on the ground reloading his weapon. In her right hand, she holds a sword, the symbol of the warrior. This personification of Paris is proud and defiant, willing to protect her citizens to the last. Behind her, a small girl facing back toward the city crouches and covers her head. The city wanted the statue to remind its residents that Paris defended itself in 1870, remaining unified in the face of an invading enemy. Doing so required choosing to overlook how that unity broke down during the Commune of 1871. See Hollis Clayson, *Paris In Despair: Art and Everyday Life under Siege, 1870–71* (Chicago: University of Chicago Press, 2002), ch.14. In the winter of 1909–1910, the National Assembly debated a bill concerning the creation of a medal to commemorate the soldiers who fought in the Franco–Prussian War. These debates again demonstrated how divisive the memory of the war was at the very moment of the flood. Some of these discussions took place in early February while the water remained high in the capital. See Karine Varley, "Under the Shadow of Defeat: The State and the Commemoration of the Franco-Prussian War, 1871–1914," *French History* 16 (2002), 323–44.

11. *Paris Inondé 1910* (Paris: Défense de Paris, 1910). See Bibliothèque Nationale, 8°Z LE SENNE 5621.

12. Henriot, "Nos Intimes," *L'Illustration,* February 19, 1910.

13. Unity was anchored in Paris's identity as the nation's capital, the stage for so much of its history as well as its most modern city. The Third Republic had been born in the midst of the most dramatic urban destruction Paris had faced since Haussmann's renovations. Large parts of the city were demolished by a combination of the Prussian siege and the subsequent fighting between national troops and the rebellious Communards. Numerous photographs of the destruction show major buildings, most famously City Hall, in ruins after being burned by Communards, who refused to let French troops recapture it. Indeed, the Republican government used these photographs as propaganda to convey how horrible they believed the radical Communards were and, by contrast, how safe and orderly the Republic was. One of the Third Republic's first tasks was to rebuild Paris in the aftermath of this widespread urban destruction and prove that, under its leadership, the city could be resilient in the wake of both foreign invasion and a bloody and divisive civil war fought out in the streets. In 1910 they sought to show it again.

14. Vanessa R. Schwartz, *Spectacular Realities: Early Mass Culture in Fin de Siècle Paris* (Berkeley: University of California Press, 1998); and Gregory Shaya, "The *Flâneur,* the *Badaud,* and the Making of a Mass Public in France, circa 1860–1910," *American Historical Review* 109 (February 2004), 41–77.

15. In his famous 1903 essay "The Metropolis and Mental Life," German sociologist Georg Simmel described the urban dweller as being so detached from others around him that he could not form any meaningful connections to them. Despite being constantly surrounded by people, Simmel claimed, "One nowhere feels as lonely and lost as in the metropolitan crowd." Georg Simmel, *The Sociology of Georg Simmel,* trans. Kurt H. Woolf (Glencoe, Ill.: Free Press, 1950), 418. To survive the mental stresses and strains of city life, the urban dweller had adopted a detached, blasé attitude that kept him safe but ultimately alone. Relationships in the city were reduced to money, and people had few meaningful interactions on any regular basis, Simmel believed. Likewise, American psychologist George Beard described the conditions of modern, urban life—the pace, the overwhelming technology, the obsession with punctuality and timekeeping, the noise, the sheer busyness—and diagnosed city dwellers as being constantly on the verge of nervous exhaustion.

16. Lawrence J. Vale and Thomas J. Campanella, eds., *The Resilient City* (New York: Oxford University Press, 2005). The essays in this excellent collection inform much of my discussion on how cities recover after a disaster.

17. Ted Steinberg, *Acts of God: The Unnatural History of Natural Disaster in America* (New York: Oxford University Press, 2000); and Kevin Rozario, "Making Progress: Disaster

Narratives and the Art of Optimism in Modern America," in Vale and Campanella, *The Resilient City.*

18. On contemporary San Francisco, see also David L. Ulin, *The Myth of Solid Ground: Earthquakes, Prediction, and the Fault Line Between Reason and Faith* (New York: Viking, 2004). In 2005, during hurricane Katrina, New Orleans became infamous for televised scenes of human suffering. But the somewhat lesser-known stories of New Orleans include the creative ways that people provided one another with aid, especially given the inability or unwillingness of government agencies to move quickly. In hotels, hospitals, and at the neighborhood level, residents of New Orleans improvised ways of helping. The self-styled "Robin Hood Looters," for instance, consisted of about a dozen friends who rescued stranded victims and searched for food and supplies among the abandoned homes, giving it to those in need. Their "looting" was not selfish but in service to the community in an effort to keep people alive. In Uptown, neighbors gathered in a school and cared for one another until help arrived, at one point evicting a group of thugs who had started vandalizing and stealing from vending machines. Local churches and mosques reached out to people in distress. An Internet domain hosting service set up a free Web-based messaging service so that people could stay in touch. In their research on these acts of spontaneous rescue during Katrina, sociologists Havidán Rodríguez, Joseph Trainor, and Enrico L. Quarantelli write: "The various social systems and the people in them rose to the demanding challenges of a catastrophe." Likewise, New Orleans journalist Jed Horne tells the stories of "an impromptu and unofficial rescue mission" in his history of the storm. Throughout southern Louisiana, "people with boats cranked them onto trailers or strapped them to the roofs of cars and trucks and headed for the disaster zone, for New Orleans. . . . An informal flotilla estimated at three hundred craft would work Katrina's aftermath in New Orleans." Even at a moment when a city seemed to be falling apart and in the absence of strong government intervention, people joined forces.

The strength of these social ties matters, especially in the city. In *Heat Wave,* his important study of Chicago deaths in the summer of 1995, sociologist Eric Klinenberg shows how individuals in neighborhoods with strong ties survived a crisis. In parts of town notorious for violence, crime, abandoned houses, and empty lots, people died from the heat at a much higher rate. Chicagoans in these areas were afraid to check on their neighbors, go to a shelter or the store, or reach out to a stranger if they needed help. By contrast, in areas with strong community networks, dense populations, and the presence of family and friends, people survived the heat wave in much greater numbers. Reflecting larger patterns of race and poverty, Klinenberg reveals that a person's vulnerability was partly determined by whether the human connections in their neighborhood were weak or strong.

Had Paris in 1910 been a far-flung, loosely connected collection of individuals deeply divided by race and class—more on the order of Los Angeles or New Orleans—how might the city's history during the flood have been different? Would it have recovered, or would the Paris of today simply not exist? Havidán Rodríguez, Joseph Trainor, and Enrico L. Quarantelli, "Rising to the Challenges of a Catastrophe: The Emergent and Prosocial Behavior Following Hurricane Katrina," *Annals of the American Academy of Political and Social Science* 604 (March 2006): 99; and Jed Horne, *Breach of Faith: Hurricane Katrina and the Near Death of a Great American City* (New York: Random House, 2006), 66. See also Douglas Brinkley, *The Great Deluge: Hurricane Katrina, New Orleans, and the Mississippi Gulf Coast* (New York: William Morrow, 2006); and Eric Klinenberg, *Heat Wave: A Social Autopsy of Disaster in Chicago* (Chicago: University of Chicago Press, 2002).

19. The French spoke of a *Union Sacrée* (sacred union) at the outbreak of the war. The experience of the fighting severely tested whether that union had ever truly been real. See Jean-Jacques Becker, *The Great War and the French People* (New York: St. Martin's Press, 1986).

20. The flood pulled the French together and reinforced national ideals of the sort described by Benedict Anderson, *Imagined Communities: Reflections on the Origins and Spread of Nationalism,* rev. ed. (London: Verso, 1991).

21. "In daily life," as historian Emmanuelle Cronier described the situation, "the dramatic context seemed to bring people together around the search for news or discussion of latest events, encouraging public expression of opinions and feelings formerly more confined to private life." Emmanuelle Cronier, "The Street," in Jay Winter and Jean-Louis Robert, eds., *Capital Cities at War: Paris, London, Berlin, 1914–1919, vol 2: A Cultural History* (Cambridge, UK: Cambridge University Press, 2007), 73–74.
22. Remy de Gourmont, *Pendant l'orage* (Paris: Champion, 1915), 123.
23. Herbert Adams Gibbons, *Paris Reborn* (New York: Century, 1915), 348.
24. Helen Davenport Gibbons, *Paris Vistas* (New York: Century Company, 1919), 165.

EPILOGUE

1. Agence France Presse, "Flood Waters Rise in Paris," December 29, 1993.
2. Alan Riding, "Fearing a Big Flood, Paris Moves Art," *New York Times,* February 19, 2003.
3. Kai T. Erikson, *Everything in Its Path: Destruction of Community in the Buffalo Creek Flood* (New York: Touchstone, 1976), 202–3.
4. Staff of the *Grand Forks Herald* and Knight-Ridder Newspapers, *Come Hell and High Water* (Grand Forks, ND: Grand Forks Herald, 1997), 6.
5. See Tricia Wachtendorf and James M. Kendra, "Considering Convergence, Coordination, and Social Capital in Disasters," Preliminary Paper #342a, University of Delaware Disaster Research Center, 2004; J. M. Kendra and T. Wachtendorf, "Reconsidering Convergence and Converger Legitimacy in Response to the World Trade Center Disaster," in Lee Clarke, ed., *Terrorism and Disaster: New Threats, New Ideas* (Amsterdam: Elsevier, 2003); Kathleen J. Tierney, "Strength of a City: A Disaster Research Perspective on the World Trade Center Attack," Preliminary Paper #310, University of Delaware Disaster Research Center, 2001; and E. L. Quarantelli, "Disaster Related Social Behavior: Summary of 50 Years of Research Findings," Preliminary Paper #280, University of Delaware Disaster Research Center, 1999.
6. Erikson, *Everything in Its Path,* 202.
7. "La lutte contre les inondations," *Journal des Debates politiques et litteraire,* January 27, 1910; and Paul Messier, "Les Inondations, leurs causes, leurs effets," *Fermes et Chateaux,* March 1, 1910, 175–76.
8. Michael D. Bess, *The Light Green Society: Ecology and Technological Modernity in France, 1960–2000* (Chicago: University of Chicago Press, 2003), 4.
9. Ibid., 66.
10. Eric Klinenberg, *Heat Wave: A Social Autopsy of Disaster in Chicago* (Chicago: University of Chicago Press, 2002); and Mike Davis, *City of Quartz: Excavating the Future in Los Angeles* (New York: Vintage, 1992).
11. Indeed, some studies suggest that such communities are precisely what people need in the event of a disaster. For her book, *The Unthinkable: Who Survives When Disaster Strikes and Why,* Amanda Ripley interviewed people who had survived everything from floods to earthquakes to hostage situations to 9/11. She found that individuals tend to help one another in disasters in part as a survival tactic but also because a sense of camaraderie emerges from the situation. One of her key tips to staying alive during a disaster is "Get to know your neighbors. They may be your key to survival. The stronger your community is, the better equipped you will be to survive a disaster." Jen Philips interview with Amanda Ripley, "Five Ways to Survive Any Disaster," *Mother Jones,* June 9, 2008, http://www.motherjones.com/interview/2008/06/five-ways-to-survive-disaster.html; Amanda Ripley, *The Unthinkable: Who Survives When Disaster Strikes and Why* (New York: Crown, 2008).

a NOTE *on the* HISTORY *of the* FLOOD

1. Marc Ambroise-Rendu, *1910 Paris inondé* (Paris: Editions Hervas, 1997), 99. My discussion of efforts to control floods is based on Ambroise-Rendu's account.

Selected Bibliography

ARCHIVAL SOURCES:

ARCHIVES DE PARIS

D3 S4 13
D3 S4 14
D3 S4 21 through 30
VD6 2101
VO NC 834
D8 S4 11
1353 W 2
1353 W 6
8 Fi

ARCHIVES NATIONALES

F7 12649
F7 12559
F10 2296
F14 14722
F14 16583
F14 16584
F14 16578
322AP 47

ARCHIVES DE LA PRÉFECTURE DE POLICE DE PARIS

DB 159
DB 160
DB 161

BIBLIOTHÈQUE HISTORIQUE DE LA VILLE DE PARIS

Files on 1910 flood

ARCHIVES HISTORIQUES DE LA DIOCÈSE DE PARIS

Files on 1910 flood

SELECTED PERIODICALS

Bulletin Municipal Officiel
Le Matin
Le Petit Journal
Le Journal
Journal des Débats
Action Française
Gil Blas
L'Illustration
Annales de Géographie
Construction Moderne
La Nature
La Génie Civil
La Vie Illustrée
Le Figaro
New York Times
London Times
Economist
Nature
Boston Daily Globe
New Orleans Times-Picayune
Washington Post
Los Angeles Times
Lancet
Scientific American

Ambroise-Rendu, Anne-Claude. *Peurs privées, angoisse publique: un siècle de violence en France.* Paris: Larousse, 1999.

Ambroise-Rendu, Marc. *1910 Paris inondé.* Paris: Editions Hervas, 1997.

Backouche, Isabelle. *La Trace du fleuve: la Seine et Paris (1750–1850).* Paris: Editions de L'EHESS, 2000.

———. "Paris sous les eaux: la grande crue de 1910." *L'Histoire* 257 (September 2001).

Barnes, David S. *The Great Stink of Paris and the Nineteenth Century Struggle against Filth and Germs.* Baltimore: Johns Hopkins University Press, 2006.

Beaudoin, François. *Paris/Seine: ville fluviale, son histoire des origines à nos jours.* Paris: Nathan, 1993.

Beaumont-Maillet, Laure. *L'Eau à Paris.* Paris: Editions Hazan, 1991.

Berlanstein, Leonard. *The Working People of Paris, 1871–1914.* Baltimore: Johns Hopkins University Press, 1984.

Berlière, Jean-Marc. *Le Préfet Lépine: vers la naissance de la police moderne.* Paris: Denoël, 1993.

Bess, Michael D. *The Light Green Society: Ecology and Technological Modernity in France, 1960–2000.* Chicago: University of Chicago Press, 2003.

Carline, Richard. *Pictures in the Post: The Story of the Picture Postcard and Its Place in the History of Popular Art.* London: Gordon Fraser, 1971.

Chrastil, Rachel. "The French Red Cross, War Readiness, and Civil Society, 1866–1914." *French Historical Studies* 31 (Summer 2008): 445–76.

Clayson, Hollis. *Paris in Despair: Art and Everyday Life under Siege, 1870–71.* Chicago: University of Chicago Press, 2002.

Cohen, Margaret. "Modernity on the Waterfront: The Case of Haussmann's Paris," in Alev Cinar and Thomas Bender, eds. *Urban Imaginaries: Locating the Modern City.* Minneapolis: University of Minnesota Press, 2007.

Commission des Inondations. *Rapports et documents divers.* Paris: Imprimerie Nationale, 1910.

Cronin, Vincent. *Paris on the Eve, 1900–1914.* New York: St. Martin's, 1990.

Dausset, Louis. *Rapport général au nom de la Commission municipale et départementale des inondations*. Paris: Conseil Municipal de Paris, 1911.

Evenson, Norma. *Paris: A Century of Change, 1878–1978*. New Haven: Yale University Press, 1979.

Exposition universelle de 1900: les plaisirs et les curiosités de l'exposition. Paris: Librarie Chaix, 1900.

Fierro, Alfred. *Historical Dictionary of Paris*. Landham, Md.: Scarecrow Press, 1998.

Findling, John E., ed. *Historical Dictionary of World's Fairs and Expositions, 1851–1988*. New York: Greenwood, 1990.

Fraser, John. "Propaganda on the Picture Postcard." *Oxford Art Journal* (October 1980): 39–46.

Gagneux, Renaud, Jean Anckaert, and Gérard Conte. *Sur les traces de la Bièvre parisienne*. Paris: Parigramme, 2002.

Gandy, Matthew. "The Paris Sewers and the Rationalization of Urban Space." *Transactions of the Institute of British Geographers* 24 (1999): 23–44.

Geary, Christraud M., and Virginia-Lee Webb. *Delivering Views: Distant Cultures in Early Postcards*. Washington, D.C.: Smithsonian Institution Press, 1998.

Gould, Roger V. *Insurgent Identities: Class, Community, and Protest in Paris from 1848 to the Commune*. Chicago: University of Chicago Press, 1995.

Greenhalgh, Paul. *Ephemeral Vistas: The Expositions Universelles, Great Exhibitions, and World's Fairs, 1851–1939*. Manchester, UK: Manchester University Press, 1988.

Harvey, David. *Consciousness and the Urban Experience: Studies in the History and Theory of Capitalist Urbanization*. Baltimore: Johns Hopkins University Press, 1985.

———. *Paris, Capital of Modernity*. New York: Routledge, 2003.

Hausser, Elisabeth. *Paris au jour le jour: les évenements vus par la presse*. Paris: Editions de Minuit, 1968.

Jackson, Jeffrey H. "Envisioning Disaster in the 1910 Paris Flood." *Journal of Urban History*. Forthcoming.

Jacobs, Jane. *Death and Life of Great American Cities*. New York: Vintage, 1992.

Jones, Colin. *Paris: Biography of a City*. New York: Viking, 2005.

Jordan, David. *Transforming Paris: The Life and Labors of Baron Haussmann*. New York: Free Press, 1995.

Kalifa, Dominique. "Crime Scenes: Criminal Topography and Social Imaginary in Nineteenth-Century Paris." *French Historical Studies* 27 (Winter 2004): 175–94.

Keller, Ulrich. "Photojournalism Around 1900: The Institutionalization of a Mass Medium," in Kathleen Collins, ed. *Shadow and Substance: Essays on the History of Photography*. Troy, Mi.: Amorphous Institute Press, 1990.

Klinenberg, Eric. *Heat Wave: A Social Autopsy of Disaster in Chicago*. Chicago: University of Chicago Press, 2002.

Lacour-Veyranne, Charlotte. *Les Colères de la Seine*. Paris: Musée Carnavalet, 1994.

Lépine, Louis. *Mes souvenirs*. Paris: Payot, 1929.

Le Roy Ladurie, Emmanuel. "Quand Paris est sous les eaux." *L'Histoire* 334 (September 2008).

Mandell, Richard. *Paris 1900: The Great World's Fair*. Toronto: University of Toronto Press, 1967.

Marchand, Bernard. *Paris: histoire d'une ville, XIXe–XXe siècle*. Paris: Editions du Seuil, 1993.

Mellot, Philippe. *Paris inondé: photographies, janvier 1910*. Paris: Editions de Lodi, 2003.

Meyer, Jonathan. *Great Exhibitions: London, New York, Paris, Philadelphia, 1851–1900*. Woodbridge, UK: Antique Collector's Club, 2006.

Nord, Philip G. *Paris Shopkeepers and the Politics of Resentment*. Princeton: Princeton University Press, 1986.

———. *The Republican Moment: Struggles for Democracy in Nineteenth-Century France*. Cambridge: Harvard University Press, 1995.

Paris 2011: La Grande inondation. Directed by Bruno Victor-Pujebet. 75 min. Studio Canal, 2006. DVD.

Pawlowski, Auguste, and Albert Radoux. *Les Crues de Paris: causes, méchanisme, histoire*. Paris: Berger-Levrault, 1910.

Pike, David L. *Subterranean Cities: The World beneath Paris and London, 1800–1945.* Ithaca: Cornell University Press, 2005.

Pinkney, David. *Napoleon III and the Rebuilding of Paris.* Princeton: Princeton University Press, 1958.

Pinon, Pierre. *Paris: biographie d'une capitale.* Paris: Hazan, 1999.

Porot, Jacques. *Louis Lépine: préfet de police, témoin de son temps (1846–1933).* Paris: Editions Frison-Roche, 1994.

Rabinbach, Anson. *The Human Motor: Energy, Fatigue, and the Origins of Modernity.* New York: Basic Books, 1990.

Rearick, Charles. *Pleasures of the Belle Epoque.* New Haven: Yale University Press, 1985.

Reid, Donald. *Paris Sewers and Sewermen: Realities and Representations.* Cambridge: Harvard University Press, 1991.

Ripley, Amanda. *The Unthinkable: Who Survives When Disaster Strikes—and Why.* New York: Crown, 2008.

Schor, Naomi. "'Cartes Postales': Representing Paris 1900." *Critical Inquiry* 18 (Winter 1992): 188–244.

Schwartz, Vanessa R. *Spectacular Realities: Early Mass Culture in Fin de Siècle Paris.* Berkeley: University of California Press, 1998.

Schwartz, Vanessa R., and Leo Charney. *Cinema and the Invention of Modern Life.* Berkeley: University of California Press, 1995.

Shaya, Gregory. "The *Flâneur*, the *Badaud,* and the Making of a Mass Public in France, circa 1860–1910." *American Historical Review* 109 (February 2004): 41–77.

Silverman, Debora. *Art Nouveau in Fin-de-Siècle France: Politics, Psychology, and Style.* Berkeley: University of California Press, 1989.

Sluhovsky, Moshe. *Patroness of Paris: Rituals of Devotion in Early Modern France.* Leiden: Brill, 1998.

Soppelsa, Peter. "The Fragility of Modernity: Infrastructure and Everyday Life in Paris, 1870–1914." Ph.D. diss., University of Michigan, 2009.

——. "Métro-Nécro: The 1903 Métro Accident and its Impact on Infrastructure and Practice, 1903–1914." Paper presented at the Society for French Historical Studies Conference, New Brunswick, NJ, March 2008.

Steinberg, Ted. *Acts of God: The Unnatural History of Natural Disasters in America.* New York: Oxford University Press, 2000.

Stovall, Tyler. *The Rise of the Paris Red Belt.* Berkeley: University of California Press, 1990.

Sutcliffe, Anthony. *The Autumn of Central Paris: The Defeat of Town Planning, 1850–1970.* London: Edward Arnold, 1970.

Ulin, David L. *The Myth of Solid Ground: Earthquakes, Prediction, and the Fault Line between Reason and Faith.* New York: Viking, 2004.

Vale, Lawrence J., and Thomas J. Campanella, eds. *The Resilient City: How Modern Cities Recover from Disaster.* New York: Oxford University Press, 2005.

Varley, Karine. "Under the Shadow of Defeat: The State and the Commemoration of the Franco-Prussian War, 1971–1914." *French History* 16 (September 2002): 323–44.

Williams, Rosalind. *Dream Worlds: Mass Consumption in Late Nineteenth Century France.* Berkeley: University of California Press, 1982.

——. *Notes on the Underground: An Essay on Technology, Society, and the Imagination.* Cambridge: MIT Press, 1990.

Wohl, Robert. *The Generation of 1914.* Cambridge: Harvard University Press, 1979.

Zeldin, Theodore. *A History of French Passions,* vol. 2., *Intellect, Taste, and Anxiety.* Oxford: Clarendon Press, 1977.

Zeyons, Serge. *La Belle Epoque: les années 1900 par la carte postale.* Paris: Larousse, 1990.

Acknowledgments

All research is a collaborative effort, and this book is no different. I would like to thank those who helped to make it possible.

Rhodes College provided financial support, including Faculty Development Endowment grants, a Spence Wilson International Travel grant, and support from the Office of the Provost, which allowed me to travel to Paris. Rhodes has also proven to be a rich intellectual environment thanks to good colleagues. Shira Malkin, with whom I co-taught a course on Paris, helped put the Seine on my map, and Katheryn Wright shared many conversations with me about the flood as well as postcard shopping in Paris. Many others, especially my colleagues in the history department, have generously read portions of this work and commented on presentations.

My agent Judith Ramsey Ehrlich, assisted through much of the process by Martha Hoffmann, worked tirelessly to give extremely constructive feedback and hearty encouragement along the way, and I am deeply grateful for her mentorship. The manuscript also benefited immensely from the remarkable editorial talents of Jean Casella, whose insightful suggestions strengthened the book significantly at a very important stage in the process. My editor at Palgrave Macmillan, Alessandra Bastagli, offered very useful comments to improve the narrative quality and overall structure of this book.

I was welcomed as a Fellow-in-Residence at the Columbia University Institute for Scholars at Reid Hall in Paris in the fall of 2007. Reid Hall provided an extremely congenial place to work and a vibrant community, and I thank Danielle Haase-Dubosc and Mihaela Bacou for their support and for creating such a wonderful space to think and write, along with my colleagues at Reid Hall for their friendship and conversation. That semester, I was also fortunate to find friends and intellectual exchange in the informal salon organized by Micah Alpaugh for members of the H-France listserv, and I'm grateful to him for bringing us all together. One of the regular participants, Wendy Pfeffer, asked many excellent questions that helped formulate my thinking, and she offered her insights on an early version of the manuscript. The H-France group allowed me to reconnect with my friend Jean Pedersen, with whom I had many wonderful conversations about the flood that further refined my writing.

I have presented portions of this work as it progressed at conferences, including the Society for the Anthropology of North America conference and two meetings of the Society for French Historical Studies. I benefited greatly from the astute comments by Rosemary Wakeman and Suzanne Kaufman. I appreciate the opportunity to share my work and the excellent questions and comments offered by fellow panelists and the audiences at these and other gatherings.

Pete Soppelsa and I have had numerous discussions about the flood since we met in the Archives de Paris, and he generously took the time to read a draft of the manuscript and to share his important research with me. Vanessa Schwartz and I struck up an ongoing dialogue about the flood, and I thank her for her encouragement and insight. Other friends, including Michael Bess, Robert Edgecombe, Michelle Pinto, and Judy Pierce, have read drafts and offered their wisdom at important moments. My research assistant, Andy Crooks, was instrumental in helping to build the Web site that accompanies this book, www.ParisUnderWater.com. Artist Danita Barrentine brought her talented eye and great skill to the Web site in order to make it work so beautifully.

History department Administrative Assistants Murfy Nix and Heather Holt have helped in countless ways that may have seemed small but have made a big difference.

The sources for this book came from a range of archives and libraries, and I thank the staffs of all, especially the very generous Geneviève Morlet at the BHVP, Abbé Philipe Ploix and Vincent Thauziès at the diocesan archive in Paris, Yvonne Boyer at the W. T. Bandy Center as well as the Special Collections Department at the Jean and Alexander Heard Library at Vanderbilt University, and Kenan Padgett in the Interlibrary Loan Department at Rhodes College's Barrett Library.

In addition to the photographs held in archival collections, there are several published volumes that contain flood photos as well as numerous Web sites that have a wide variety of flood imagery. The best Web site remains http://lefildutemps.free.fr/crue_1910/ created by Chantal Leduc and the late Gilles Pagandet. Although I never met either, I thank them for putting so much time and energy into preserving and sharing the imagery of the 1910 flood.

Novelist Sarah Smith is one of the few people in the United States to have seriously dealt with the flood in her writing, and I am grateful that she pointed me in some good directions early in my research.

As always, my family has been so supportive of my work, and I thank them for their continued love and interest in what I do. In particular, I often think how very different, and much less rich, my life would be without the wonderful stories that my grandparents, Clyde and Marie Caraway, brought back with them from their adventures abroad. Most of what I study probably had its genesis in our many Saturdays together.

The biggest thanks of all goes to my wife, Ellen. She was there with me in the sewers of Paris when I first heard about the flood of 1910, and she has lived with the project from beginning to end. She has traveled, listened, talked, read, and prodded along the way. She was the one who really helped me to see the value of the flood photographs and played a crucial role in making sense of them. More than any other collaborator, she is the most important one of all, both in this book and in my life. I dedicate this book to her.

Index